CONCORDIA UNIVERSITY

3 4211 00139 1583

D1507030

Leader of the fast-growing Nazi Party, Adolf
Hitler salutes his goose-stepping Brownshirts—
part of an enormous crowd of followers
who assembled in Brunswick on October 18,
1931, to show off their strength in strife-
torn, Depression-weary Germany. Fifteen
months later, Hitler climbed to power as
Chancellor of the Reich, inaugurating a reign
of violence and conquest that lasted 12 years.

THE NAZIS

Other Publications:
THE EPIC OF FLIGHT
THE GOOD COOK
THE SEAFARERS
THE ENCYCLOPEDIA OF COLLECTIBLES
THE GREAT CITIES
HOME REPAIR AND IMPROVEMENT
THE WORLD'S WILD PLACES
THE TIME-LIFE LIBRARY OF BOATING
HUMAN BEHAVIOR
THE ART OF SEWING
THE OLD WEST
THE EMERGENCE OF MAN
THE AMERICAN WILDERNESS
THE TIME-LIFE ENCYCLOPEDIA OF GARDENING
LIFE LIBRARY OF PHOTOGRAPHY
THIS FABULOUS CENTURY
FOODS OF THE WORLD
TIME-LIFE LIBRARY OF AMERICA
TIME-LIFE LIBRARY OF ART
GREAT AGES OF MAN
LIFE SCIENCE LIBRARY
THE LIFE HISTORY OF THE UNITED STATES
TIME READING PROGRAM
LIFE NATURE LIBRARY
LIFE WORLD LIBRARY
FAMILY LIBRARY:
   HOW THINGS WORK IN YOUR HOME
   THE TIME-LIFE BOOK OF THE FAMILY CAR
   THE TIME-LIFE FAMILY LEGAL GUIDE
   THE TIME-LIFE BOOK OF FAMILY FINANCE

Previous World War II Volumes:
Prelude to War
Blitzkrieg
The Battle of Britain
The Rising Sun
The Battle of the Atlantic
Russia Besieged
The War in the Desert
The Home Front: U.S.A.
China-Burma-India
Island Fighting
The Italian Campaign
Partisans and Guerrillas
The Second Front
Liberation
Return to the Philippines
The Air War in Europe
The Resistance
The Battle of the Bulge
The Road to Tokyo
Red Army Resurgent

WORLD WAR II · TIME-LIFE BOOKS · ALEXANDRIA, VIRGINIA

BY ROBERT EDWIN HERZSTEIN
AND THE EDITORS OF TIME-LIFE BOOKS

THE NAZIS

Time-Life Books Inc.
is a wholly owned subsidiary of
TIME INCORPORATED

Founder: Henry R. Luce 1898-1967

Editor-in-Chief: Henry Anatole Grunwald
Chairman of the Board: Andrew Heiskell
President: James R. Shepley
Editorial Director: Ralph Graves
Vice Chairman: Arthur Temple

TIME-LIFE BOOKS INC.

Managing Editor: Jerry Korn
Executive Editor: David Maness
Assistant Managing Editors: Dale M. Brown
(planning), George Constable, George G. Daniels
(acting), Martin Mann, John Paul Porter
Art Director: Tom Suzuki
Chief of Research: David L. Harrison
Director of Photography: Robert G. Mason
Senior Text Editor: Diana Hirsh
Assistant Art Director: Arnold C. Holeywell
Assistant Chief of Research: Carolyn L. Sackett
Assistant Director of Photography: Dolores A. Littles

Chairman: Joan D. Manley
President: John D. McSweeney
Executive Vice Presidents: Carl G. Jaeger,
John Steven Maxwell, David J. Walsh
Vice Presidents: Nicholas Benton (public relations),
Nicholas J. C. Ingleton (Asia), James L. Mercer
(Europe/South Pacific), Herbert Sorkin (production),
Paul R. Stewart (marketing), Peter G. Barnes,
John L. Canova
Personnel Director: Beatrice T. Dobie
Consumer Affairs Director: Carol Flaumenhaft
Comptroller: George Artandi

WORLD WAR II

Editorial Staff for The Nazis
Editor: Gerald Simons
Picture Editor/Designer: Raymond Ripper
Text Editors: Brian McGinn, Robert Menaker,
Mark M. Steele
Staff Writers: Kathleen Burke, Peter Kaufman,
John Newton, Teresa M. C. R. Pruden
Researchers: Charlie Clark, Elizabeth Ajemian,
Kristin Baker, LaVerle Berry, Loretta Y. Britten,
Jane Edwin, Lucinda Moore, Sara Schneidman,
Cronin Buck Sleeper
Art Assistant: Mary L. Orr
Editorial Assistant: Connie Strawbridge

Special Contributors
Robin Richman (pictures), Champ Clark (text),
Paula York (research)

Editorial Production
Production Editor: Douglas B. Graham
Operations Manager: Gennaro C. Esposito,
Gordon E. Buck (assistant)
Assistant Production Editor: Feliciano Madrid
Quality Control: Robert L. Young (director),
James J. Cox (assistant), Daniel J. McSweeney,
Michael G. Wight (associates)
Art Coordinator: Anne B. Landry
Copy Staff: Susan B. Galloway (chief),
Sheirazada Hann, Victoria Lee, Barbara F. Quarmby,
Celia Beattie
Picture Department: Alvin L. Ferrell

Correspondents: Elisabeth Kraemer (Bonn); Margot
Hapgood, Dorothy Bacon, Lesley Coleman (London);
Susan Jonas, Lucy T. Voulgaris (New York); Maria
Vincenza Aloisi, Josephine du Brusle (Paris); Ann
Natanson (Rome). Valuable assistance was also
provided by: Wibo van de Linde (Amsterdam); Helga
Kohl, Martha Mader (Bonn); David Schrieberg
(Jerusalem); Brian L. Davis (London); Felix Rosenthal
(Moscow); Carolyn T. Chubet, Miriam Hsia,
Christina Lieberman, Villette Harris (New York);
Mimi Murphy (Rome).

The Author: ROBERT EDWIN HERZSTEIN is a Professor of European History at the University of South
Carolina. Since receiving his Ph.D. at New York University in 1964, he has authored The War That Hitler
Won, Adolf Hitler and the German Trauma, and
Western Civilization, and has edited Adolf Hitler and
the Third Reich.

The Consultant: COLONEL JOHN R. ELTING, USA
(Ret.), is a military historian and author of The Battle
of Bunker's Hill, The Battles of Saratoga and Military
History and Atlas of the Napoleonic Wars. He edited
Military Uniforms in America: The Era of the Ameri-
can Revolution, 1755-1795 and Military Uniforms in
America: Years of Growth, 1796-1851, and was asso-
ciate editor of The West Point Atlas of American Wars.

Library of Congress Cataloguing in Publication Data

Herzstein, Robert Edwin.
    The Nazis.

    (World War II; 21)
    Bibliography: p.
    Includes index.
    1. World War, 1939-1945—Germany.
2. Germany—Politics and government—1933-1945.
I. Time-Life Books.   II. Title.   III. Series.
D757.H397   940.53'43   79-24323
ISBN 0-8094-2536-X
ISBN 0-8094-2535-1 lib. bdg.

For information about any Time-Life book, please write:

Reader Information
Time-Life Books
541 North Fairbanks Court
Chicago, Illinois 60611

© 1980 Time-Life Books Inc. All rights reserved.
No part of this book may be reproduced in any form or by any
electronic or mechanical means, including information stor-
age and retrieval devices or systems, without prior written per-
mission from the publisher, except that brief passages may be
quoted for reviews.
First printing.
Published simultaneously in Canada.
School and library distribution by Silver Burdett
Company, Morristown, New Jersey.

TIME-LIFE is a trademark of Time Incorporated U.S.A.

CONTENTS

HITLER'S ARTFUL SPECTACLES

REKINDLING PRIDE WITH PAGEANTRY

Deputy Führer Rudolf Hess (left) and architect Albert Speer (second from left) listen as Hitler outlines plans for the 1934 Nuremberg rally.

"I'm beginning to comprehend some of the reasons for Hitler's astounding success," wrote American journalist William L. Shirer from Berlin in September 1934. "He is restoring pageantry and color and mysticism to the drab lives of twentieth-century Germans." Indeed he was. Hitler's Nazi Party, empowered in 1933 to lead the nation, had made a fine art of staging enormous spectacles that inspired a new sense of national pride.

In Nuremberg each September hundreds of thousands of Germans cheered as battalions of storm troopers goose-stepped through the streets to the martial music of brass bands. At the 1937 rural Harvest Day festival, a great mass of farmers thrilled to the sight of a mock tank battle that attested to the Wehrmacht's increasing strength. At night the spectacles were crowned by the surrealistic splendor of 100 or more searchlights sending their beams 20,000 feet into the air. "The effect," wrote the British Ambassador, "both solemn and beautiful, was like being in a cathedral of ice."

At each grandiose festival, the main attraction was Hitler, the man who made the Nazi magic work. He presided over the exhibitions and parades, and took the adoring salutes of the marchers. Then, invariably, he excited the crowds and the nation with variations on the speech that had swept him to power—a vigorous attack on the Bolsheviks, the Jews, and the nations that had imposed the humiliating Versailles Treaty on Germany at the close of World War I.

Above all, Hitler pledged a greater, stronger Germany—and the extravagant spectacles were intended to prove to the people that he was making the promise come true. Under his leadership, he was saying, Germany had recovered from the political chaos and economic ruin of the '20s, and was regaining its rightful place among the great powers.

While they inspired the Germans, the Nazi spectacles stunned the rest of the world. Many correspondents sent home stories that spoke apprehensively of Germany's growing armed forces. "All the talk here has been of peace," wrote The New York Times reporter as early as 1933, "yet the atmosphere has been far from peace-loving."

The Führer dedicates the Volkswagen factory in June of 1938 with a promise to manufacture a "people's car" for every German citizen. It was rumored that Hitler himself had helped to design the prototype (foreground) and that the vehicle could easily be converted to a light tank.

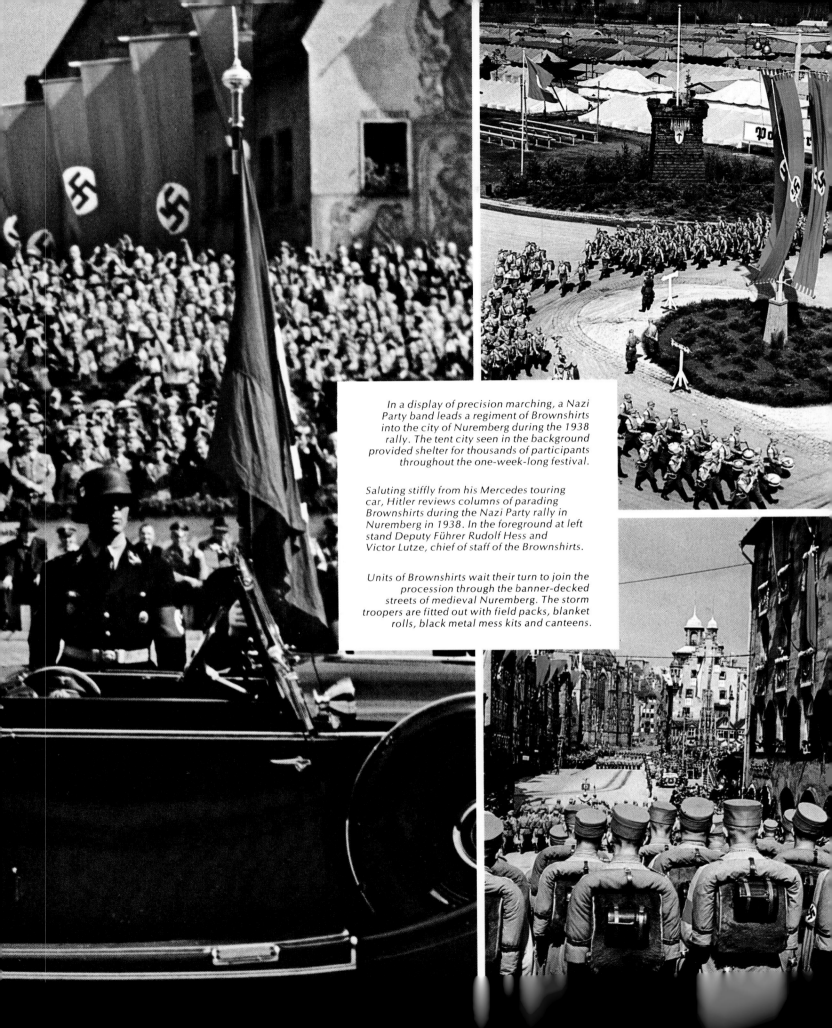

In a display of precision marching, a Nazi Party band leads a regiment of Brownshirts into the city of Nuremberg during the 1938 rally. The tent city seen in the background provided shelter for thousands of participants throughout the one-week-long festival.

Saluting stiffly from his Mercedes touring car, Hitler reviews columns of parading Brownshirts during the Nazi Party rally in Nuremberg in 1938. In the foreground at left stand Deputy Führer Rudolf Hess and Victor Lutze, chief of staff of the Brownshirts.

Units of Brownshirts wait their turn to join the procession through the banner-decked streets of medieval Nuremberg. The storm troopers are fitted out with field packs, blanket rolls, black metal mess kits and canteens.

Linking arms across an immense athletic field, thousands of members of the League of German Girls dance in celebration of "faith and beauty" during the Nazi Party rally at Nuremberg in 1939. This particular performance required long and meticulous advance preparation: The women who participated had been selected from local chapters months ahead of time and had spent almost every evening thereafter in rehearsal.

Performing at the Nuremberg rally, young men demonstrate their strength and skill in a precision drill with heavy poles. The colossal stadium, designed in 1934 by Hitler's leading architect, Albert Speer, had two adjoining grandstands, one a quarter of a mile long, and seats for 124,000 spectators.

At left, the many medals and awards won by
Adolf Hühnlein, head of the National Socialist
Motor Corps, are displayed at his funeral on
June 21, 1942, by a pair of Brownshirts standing
in front of an elaborate display of shrubbery
and flowers. The Nazi Party usually saluted its
departed leaders with floral arrangements,
music by Wagner, and lengthy eulogies that
were specially written for the occasion
by Joseph Goebbels' Ministry of Propaganda.

Nazi representatives turn out in full regalia
on April 17, 1944 (right), to mark the passing of
Adolf Wagner, Gauleiter of Munich-Upper
Bavaria. The funeral, held in the cavernous
Kongresssaal of Munich's Deutsches Museum,
featured the trappings and symbols of the
party: the swastika draped over the coffin, the
standards emblazoned with ''Deutschland
Erwache'' (''Germany, Awake!''), the Nazi eagle.

AN AWESOME DISPLAY OF MILITARY MIGHT

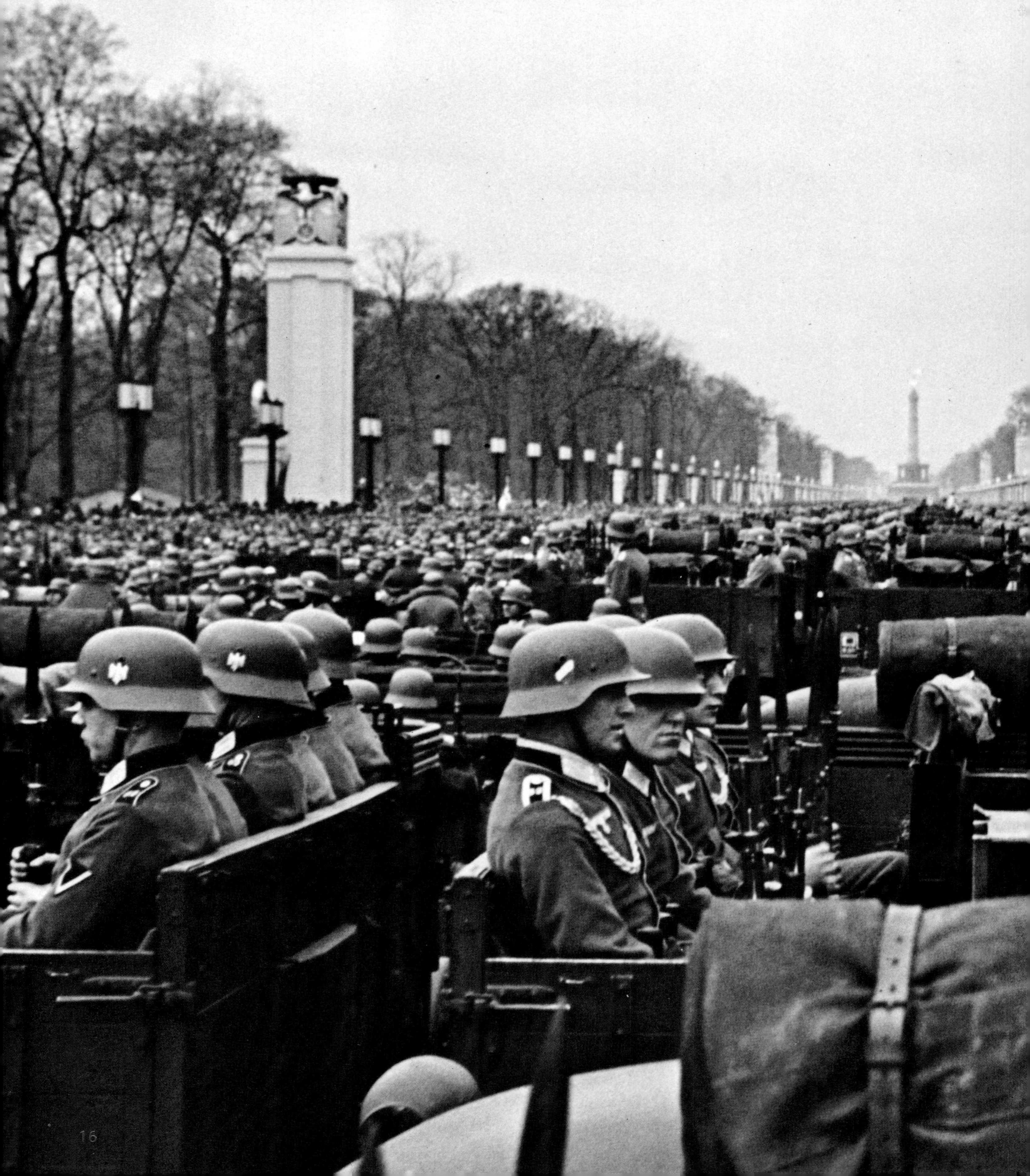

Trucks filled with Wehrmacht infantrymen assemble in the Tiergarten, Berlin's sprawling central park, for a parade honoring Hitler on his 50th birthday, April 20, 1939. The trucks, along with columns of tanks and artillery, rumbled past the Führer's reviewing stand, while great formations of Luftwaffe warplanes droned overhead. This intimidating show of German power was witnessed by two million Berliners and many representatives of foreign nations. After the parade, the visiting dignitaries—including the American Chargé d'Affaires—signed their names in Hitler's birthday register as a matter of course.

17

1

It was 6 o'clock on the evening of July 19, 1940, an hour of exultation for the Reich that Adolf Hitler had proclaimed would last 1,000 years. France had capitulated nearly a month before, and this was to be the Führer's first public appearance since the surrender ceremony in the forest of Compiègne. "It seemed to all of us," recalled architect Albert Speer, whom Hitler had ordered to draw plans for a grandiose new Berlin, "that with every passing month we were almost effortlessly drawing nearer to the reason for the arches of triumph and the avenues of glory."

Now, Hitler was to speak before the Reichstag, and the occasion had been invested with all the symbolic panoply that the ceaselessly agile mind of Dr. Joseph Goebbels, among other things the Gauleiter of Berlin, could conjure. Just yesterday, by his edict, all Berlin's schools, shops and offices had been closed, a million Nazi swastika flags had been distributed and church bells had chimed as German troops marched through the city's Brandenburg Gate—victorious for the first time since 1871.

For Goebbels, the victory parade had very nearly ended in disaster: A cavalry horse, driven wild by the clash of cymbals and the blare of trumpets, had backed into the reviewing stand, lashed out with its hoofs and come within inches of ending the career of Nazi Germany's Minister of Popular Enlightenment and Propaganda.

But that incident was almost completely forgotten by the time the political and military leaders of the Third Reich began arriving at the Kroll Opera House to hear Hitler's speech. Searchlights crisscrossed the night sky on this mellow summer evening. Crowds lined the Unter den Linden boulevard. The throaty roar of motorcycle escorts, the pop and glare of flash bulbs and the roll of drums ushered in the sleek black Mercedes that disgorged Nazi dignitaries in front of the immense building. Some 600 Reichstag deputies were in attendance, many of them "Old Fighters" from the early struggles for control of Germany's streets and meeting halls. All owed their prominence to Hitler's appointment and all wore red, white and black swastika bands on their arms as a sign of their allegiance.

With the politicians came the triumphant German military: admirals, their shoulders glittering with gold braid, and generals, their field-gray uniforms trimmed with crimson, their chests ablaze with decorations. Then came the party

THE NEW MEN OF POWER

functionaries, their arms raised in the Nazi salute as they entered the building. The salute was required of Nazis; failure to render that homage could bring heavy punishment.

One by one, arms stiffly outstretched, the nabobs of Nazism stalked into the opera house. Cheers rose from the multitude as Hitler's principal lieutenants arrived: Goebbels, a tiny (barely five feet tall) man with a crippled right foot; Reichstag President and Luftwaffe chief Hermann Göring, of average height but Gargantuan in girth and weighing around 300 pounds; Foreign Minister Joachim von Ribbentrop, wanly handsome, head held high; Deputy Führer Rudolf Hess, eyes burning in deep, dark sockets; SS chief Heinrich Himmler, looking perfectly harmless despite his cap with its skull-and-crossbones insignia; party ideologue Alfred Rosenberg, tall and dour, the "philosopher" of anti-Semitism; and, wobbling slightly in his chronic state of inebriation, Robert Ley, chief of the German Labor Front.

Almost certainly lurking somewhere in the shadows was Martin Bormann, the assistant to Deputy Führer Hess and the man who would soon take power over the Nazi Party organization. Wherever Hitler went, there too went Bormann, jotting down the dictator's every word on white index cards, of which he carried an endless supply. Bormann's presence on this particular occasion went unremarked. But then, nobody ever noticed Martin Bormann; as late as 1941 his name was virtually unknown in the Reich.

These were the Nazis, Germany's new men of power, the self-made leaders of the Third Reich at their zenith, lords and masters of continental Europe from the Atlantic to the Baltic and from the North Cape to the Mediterranean. By normal standards, they were failures in their private lives, eccentric in their actions and outlooks, and as unlikely a lot of individuals as had ever been gathered together. Yet their personal shortcomings could have mattered to few in the throng outside the Kroll Opera House, cheering and even weeping for joy in the moment's emotion. For to Germans as a people, this was the hour of redemption from nearly two decades of national humiliation and deprivation. And these were the men who had brought it about.

Inspired by a single charismatic figure, the Nazi leaders were perhaps the boldest gamblers in the history of humankind—brilliant in the play of power, bluffers on the grand scale. They knew the consequence of defeat. "May God help us," Göring once said, "if we lose this war." Yet the stake was nothing less than world empire. Before they were done, the Nazis would carry conflict to the deserts of Africa, the shores of the Americas and the banks of the Volga—all in pursuit of the German dream of *Lebensraum*.

In their colossal wager the Nazis, through the organization of their National Socialist Party, would reach with repressive hands into every corner of German life, subverting justice and the rule of law. They had already replaced traditional workers' rights with the spurious promise of a blue-collar paradise, brought into ideological thrall the flower of German youth from cradle to the age of conscription, and held absolute sway over the arts and the professions.

Soul and sinew of the Nazi system was a state within a state—the black-uniformed Schutzstaffel, or SS, with its remorseless devotion to the obliteration of all enemies, real or fancied, at home or abroad. Its leader, Heinrich Himmler, would infiltrate the German Army with dozens of divisions of fanatically politicized fighting men. He would create a bureaucracy of terror at the center of which was a network of concentration camps—and he would soon place genocide on an assembly-line basis.

Indeed, for the Nazis genocide was the inevitable result of the ideal of Aryan supremacy, which provided the heartbeat of their ideology. Founded on the smoldering coals of a classical anti-Semitism, fanned by the pseudo philosophies of such men as Alfred Rosenberg, and bursting into full flame in the instinctive hatreds of Adolf Hitler, Nazi racism would lead to a holocaust unparalleled in the long history of human inhumanity.

Hand in hand with the liquidation of Jews went the ruthless exploitation of both the human and material resources of subjugated lands. In the swathes cut by surging German armies, party leaders carved out baronies for themselves. For the profit of the Greater German Reich, entire factories would be dismantled and shipped to the fatherland, while untold millions would be forced into slave labor.

None of it, of course, could have transpired without the German Army, soon to be commanded personally by Hitler, at first with intuitive genius and later in disastrous frenzy. Beguiled by Hitler's appeals to patriotism and by his pledge to redeem the shame of Versailles, the Wehrmacht officer corps had acquiesced in his assumption of power. Rarely have men paid so dearly for their fecklessness. The generals would suffer personal insult beyond the limits of endurance; some would be banished from command and degraded in rank; many would be required on peril of their lives to obey orders that could only result in carnage for their own troops. And when, as the end inexorably neared, German officers would attempt to assassinate their Führer, reprisal would be so swift, so merciless and so far-reaching as to make clear, once and for all, that the downfall of Nazi Germany would be wrought not from within but on the battlefield.

But this night in July 1940 was not one for premonitions of doom. It was instead an occasion for the pinks and whites and yellows and crimsons of the floral arrays within the opera house, for the great copper eagle that loftily surveyed the scene, for the vast swastika banners sweeping from ceiling to floor and for the roars of *"Sieg heil! Sieg heil! Sieg heil!"* as at long last the Führer of Germany's New Order took his place on the dais.

During his lifetime, Adolf Hitler spoke before audiences totaling an estimated 35 million people. He was one of the supreme orators of history; many of his chief followers had become his disciples by no more than the happenstance of hearing him speak. Tonight he was in good form. He rarely shouted and not once did he burst into the hysterical shrieks that so often marked his speeches. He used his hands, graceful and delicate, to help weave his spell.

"In the middle of the tremendous struggle for freedom and the future of the German nation," he began, "I have called you into session to give our own people insight into the unique historic events that we have experienced, and to thank our well-deserving soldiers." Hitler recited the litany of Allied perfidy and German heroism. The Poles had defied him; the French had sent "Negro soldiers" into battle against him; the Jewish world was determined to enslave Germany; the Allies had deceived Germany into defeat in 1918. Hitler went on to painstakingly detail the recent German conquest of Norway, which he termed "the most daring operation in Germany's military history. All of the units of our young Reich Navy have achieved everlasting glory."

Then he recounted the magnificent blitzkrieg in the West. He related the swift fall of Belgium and Holland, described how "in an intense envelopment, the Army had stormed behind the back of the Maginot Line," how both the French Army and the British Expeditionary Force had been obliterated in France, and how "here the German leadership shone forth in splendor." These gains, he cried, were "the

most sweeping military advances in world history. The entire German race can take an equal part in this glory. The Greater German Reich, coming out of this war, will be holy and dear not only for the generations living today but also for those to come, by this heroic action of all Germans.''

Hitler turned now to his colleagues. It was time to pay brief compliments to his functionaries in the Nazi hierarchy. Rudolf Hess had been ''one of the most loyal fighters for the creation of the present state and its Wehrmacht since the beginning of the movement.'' Robert Ley was ''the guarantee of the attitude of the German working class!'' Joachim von Ribbentrop was Hitler's ''dear party comrade.''

And then came Hermann Göring's great moment of glory. Throughout Hitler's speech, Göring had been seated above and to the rear of the speakers' podium on the thronelike edifice that was his by right of his role as the Reichstag President. In addition to that position and his job as Luftwaffe chief, Göring was Chairman of the Council of Ministers for the Defense of the Reich, Air Minister, Plenipotentiary of the Four-Year Economic Plan, Premier of Prussia, President of the Prussian State Council, Police General, Reich Forest Master and Reich Master of the Hunt.

More honors were about to be his. The Führer declared: ''As the sole creator of the Luftwaffe, Field Marshal Göring has already contributed the most to the build-up of Germany's armed forces. So far during the course of the War, he has, as leader of the Luftwaffe, achieved victory. His merits are unique.'' Hitler thereupon named Göring the only Reich Marshal of the Greater German Reich and bestowed upon him one of the highest military decorations, the Grand Cross of the Iron Cross.

There was more to come in Adolf Hitler's demonstration of largesse. Next, 12 generals were appointed field marshal, each beaming gratefully as he arose and saluted from the balcony. They were Walther von Brauchitsch, Commander in Chief of the Army; Wilhelm Keitel, Chief of the High Command of the Armed Forces; three of Göring's Luftwaffe generals, Erhard Milch, Albert Kesselring and Hugo Sperrle; three Army group commanders, Gerd von Rundstedt, Fedor von Bock and Wilhelm Ritter von Leeb; and four Army commanders, Wilhelm List, Günther Hans von Kluge, Erwin von Witzleben and Walther von Reichenau. ''By declaring

these promotions,'' the Führer said, ''I am honoring the collective armed forces of the Greater German Reich.''

There was curiously little cheering as the 51-year-old Führer spoke of his victories and bestowed his favors. The crowd at last came to life with a great roar of triumph when Hitler concluded with a stirring tribute to Germany's heroic dead, ''who gave their souls for the freedom and future of our people and for the eternal greatness of the Greater German Reich. Germany, *Sieg heil!*''

But for most of the time Hitler was speaking, the audience sat as if mesmerized—not so much by the words as by the man himself. Everyone in the opera house was familiar with the story, already beginning to merge into myth, of Adolf Hitler and of the circumstances surrounding his rise to power. But few understood the complexities of the man, or of the party he had forged.

He had, by a stroke of geographic ill fortune, been born on the Austrian side of the Austro-German frontier, the son of a low-ranking customs official. He had dreamed of becoming a great artist, and upon the death of his beloved mother when he was 19, he had set off for Vienna with, in his own words, ''a suitcase full of clothes in my hand and an indomitable will in my heart.''

According to Hitler's own account, the next four years were abysmal ones. He was penniless, and he knew no trade. He bounced from one odd job to another—beating carpets, shoveling snow, manhandling railway luggage—meanwhile living in cheap rooming houses and men's hostels, finding meager nourishment in soup kitchens and occasionally peddling a sketch of such Viennese landmarks as St. Stephen's Cathedral and the Palace of Schönbrunn. Actually, Hitler exaggerated his hardships in an effort to appeal to German workers and Socialists. He did not take a steady job because he had enough money from his family estate to get by without one.

For the young Adolf Hitler, the Great War came as a blessed release. A passionate German nationalist from an early age despite his Austrian birth, he joined the German Army; he was a good soldier, and beyond any question a brave one. Corporal Hitler was twice wounded and twice decorated for his courage in action; the second award, the Iron Cross, First Class, was rarely given to enlisted men. When the War's end came, Hitler was in a military hospital,

Hitler, Martin Bormann and staff officials admire an elaborate model of a triumphal arch that the Führer intended to build in Berlin when the city became ''Germania,'' the capital of all Europe. Hitler appropriated billions of reichsmarks to grace his dream capital with monuments, but most of the money was eventually diverted to wartime emergencies.

temporarily blinded from a gas attack at Ypres the month before. By his own subsequent account, he flung himself onto his bunk in despair at the news of armistice. ''Did all this happen,'' he asked himself, ''so that a gang of wretched criminals could lay hands on the fatherland?''

Hitler went to Munich. And it was there that he met his destiny in a smoke-choked beer cellar, where a pitiable little group of right-wingers calling themselves the German Workers' Party held their dreary meetings. In September 1919, Hitler, now employed by the German Army's Political Department, was sent to investigate this noisy nest, which his superiors suspected of being subversive. ''This was a time,'' Hitler later recalled, ''in which anyone who was not satisfied with developments felt called upon to found a new party. Everywhere these organizations sprang out of the ground, only to vanish silently after a time.''

Despite his air of disdain, Hitler was fascinated by politics, and the German Workers' group provided a platform of sorts. He not only joined the party but, by application of his frenetic energies and burgeoning oratorical powers, quickly took it over. In April 1920, he renamed it the National

Socialist German Workers' Party—which in German is Nationalsozialistische Deutsche Arbeiterpartei, or Nazi for short. Its name notwithstanding, the organization was neither a workers' party nor a Socialist one—except, perhaps, as defined by Hitler. His definition of Socialism had a grand irrelevance: ''Whoever has understood our great national anthem, 'Deutschland, Deutschland über Alles,' to mean that nothing in the wide world surpasses in his eyes this Germany—people and land—that man is a Socialist.'' In the post-World War I economic, political and social chaos of a defeated Germany, when only love of country and desire for its redemption remained constant, Hitler thus staked out for himself and his party the broadest possible territory.

Though the early Nazi Party attracted some working-class members, it was not a party of the laboring man. In 1935, only 30 per cent of its membership consisted of workers —against more than 50 per cent white-collar employees, civil servants, shopkeepers and other self-employed independents, all thoroughly middle class.

This middle class, caught in the age-old squeeze between the very rich and the very poor, suffered greatly during the

agony of Germany's defeat and the economic repressions of the Versailles Treaty. Hitler himself knew little and cared less about economics as such. Yet with his every political instinct, he knew that his National Socialist Party could feed and fatten on the human misery caused by economic deprivation—and the Nazi rise to power ran in direct opposition to the plunging economic graphs of postwar Germany.

In April of 1921, the Allied powers finally finished totting up their reparations bill and presented it to Germany in the staggering sum of 132 billion gold marks. The mark, normally valued at four to the dollar, fell almost instantly to 75. It kept on plummeting—until, by the end of the awful year of 1923, a single U.S. dollar was worth an incredible four *billion* German marks. German salaries and wages were worthless, purchasing power was nil, the life savings of the middle class had vanished, unemployment passed one million, hundreds of thousands stood in bread lines—and Adolf Hitler tasted opportunity.

"The government," said Hitler, "calmly goes on printing these scraps of paper because if it stopped that would be the end of the government. The swindle would at once be brought to light." His view of the future was dire: "Believe me, our misery will increase. If the horrified people notice that they can starve on billions, they must arrive at this conclusion: We will no longer submit to a state that is built on the swindling of the majority."

Hitler reached eagerly for power, too eagerly, and if the effort was in some ways comedic, it was deadly enough in its purpose and outcome.

On the evening of November 8, 1923, while Bavarian State Commissioner Gustav Ritter von Kahr was making a political speech in Munich's sprawling Bürgerbräukeller, some 600 Nazis and right-wing sympathizers surrounded the beer hall. Hitler burst into the building and leaped onto a table, brandishing a revolver and firing a shot into the ceiling. "The National Revolution," he cried, "has begun!"

Then, while Hermann Göring remained to assure the astounded audience that Nazi intentions were entirely benign, Hitler at revolver's point herded Kahr, along with the head of the Bavarian state police and the Bavarian commander of the Army, into an adjoining room. There, he urged his prisoners to recognize him as the new head of the Bavarian state government. The three were reluctant even to speak to him.

Leaving them under guard, Hitler returned to the main hall. "The Bavarian Ministry," he shouted, "is removed!" The first task of his new government, he said, would be "to organize the march on that sinful Babel, Berlin, and save the German people. Tomorrow will find either a national government in Germany or us dead!"

Hitler was running a bluff—and it seemed for a brief while that it had worked. The three prisoners, hearing cheers from the people in the hall, pretended to acquiesce to Hitler's demands. At that point, informed that fighting had broken out in another part of the city, Hitler rushed to that scene. His prisoners were allowed to leave, and they set about organizing defenses against the Nazi coup, or *Putsch.*

Hitler was of course furious. And he was far from finished. At about 11 o'clock on the morning of November 9—the anniversary of the founding of the German Republic in 1919—3,000 Hitler partisans again gathered outside the Bürgerbräukeller. The unruly procession then headed for the center of Munich, led by Hitler, Göring and General Erich Ludendorff, the famed old Quartermaster General of World War I, now a Nazi showpiece.

Confronted on the way by a police line, Göring stepped forth from the mob and threatened to shoot hostages who had been taken by the Nazis during the night. The police moved aside and the marchers strode on. But as they began to emerge from a narrow street onto Munich's broad Odeonsplatz, they were again stopped by police. "Don't shoot!" cried one of Hitler's bodyguards. "His Excellency Ludendorff is coming!" Adolf Hitler wildly waved his revolver. "Surrender!" he shouted. "Surrender!"

To this day, no one knows who fired the first shot. But a shot rang out, and it was followed by fusillades from both sides. Hermann Göring fell wounded in the thigh and both legs. Hitler flattened himself against the pavement; he was unhurt. General Ludendorff continued to march stolidly toward the police line, which parted to let him pass through (he was later arrested, tried and acquitted). Behind him, 16 Nazis and three policemen lay sprawled dead among the many wounded.

After a trial that he managed to turn into a platform for his political views, Hitler was sentenced to five years in prison.

Smoke billows from Berlin's Reichstag, devastated by a fire of undetermined origin on the night of February 27, 1933. The Nazis, who were immediately suspected of setting the blaze to create chaotic conditions that they could then exploit, rushed to pour verbal fuel on the flames. In angry speeches, Hitler blamed the Bolsheviks, and Göring demanded that Communist deputies "be strung up this very night."

He served nine months, and he used the time to dictate *Mein Kampf,* a remarkable blueprint of Germany's future under the Nazi regime.

Abortive though the renowned Beer Hall Putsch was, the Nazis learned from it a lesson that would take them to eventual power. Said Göring: "We shall plan no more putsches. We shall merely make the situation so bad internally that the people will clamor for National Socialist rule."

And many did, fomenting riot, brawling in the streets, breaking up opposition political meetings and generally creating as much chaos as possible. Yet economic circumstances turned against them. Hitler had scarcely begun serving his jail term when an extraordinary man with a remarkable name—Hjalmar Horace Greeley Schacht (his parents had lived in the United States and had taken a liking to the famous newspaper publisher)—was called into government to tackle Germany's currency problems.

Schacht's solution was a work of imaginative genius. To pay German reparations, he borrowed from the nations to whom the reparations were owed; these nations had no choice but to lend the money, for an insolvent Germany could never be expected to pay a penny of its debts. Schacht also reformed German currency, basing its value on German productivity rather than gold. The effect was felt almost immediately, and the improving economy was disastrous for the National Socialists: In the elections of May 1924, they had won about two million votes; by December they were below one million.

Between 1924 and 1930, Schacht borrowed some seven billion dollars. The country's industrial output rebounded and in 1928, for the first time since the War, unemployment fell below one million, to 650,000. In the national elections that year, the National Socialist Party received a paltry 810,000 votes out of 31 million and elected only 12 deputies to the Reichstag.

Then came the Crash.

The Great Depression that followed the Wall Street disaster of October 24, 1929, afflicted nations throughout the world—but none more so than Germany with its ramshackle economy. By 1930, Germany's loan sources had dried up, exports had dwindled drastically, factories and banks had closed, millions had lost their jobs, the bread lines had reappeared—and Adolf Hitler was delighted. "Never in my life," he wrote, "have I been so well disposed and inwardly contented as in these days. For hard reality has opened the eyes of millions of Germans."

To a desperate Germany, Hitler offered crude solutions: He would unilaterally end reparations and refuse to repay the debts incurred by Schacht; he would crush the Jew, whose greed was the cause of all economic evil; he would provide every German with food and a job. He promised nonpartisan politics, a Germany where people worked together, a Germany to be proud of.

From their depths, the German people responded. In the elections of 1930, only two years after its dismal showing in 1928, the National Socialist Party won more than 6.4 million votes and sent 107 deputies to the Reichstag.

Hitler may not have understood economics, but he was keenly aware that he would need money to finance his final lunge for power. "In the summer of 1931," recalled Otto Dietrich, Reich press chief, "the Führer suddenly decided to concentrate systematically on cultivating the influential industrial magnates." His instrument was a sottish little man named Walther Funk, who would rise to become president of the Reichsbank and Minister of Economics during Hitler's rule. Funk resigned from his job as editor of a Berlin financial newspaper and set out to persuade industrialists and bankers that Hitler was, in Funk's words, "an enemy of state economy and that he considered free enterprise and competition as absolutely necessary."

Funk succeeded in winning the Nazis a share of the funds large companies donated to all acceptable political parties. Money was soon pouring into Nazi coffers from such men as Fritz Thyssen, head of the German steel trust; Georg von Schnitzler of the I. G. Farben chemical cartel, and Baron Kurt von Schröder, representing Cologne banking interests.

In the elections of July 31, 1932, Adolf Hitler's National Socialist Party won 13.7 million votes and 230 seats in the Reichstag, making it by far Germany's largest political party—and opening wide the gateway to power.

Power. The word throbs throughout the history of the Nazi Party. Beyond the ancient German creed of anti-Semitism and a yearning for *Lebensraum,* National Socialism had scarcely any ideology. What it had instead was an intoxication with power.

Marching in the front row of a troop of "Old Fighters," Hitler leads a Munich parade reenacting the 1923 Beer Hall Putsch. The ceremony was repeated every year, but with one small detail always omitted: Soon after the police had fired on the rebellious Nazis and their sympathizers, Hitler fled, while 16 of his followers were killed or mortally wounded.

To Hitler, power was force and power was struggle. "Only force rules," he said in a 1938 speech at Essen. "Force is the first law." The very existence of the human race, he believed, is "bound up in three things: Struggle is the father of all things, virtue lies in blood, leadership is primary and decisive." The tool of power was terror, both spiritual and physical.

In a seminal passage of *Mein Kampf*, Hitler wrote of the spiritual terror that Nazism must exert, "particularly on the bourgeoisie, which is neither morally nor mentally equal to such attacks"; at a given sign, he said, Nazism would unleash "a veritable barrage of lies and slanders against what-

ever adversary seems most dangerous, until the nerves of the attacked persons break down. This is a tactic based on precise calculation of all human weaknesses, and its result will lead to success with almost mathematical certainty." Equally valuable in its results, wrote Hitler, was "physical terror toward the individual and the masses." Suffering its effects, he said, "the defeated adversary in most cases despairs of the success of any further resistance."

Hitler radiated power—and inspired fear. Whatever Hermann Göring's faults, the man possessed abundant courage. And yet he once confessed: "Every time I face Hitler, my heart falls into my trousers." After witnessing one of the

Führer's frequent rages, Göring said, "I couldn't eat anything again until midnight, because before then I would have vomited in my agitation."

Thus, by the extraordinary power of his personality, Hitler stood as the sole repository and dispenser of power in Nazi Germany. "I lead the movement alone," he said. So he did—and the men around him knew it. Said Hans Frank, the Nazi overlord of Poland, not long before his belief in Hitler's destiny carried him to the gallows as a convicted war criminal: "It was Hitler's regime, Hitler's policy, Hitler's rule of force, Hitler's victory, Hitler's defeat—nothing else." In his war-crimes trial, Rudolf Hess peered through the mists of his madness and said, "It was granted to me for many years to live and work under the greatest son whom my nation has brought forth in the thousand years of her history." Heinrich Himmler saw in Hitler's orders "the binding decisions of the Germanic race's Führer, pronouncements from a world transcending this one."

But it remained for Göring to put his finger on the true rationing of power as between Hitler and his immediate underlings. "Anyone who knows how it is with us," said Göring, "knows that we each possess just so much power as the Führer wishes to give."

In that sense, Hitler was most generous. He himself found day-to-day administration a drudge, and he was more than willing to parcel out power. Hitler was delighted by the ensuing free-for-all among his lieutenants; indeed, said Speer, he "watched any efforts at rapprochement with keen suspicion" as a possible threat to his own position.

Hitler did, of course, retain for himself the role of supreme arbiter, sometimes stepping in to settle disputes of astounding triviality. For example, in 1939, after Ribbentrop signed a treaty relating to the German-Russian division of ravaged Poland, Josef Stalin as a gesture of good will gave to the Nazi Foreign Minister a huge hunting preserve on the Soviet side of the new frontier. Göring, whose greed knew no bounds, was furious, claiming that Stalin had surely intended the land to be a gift to the German state. In that case, he insisted, the preserve would fall under his own jurisdiction as Reich Master of the Hunt. Hitler decided in Göring's favor, reducing Ribbentrop to futile rage.

Thus, the Nazi state, which presented to the outside world a national monolith more massive than any hitherto known to man, was in reality a hodgepodge of overlapping jurisdictions, contested responsibilities, murderous rivalries and searing hatreds. Göring loathed Goebbels, Goebbels loathed Rosenberg, Rosenberg loathed Ley and Bormann—and everybody loathed Ribbentrop. Speer wrote of "that profligate Göring, that fornicator Goebbels, that drunkard Ley, that vain fool Ribbentrop." Himmler called Goebbels a "repulsive Levantine." Goebbels referred to Alfred Rosenberg as "Almost Rosenberg" because he had "managed to become a scholar, a journalist, a politician—but only almost." Said Goebbels of Ribbentrop: "He married his money and he swindled his way into office."

Hitler knew full well that his minions were deeply flawed, and he was content. "I do not," he once said, "consider it to be the task of a political leader to attempt to improve upon, or even to fuse together, the human material lying ready to his hand." He let his subordinates run—and run they did, each of them wielding prodigious power according to individual purpose and motive.

To Hermann Göring, aged 47 at the time of his opera house awards, power was the means to indulge a body abused and a soul embittered. Fat, seemingly jolly and able to laugh at himself, Göring was, next to Hitler, the most popular of the German leaders. "The people want to love," he explained, "and the Führer was often too far from the broad masses. Then they clung to me." But though they liked him, Germans also enjoyed poking fun at his oddities, and they chortled with glee when word got out of the innocent remark of visiting Queen Rambi Barni of Siam. "He must be a very rich man," said the Queen after meeting Göring, "to be able to afford so much rice. Or is it potatoes?"

But Göring was no joke. Under the layers of fat lay a fiercely combative spirit. The son of a retired provincial governor in German Southwest Africa, Göring became a World War I flying ace, accounting for 22 enemy planes, winning the Pour le Mérite, Germany's highest award for valor, and ending the conflict as the last commander of the Richthofen squadron—the famed Flying Circus.

Postwar Germany paid little homage to war heroes. Rootless and disgruntled, Göring became an itinerant commercial pilot. In that capacity he frequently traveled to Sweden, and there he met and married the wealthy Baroness Karin von Fock-Kantzow. Though her fortune was certainly no obstacle to Göring's affections, there is no question that he loved her; she was probably the only person other than himself for whom he felt the slightest tenderness. In sentimental memory after her death, Göring would name his estate Karinhall—and live there with his second wife, the celebrated actress Emmy Sonnemann, whose marriage to Göring was the greatest social extravaganza in the history of the Third Reich.

Out of curiosity, Göring one evening in 1921 dropped in on the Munich beer cellar where Hitler was speaking and was entranced by the would-be Führer's visions of power. Some time later, when Göring volunteered to command a squad of Nazis, Hitler was equally enthusiastic. "Splendid!" he cried. "A war ace with the Pour le Mérite—imagine it! Excellent propaganda!"

It was in his new role that Göring found himself marching in the front ranks of the Nazis during the Beer Hall Putsch. To help the wounded Göring escape the retributive round-up that followed, friends bore him on a stretcher through the Alpine passes to Innsbruck, his wife trudging along behind. Frail at best (she was an epileptic), Karin was so weakened from the ordeal that she contracted tuberculosis, and was an invalid until her death eight years later.

It was all too much for Göring. To ease the agony of his infected wounds and his troubled mind, he sought refuge in morphine, became addicted, suffered mental breakdowns and spent much of the time from 1924 to 1926 shuttling in and out of Swedish asylums. Although he would rely upon morphine for the rest of his life, by the time he returned to Germany under an amnesty granted in 1927, he was sufficiently recovered from his mental turmoil to resume his position as a valued Hitler lieutenant. And when Germany began to rearm, Göring was the obvious choice to build and command the Luftwaffe, which was so vital to Hitler's plans for conquest.

To Paul Joseph Goebbels, aged 42, power offered the opportunity to manipulate a humanity that had derided him. As he gratefully expressed it in a newspaper article, Hitler gave him the chance to "unleash volcanic passions, outbreaks of rage, to set masses of people on the march, to organize hatred and despair with ice-cold calculation."

Life had been far from kind to Goebbels. Born to a piously Catholic working-class Rhineland family, he had excelled in his studies, perhaps to compensate for his grotesquely clubbed foot. In later years he would intimate that his deformity was a battle wound—"Those of us shot up in the War," he would say—even while confiding his inner hurt to his diary: "My foot troubles me badly. I am conscious of it all the time, and that spoils my pleasure when I meet people." In fact, caught up by patriotic fervor, he had tried to enter the Army during World War I; enlistment officers took one look at his foot and his puny frame and laughed in his face. Goebbels went home, locked himself in his room, and wept for hours.

By dint of his parents' scrimping and a series of Catholic scholarships, Goebbels attended not only one but eight universities, concentrating on philosophy, history, literature and art and virtually becoming a career student before he finally got his Ph.D. He wrote an autobiographical novel, *Michael*, which publishers rejected for years. He authored two plays; no producer would touch them. He tried his hand at journalism; the daily *Berliner Tageblatt* turned down scores of his articles.

In June 1922, Goebbels was one of Germany's angry, at-loose-ends millions when he happened to hear Hitler speak at the Circus Krone in Munich. At that moment, wrote Goebbels, "I was reborn." He nevertheless soon fell out with Hitler, demanding that the party take a radical anti-capitalist approach and, when it refused, denouncing its leader as "the petty bourgeois Adolf Hitler." But a short while later, Hitler, obviously having spotted something he needed within the little man, went out of his way to embrace Goebbels after a speech. That night Goebbels' diary entry read: "Adolf Hitler, I love you."

Goebbels was an astonishingly gifted propagandist, if only because he was utterly uninhibited by considerations of truth. The truly great man, he said, "contents himself with saying: It is so. And it is so." Within two months after he became Hitler's Propaganda Minister on March 13, 1933, Goebbels staged an event not seen in Western Europe since the Inquisition. After a torchlight parade on Berlin's Unter den Linden, thousands of students flung into flames the works of such "degenerate" authors as Thomas Mann and Stefan Zweig, Jack London and H. G. Wells and Helen Keller, Zola and Freud and Proust. "The soul of the German people can again express itself," cried Goebbels at the book burning. "These flames not only illuminate the final end of an old era; they also light up the new."

On September 22, 1933, the Reich Chamber of Culture, with Goebbels at its head, was established not only to determine the nation's "line of progress, mental and spiritual, but also to lead and organize the professions." Subchambers were set up to control the press, music, the theater, radio, literature and motion pictures. All practitioners in those fields were required to join the subchambers, whose directives had the status of law. Those suspected of "political unreliability"—and Goebbels, of course, was the judge—could be deprived of their livelihood.

Goebbels was married, unhappily, to a handsome but rather stupid woman who gave him six children. "Thank God," he said in a moment of candor, "they have her looks and my brains. How terrible it would be if it had turned out the other way around." As "Protector of the German Film," Goebbels had access to scores of actresses, and he entered into a tempestuous affair with a beautiful Czech, Lida Baarova. This was the sort of scandal Hitler could not tolerate. He ordered Goebbels to choose between Baarova and continued power in government.

Goebbels chose power. And he would remain with Hitler until the day he met the fate predicted in his diary: "Such is life: many blossoms, many thorns, and—a dark grave."

Joachim von Ribbentrop became a Nazi rather late in the game. The son of a junior-grade Army career officer, Ribbentrop served as a lieutenant during World War I, and in 1918, thanks to a change in German law, took his title, "von," from a distant relative with noble credentials. After the War, he hung on the fringes of what passed in Berlin for café society, eventually marrying the daughter of a wealthy wine merchant. The bride's parents were evidently less than pleased. "Odd," his mother-in-law later remarked, "that my most stupid son-in-law should have gone the furthest." But Ribbentrop did have a blotter-like facility for soaking up languages, and his father-in-law set him to selling the family product abroad, a position that Ribbentrop elevated to style himself an "international businessman."

He met Hitler for the first time in August 1932, through the auspices of a wartime acquaintance turned Nazi. In Jan-

THE SWASTIKA: A GOOD-LUCK SIGN THAT

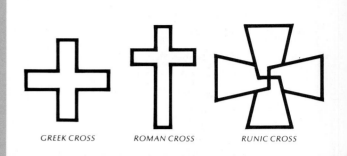

GREEK CROSS   ROMAN CROSS   RUNIC CROSS

When Adolf Hitler, the frustrated artist, was put in charge of propaganda for the fledgling National Socialist Party in 1920, he realized that the party needed a vivid symbol to distinguish it from rival groups. Therefore he sought a design for a party flag that would attract the masses.

Hitler was finally inspired by a sketch from a dentist in Starnberg, whose flag, he later claimed, "was not bad at all and quite close to my own." The background of the flag was red, and Hitler insisted that "to win over the worker" the color must be bolder than the red in the Communists' hammer-and-sickle banner. The Nazi Party emblem was to be the swastika.

Hitler had a convenient but spurious reason for choosing the hooked cross. Like other crosses (above), it had been used as a sun symbol or good luck sign by many ancient peoples, including the Aryan nomads of India in the Second Millennium B.C. In Nazi theory, the Aryans were the Germans' ancestors, and Hitler concluded that the swastika had "been eternally anti-Semitic," and would be the perfect symbol for "the victory of Aryan man."

In spite of its fanciful origin, the swastika flag was a dramatic one, and it did precisely what Hitler intended from the day in 1920 when it was first unfurled in public. Anti-Semites and unemployed workers rallied to the banner, and even Nazi opponents were forced to acknowledge that the swastika had a "hypnotic" effect. "The hooked cross" wrote correspondent William Shirer, "seemed to beckon to action the insecure lower-middle classes which had been floundering in the uncertainty of the first chaotic postwar years."

BECAME AN ANTI-SEMITIC SYMBOL

The first swastika flag has a white circle—for racial purity.

The Nazi Storm Troop standard bears a swastika and the slogan "Germany Awake!"

Nazis hail the "blood flag" in Braunschweig in 1931.

Three huge banners, hung above the Nuremberg stadium at the 1938 Nazi Party rally, show the evolving flag with the swastika given a quarter turn.

uary 1933, he offered his fashionable Berlin home at 7-9 Lentze-Allee for the secret political negotiations that led to Hitler's assumption of power. Then, with pretensions of becoming the Third Reich's Foreign Minister now that Hitler was in control, he set up his own unofficial ministry, dubbed the "Ribbentrop Bureau," and spent the next three years competing with Germany's official diplomatic establishment. He frequently traveled abroad as a good-will ambassador for the Führer, sounding out Western diplomats on such matters as rearmament, and cultivating friends in the foreign press.

His expectations were whetted in 1936, when Hitler designated him Ambassador to the Court of St. James's. But Ribbentrop appalled the British. In London, he outraged court society by snapping a Nazi salute at the King of England, and commuted home with such frequency that the humor magazine *Punch* labeled him the "Wandering Aryan."

It was characteristic of Adolf Hitler to view success with suspicion and to reward failure with preferment. In 1938, Ribbentrop was given his heart's desire. Once he was named Foreign Minister, he infuriated Hitler's other satraps by proving himself the most perfect toady of them all. Taking over the former palace of the Reich President as his official residence, he ordered an expensive renovation. When the building was nearly completed, Hitler came by to inspect it—and murmured a few words of dissatisfaction. Ribbentrop thereupon tore down the entire edifice and rebuilt according to the Führer's known Gothic tastes.

But though Ribbentrop was the target of vicious sniping by the Nazi hierarchy, Hitler kept him in favor and power, perhaps because the two shared a predilection for double-crossing the enemy. "When the War is over," Ribbentrop once boasted, "I shall have a finely carved chest made for myself. I shall put in it all the state agreements and other contracts between governments that I have broken during my period of office and shall break in the future." Chortling, Hitler replied: "And I shall send you a second chest when the first one is full."

Heinrich Himmler, aged 39, and Alfred Rosenberg, 47, were as dissimilar as two men could be. Yet each in his own way sought power in the pursuit of a vision of racial purity.

Himmler was the grandson of a Bavarian police official and the repressed son of an authoritarian headmaster. Gray-blue eyes gazing lifelessly from behind a pince-nez, a tiny mustache tucked between well-formed nose and colorless lips, pasty-pale, blue-veined hands resting before him on a tidy desk, Himmler was the personification of the impersonal, clinical killer.

How he met Hitler is uncertain. When World War I ended, Himmler was still an Army officer candidate, untested in combat; during the next few years he was active with one or another of the "free corps" of demobilized soldiers then causing trouble throughout Germany. He was in the Nazi ranks during the 1923 Beer Hall Putsch—but his part in that affray was so insignificant that Himmler was not even deemed worth throwing in jail. He went to work for the party in an office job in Landshut and later supplemented his meager salary as a part-time chicken farmer. To the helter-skelter Nazis, Himmler's acknowledged administrative talents were welcome: In 1925 he became deputy gauleiter of Upper Bavaria and Swabia, moving steadily up to deputy Reich propaganda chief. In 1929, Hitler appointed him Reichsführer-SS, and seven years later he became the chief of all German police forces.

Somewhere in the chill crypts of his being, Himmler had developed a theory: By a process of systematic extermination of inferior peoples, accompanied by the scientific breeding of a master race of "sacred" Germanic blood, the Third Reich could, in exactly 120 years, develop a people "authentically German in appearance," displaying the desired physical characteristics—the Nordic ideal of the tall, blond, blue-eyed, fair-skinned master race. In his striving toward that goal, Heinrich Himmler would write his own bloodstained pages in the history of Nazi Germany.

If Himmler's mind was a filing cabinet, Rosenberg's was a ragbag. The son of a shoemaker, Rosenberg grew up in Estonia, received a degree in architecture at the University of Moscow and then moved to Munich in 1918. There he frequented grubby cafés; one night in 1919, the young Adolf Hitler listened enthralled until dawn while Rosenberg, in his guttural Baltic accents, spewed forth a pastiche of anti-Semitic notions.

In fact, Hitler needed no encouragement in his hatred for Jews: His was the visceral instinct of a have-not seeking a scapegoat. During his vagabond Vienna days, he recalled, "wherever I went, I began to see Jews, and the more I saw, the more sharply they became distinguished in my eyes from the rest of humanity. Was there any form of filth or profligacy, particularly in cultural life, without at least one Jew involved in it? If you cut even cautiously into such an abscess, you found, like a maggot in a rotting body, often dazzled by the sudden light—a kike!"

In 1923 Rosenberg's loyalty and commitment to Hitler won him the editorship of the Nazi Party newspaper, *Völkischer Beobachter,* and during the next several years he summed up his racial credo in a muddled tome called *The Mythos of the Twentieth Century.* Hitler, while applauding Rosenberg's sentiments, seems to have found the book heavy going. He praised the magnum opus to Rosenberg's face as "a very intelligent book." But behind the man's back he dismissed it as "stuff nobody can understand," written by "a narrow-minded Baltic German who thinks in horribly complicated terms."

Robert Ley, aged 50, the alcoholic, stammering son of a Rhineland peasant, enjoyed power in the manner of a big-city political boss—which he was. A college-educated air-force pilot during World War I, Ley was twice shot down, the second time ending up badly wounded behind French lines. And it was in a prisoner-of-war camp, organizing inmate committees to make demands of their French captors, that Ley discovered his true talent. Upon his release, he went home to the Rhineland, and within a few months he had turned the working classes of Cologne into a potent political force.

At the time of the 1923 Putsch, Ley had yet to meet Hitler. But Nazi ruthlessness appealed to him, and after Hitler was freed from prison Ley brought his Cologne organization into the party. By 1933, he was the obvious choice to become head of the newly formed German Labor Front, which was designed to replace the traditional labor unions and take control of the workers' movement.

The established union leaders were understandably suspicious of the new Nazi labor organization. But Hitler and his men were expert at disposing of such problems. May Day 1933 was declared a national holiday and labor leaders from all over Germany were flown to Berlin to celebrate the occasion. The Nazis used their absence from home to seize union headquarters and appropriate union funds. In Berlin, the union leaders themselves were arrested, and many were sent to concentration camps as a clear and present danger to the state.

Three weeks later, Hitler decreed an end to collective bargaining in Nazi Germany; henceforth, stooges appointed as trustees by Labor Front leader Ley would "regulate labor contracts" (with wages frozen at Depression levels) and "maintain labor peace."

Robert Ley now held labor in his clutch, yet like any good political boss, he still felt a need to divert his constituency. "It is more important," he said, "to feed the souls of men than their stomachs." In the business of soul feeding, Ley was sincere and tirelessly inventive. He set up a super-agency called *Kraft durch Freude* ("Strength through Joy"), which sponsored bockwurst-and-beer socials, sent art exhibits to the hinterlands, promised "people's cars" to every worker (in the event, the Volkswagen did not get off the production line until after the War had ended) and operated a giant travel bureau that ran its own fleet of tourist liners and took German workers at cost to faraway places. In 1938 alone, some 10 million citizens enjoyed Strength-through-Joy vacation trips.

And then there was Rudolf Hess.

Of all the Nazi leaders, only Hess was selfless in his ambitions. "Hitler is Germany," he had said. "Germany is Hitler." Power and might for this dual entity was all Hess sought from life. And for the excess of his devotion he would be branded traitor by the man about whom his universe revolved.

Hess was born in Alexandria, Egypt, on April 26, 1894, the son of a German wholesale merchant. A morose boy, he became a morose man. During the Great War he was wounded near Verdun, was hospitalized for a while, and was then sent to the Rumanian front, where he was shot through a lung. While convalescing, he became interested in aviation, and shortly before the Armistice, he returned to combat as a flier—a skill that would one day transport him into disgrace.

Amid the ashes of Germany's defeat, Hess was gloomier than ever—until, one glorious day in 1920, he heard Hitler speak. His wife, Ilse, later recalled how Hess rushed into their rooming house in the town of Schwabing near

Munich, laughing hysterically and shouting, "The man! The man! The man!"

From that day, Rudolf Hess was Hitler's slave, marching in the Beer Hall Putsch and then accompanying Hitler to the Landsberg Fortress prison, where he served as stenographer while his master dictated *Mein Kampf*. Upon the Nazi assumption of power, Hitler designated Hess Deputy Führer, first in the line of succession, and placed him in charge of the party organization, giving him "the power to make decisions in my name in all questions relating to the conduct of the party."

Hess was responsible for at least 19 departments, involving such diverse areas as racial hygiene, unemployment, schools, Nazified art and the organization of Germans living outside the Reich. He was also responsible for cosigning vicious decrees against the Jews and anyone opposed to the state, the Führer or the party. Through Hess, Hitler intended to keep a check on other Nazi leaders.

But Hess was exceedingly peculiar and becoming more so. He turned to the pseudo sciences that flourished in postwar Germany. He had astrologers lay out his charts by the stars and he consulted various fortunetellers about his own fate and that of his country. He believed in "biodynamic" vegetarian diets and in "terrestrial radiations" that affected human behavior. He thought that evil spirits had been sent to plague him by Jews, but he concluded that they could be removed from his body by magnets. When Hess's son was born in 1937, the happy father asked that each of Germany's gauleiters, or district leaders, send samples of dirt to be placed under the crib, thereby making the infant a true child of Germany.

Before long, all this began to grate on Hitler. "With Hess," he complained, "every conversation becomes an unbearably tormenting strain." And slowly but surely, the man whom Hitler had once affectionately called *"mein Rudi, mein Hesserl"* was removed to the periphery of favor. Although Hess remained in command of the party apparatus, Hitler avoided him, rarely speaking to him except at party rallies and other formal occasions. In 1938, Hermann Göring replaced Hess as next in the line of succession. And Hess, now a notch lower, could sense from below the silent gray presence of his assistant, Martin Bormann, gathering up the strings of power within the Nazi Party organization.

But loyal Hess was and loyal he would remain. Indeed, he wished only to demonstrate his faith and regain Hitler's favor—and on the occasion of Hitler's victory speech in the Kroll Opera House, the muddled mind of Rudolf Hess sensed an opportunity.

In a segment of that speech, Hitler had intermingled personal insult toward Winston Churchill and other British leaders with an offer of peace toward England.

"From Britain," Hitler had said, "I now hear only a single cry—not of the people but of the politicians—that the War must go on. I do not know whether these politicians already have a correct idea of what the continuation of this struggle will be like. They do, it is true, declare that they will carry on from Canada. I can hardly believe that they mean by this that the people of Britain are to go there. The people, I am afraid, will have to remain in Britain.

"Believe me, gentlemen, I feel a deep disgust for this type of unscrupulous politician who wrecks whole nations. Mr. Churchill ought perhaps, for once, to believe me when I prophesy that a great empire will be destroyed—an empire that it was never my intention to destroy or even to harm."

And then the hypnotic voice announced:

"In this hour I feel it to be my duty before my own conscience to appeal to reason and common sense in Great Britain as much as elsewhere. I consider myself in a position to make this appeal since I am not the vanquished begging favors, but the victor speaking in the name of reason.

"I can see no reason why this War must go on."

Listening raptly, Rudolf Hess was confirmed in an idea that he had been harboring for several weeks—to appeal to the British himself. If the British turned down Hitler's offer (as, in fact, they soon did), why should not he, the Führer's most faithful follower, undertake an unofficial mission as emissary to the enemy? Perhaps he could by personal diplomacy win the British over to reason. Indeed, Hess had already mentioned such a notion to Hitler in vague terms—and had received an equally vague reply.

In the weeks that followed, the idea took shape. Night after night once his wife had retired, Hess would reread a passage from *Mein Kampf* in which Hitler had said: "If we look about us for European allies, there remain only England and Italy." He read too the predictions of the 16th Century

Serving sentences in Landsberg Fortress prison for the 1923 Putsch, Hitler and Rudolf Hess (second from right) pose comfortably with three Nazi cronies for a photograph taken by Hess's girl friend. Because the prison guards were Nazi sympathizers, they allowed Hitler to receive unlimited visitors, have flowers in his cell and eat specially prepared meals. The Führer spent his time there reading, laying plans to seize power after his release and dictating his autobiography, Mein Kampf.

French seer Nostradamus, finding insights into the present struggle between Germany and Great Britain: "Those a long time besieged in the Isles / Will take vigorous action against their enemies."

Could all this mean that the War would drag on indefinitely, that the Reich would be unable to break the British will to fight?

By September, Hess had decided on his course of action. He felt that he had a good connection with the English aristocracy. He had met the Duke of Hamilton at the Olympic Games in Berlin in 1936; the Duke had been gracious and Hess believed that he was friendly toward Germany. Hess had recently been told that the Duke had access to Churchill and the King. Acting on his own, so that if the mission failed Hitler would not be deemed responsible, Hess would fly to England in quest of the peace his Führer seemed to desire so greatly.

By the autumn of 1940, Hess was ready to take a first step. In order to carry out his mission, the onetime World War I flier needed a plane—preferably a twin-engined Messerschmitt-110, Germany's newest and fastest long-range fighter. He approached General Ernst Udet, Göring's highly regarded chief of supply and procurement for the Luftwaffe, and requested such a machine for the purpose of "training flights." Udet was polite in his reply but said that he must first receive permission from the Führer. Hess decided not to force the issue, for Hitler had forbidden his top lieutenants to risk accident by piloting their own planes.

Like many disturbed persons with a driving sense of mission, Hess could be cunning. He journeyed to Augsburg and there sought a plane from his old friend Professor Willy Messerschmitt, the famous aircraft designer. The professor was somehow persuaded to give Hess his plane, equipped with auxiliary fuel tanks.

In a flurry of activity, Hess started to obtain weather reports on North Sea conditions aloft. He practiced reading radio directional signals from the Luftwaffe transmitter in Kalundborg, Denmark; they would be critical for any overwater flight. He posted a map of northern Europe on the wall of his bedroom, and studied the checkpoints on a route northwest from Augsburg.

During the winter, Rudolf Hess made about 20 training

flights out of Augsburg. By spring he was fully proficient.

In his study one night in January 1941, Hess wrote the most important letter of his life. Then he journeyed to Augsburg and before taking off he gave a copy to his adjutant, Captain Karlheinz Pintsch, with instructions that it was to be handed personally to Adolf Hitler if Hess did not return to the airfield within four hours.

Late that afternoon, Rudolf Hess strapped himself into the Me-110, taxied out to the runway and climbed into the sky. Everything went smoothly for a few hours—but then an aileron jammed. With difficulty, Hess turned around and returned to Augsburg, where he landed safely. From the look on Pintsch's face, he could tell that the adjutant had opened and read the letter. Hess said, ''You mustn't say a word about what has transpired today!'' Pintsch swore that he would not mention the letter or Hess's flight.

In the weeks that followed, Hess tried to relax. He spent an unusual amount of time with his son and even asked that pictures be taken of the two of them—a surprising request, because he had always been reluctant to be photographed. On one occasion, he took a book Ilse was reading and leafed through the pages—which seemed to confirm his mystical insights. The volume was the *Pilot's Book of Everest,* the story of the Duke of Hamilton's flight over Mount Everest a few years before. Hess stared at a photo of the Duke, then returned the volume to Ilse, remarking only that he had met Hamilton in Berlin in 1936.

On May 1, Hess returned to Augsburg, where he gave a long May Day speech praising German workers and spoke warmly of his personal relationship with Messerschmitt and his firm. Three days later he was summoned to Berlin for a special session of the Reichstag. This could only have made him uneasy. He would have to sit next to Adolf Hitler on the government bench.

By now, he had decided to make another attempt on May 10, a Saturday. After lunch that day, Hess changed into the Luftwaffe pilot's uniform he had worn while on his training mission. He got into his Mercedes and ordered his chauffeur to drive swiftly to Augsburg. The few attendants and officials present at the Messerschmitt field had seen Hess there many times before. He climbed into the cockpit of the Me-110 and took off at 6:10 p.m.

Hess flew north over Germany to the North Sea and then headed west. As he crossed the coast of Scotland, he managed to slip past the British coastal patrol by ducking into the clouds. He flew onward to Lanarkshire, Scotland, and circled to identify what he thought was the Duke of Hamilton's residence.

Five hours after takeoff, Rudolf Hess bailed out of the plane and landed by parachute in a farmer's field near the village of Eaglesham, 12 miles from the Duke of Hamilton's estate. He was immediately taken captive by the farmer; later, the British authorities, at his request, allowed him to see the Duke. Gravely, the Deputy Führer explained to that nonplused gentleman that he was on a mission of humanity and that the Führer wished to stop the fighting. The British were incredulous, and as they listened to Hess they quickly became convinced that he was mad. They took him away to London, and delayed announcement of his arrival for two days—while the Nazi leaders were left to sweat.

On Sunday morning, May 11, the sun shone brilliantly through the large picture window in the spacious living room of the Berghof, Hitler's Bavarian retreat. In the distance shimmered the peaks of the Alps. Though he had come to the Berghof for relaxation, Hitler still followed the military reports with avid interest. It was good to hear that London was in flames, with only modest Luftwaffe losses.

Albert Speer, who was waiting in the anteroom, noticed that two of Hess's adjutants, Karlheinz Pintsch and Alfred Leitgen, were standing there pale and frightened. Pintsch reported to Albert Bormann, Martin's brother and one of Hitler's assistants, that he had a letter for the Führer from Rudolf Hess. Bormann scowled. Surely these men knew that Hitler did not like to receive letters from the old party fighters, who were always requesting favors and making complaints. Hess's thoughts, in particular, were no longer of pressing interest to Hitler. But Captain Pintsch was insistent, and Bormann took the letter to the Führer.

Hitler read it and emitted what Speer called "an inarticulate animal-like outcry." Summoning Pintsch, Hitler furiously demanded if he knew what Hess had written. "Yes, my Führer," Pintsch said. Hitler screamed, "Arrest him!"

The Führer stormed back and forth yelling for Martin Bormann. Then he cried, "I've got to talk to Göring right away." Field Marshal Keitel, who was present, had suffered through many Hitler outbursts, but he had never seen anything like this. He stood at attention, awaiting orders. The whole Berghof came alive as Hitler summoned the Nazi old guard to the mountaintop. "Get me Udet and Ribbentrop. Where's Bormann? Get him in here immediately!"

Hitler calmed down a bit as Martin Bormann appeared; at least one man was reliable. "Oh, my God, my God! Hess has flown to England! Get Udet on the telephone!" While awaiting the aviator's voice, Hitler began to talk as if there were no one else present. "I can't recognize Hess in it. It's a different person. Something must have happened to him—some mental disturbance."

When he finally had Udet on the telephone, Hitler demanded what the chances were that Rudolf Hess might successfully fly the 800 miles from Augsburg to England. Udet assured him that Hess was bound to fail. Hitler relaxed a little more and said, "Let's hope he crashes into the sea!"

Hitler looked at the letter again, reading more carefully: "My Führer, when you receive this letter I shall be in England." Hess explained his peace mission, and concluded: "And if, my Führer, this project, which I admit has but very small chance of success, ends in failure and the fates decide against me, it will always be possible for you to deny all responsibility. Simply say I am crazy."

An adjutant now entered and told Bormann that Ilse Hess was on the telephone, saying she was worried about her husband. Bormann left the room and spoke to Frau Hess. He gave her no information, but he told her to remain calm.

Bormann returned to find Hitler immersed in self-pity. "Who will believe me," the Führer groaned, "when I say that Hess did not fly there in my name, that the whole thing is not some sort of intrigue behind the backs of my allies?" Hitler turned to Bormann and said, "We had better send Ribbentrop to Rome right away."

After a sleepless night, Hitler met his gathering paladins. The group assembled in the living room. Nobody seemed to know what to do. After much discussion Hitler issued a communiqué informing the world that Hess, in an unauthorized plane flight, had doubtless met with an accident and had left behind a letter "showing traces of a mental disturbance that justifies the fear that Hess was the victim of hallucinations."

Later, after the British had announced that Hess was being held captive in England, Hitler felt obliged to make an even stronger announcement. Reich press chief Otto Dietrich, recalling Hess's fascination with the occult, said, "My Führer, may I suggest that we allude to astrologers, mesmerists, delusions in our communiqué?" Hitler liked the words and endorsed the thesis.

Hitler then issued a flurry of orders. "Bormann, summon all the Reichsleiters and gauleiters here for a meeting." "Have Ribbentrop report directly to me after his conversations with Mussolini." "Inform me immediately of any word from England." "Arrest or hold for questioning all astrologers, seers, necromancers, and others who may have had a hand in this affair!"

Bormann turned to carry out the instructions. But Hitler recalled him and ordered him to bring in a secretary. She took down yet another, far more momentous order:

"The former office of Deputy to the Führer henceforth is to be known as the Party Chancellery. It is to be under my personal command. Its chief executive officer is Reichsleiter Martin Bormann."

Effective control of the Nazi Party had just been turned over to the man who would prove to be the most skillful of Hitler's lieutenants in accumulating and wielding power.

NAZIFYING A NATION

om a window in the Chancellery, newly appointed Chancellor Adolf Hitler waves to a saluting crowd of Berliners on his first day in power, January 30, 1933.

A PARTY LED BY FINGERSPITZENGEFÜHL

The National Socialist German Workers' Party almost died a-borning in 1919. It numbered only a few dozen grumblers; it had no organization and no coherent political ideas. Just 14 years later, the Nazi Party was legally governing a nation of 66 million Germans—and was busily legalizing an absolute dictatorship.

This political miracle was the work of one man, Adolf Hitler, who took over the party in 1920. Hitler had what the Germans called *Fingerspitzengefühl,* or fingertip touch—an uncanny sense of political tactics and timing. With this gift, he swiftly adapted to changing conditions and turned adversity to his party's advantage. Without this gift, his powerful oratory and dynamic leadership would have failed—and there would have been no Third Reich.

Hitler despised parliamentary government and was, at first, determined to take power by force, marching on Berlin much as his idol Mussolini had marched on Rome. But he quickly learned through an abortive putsch that what might succeed in Italy would fail in Germany. Each country, he admitted, "must evolve its own methods of regeneration." For Germany, the methods must be legal, to appeal to the burgher as well as the revolutionary.

Hitler detested electioneering—"passing a magnet over a dunghill," he called it—but he tirelessly crisscrossed the country wooing voters. Though he often shifted party strategy, he never allowed Nazi ideology to waver. Over and over again, at mass rallies, in homes, workshops and board rooms, he hammered away at his favorite themes: love of fatherland, hatred of the "criminals" who had "stabbed the nation in the back"—i.e., the German leaders of the Weimar Republic who had submitted to the Versailles Treaty. Hitler continually sounded the same fist-shaking challenge: "German misery must be broken with German steel."

Hitler thus made himself recognized as the voice of German nationalism. And in January 1933, when he became Chancellor, millions of Germans believed in their government for the first time since the Great War. "Everyone felt," a supporter fondly recalled, "that things would get better."

Adolf Hitler in slouch hat and trench coat chats with General Erich Ludendorff and other defendants during a court recess in their 1924 putsch trial.

Surrounded by adoring Berliners, Hitler heads for his limousine during the Nazis' 1934 May Day festival, organized to honor "workers of head and hand."

In spite of the freezing weather, 20,000 spectators gather on Munich's Märzfeld parade grounds in 1923 to watch the first Nazi trooping of the colors.

BOISTEROUS, VIOLENT BAVARIAN DAYS

In late January of 1923—hard times for Germany and therefore favorable for protest—the fledgling Nazi Party held its first big rally in Munich. Fearing a clash between the boisterous Nazis and other political groups, Munich officials had prohibited demonstrations. But Hitler defied the authorities, and they backed down.

Party members descended on the Bavarian capital from all parts of Germany to hear Hitler and to enjoy the band music, folk dancing and comedians. Swastika banners flew everywhere as Hitler's 6,000 SA storm troopers passed in review.

The rally was a marvelous attention-getter. Over the next few months, party membership leaped by 35,000 and the SA rolls reached 15,000. "The swastika will be the national symbol," trumpeted the party paper. "The German freedom movement is on the march." But this success was misleading. The Nazis' new popularity led to Hitler's Beer Hall Putsch to seize the Bavarian government. It failed. Hitler was imprisoned and the party was banned.

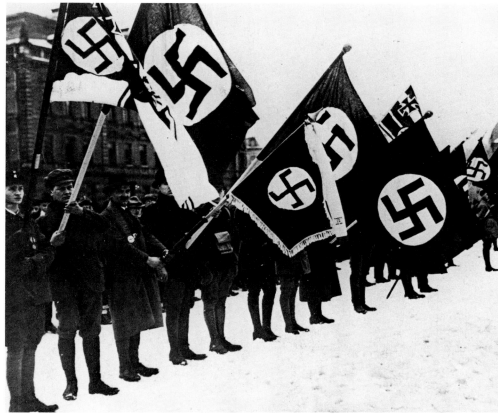

SA men wearing homemade uniforms dip their pennants during a ceremony consecrating new flags.

"Adolf Hitler speaking on Germany's future and our movement," says a poster advertising a Nazi meeting. It added, "No Jews allowed."

Bareheaded in the snow, Hitler condemns the government for having accepted the Versailles Treaty.

Carrying a banner with the slogan "Death to Marxism," disciplined SA troopers parade past Hitler (circled) in Weimar in 1926.

Hitler, flanked by key party officials, presides at a gathering with Nazi gauleiters at the party's headquarters in Munich.

TWO YEARS OF SILENCE AND REORGANIZATION

"This wild beast is checked," boasted the Prime Minister of Bavaria after Hitler's release from prison in December 1924. "We can loosen the chain." But while the Nazi Party was again permitted to function, Hitler remained on a leash, enjoined against addressing public meetings for two years.

The movement floundered, in part because improvement in economic conditions took the sting out of Nazi protest. At this juncture Hitler charted his new route to power—through the electoral process, not armed coups. He used the years of silence to form a solid party apparatus.

He tightened his hold over the large, unruly SA. He gave the gauleiters new importance as political bosses and made them responsible for local indoctrination and membership drives. He recruited bureaucrats to run party headquarters. He obeyed the ban on public speaking, but politicked vigorously at private gatherings.

By 1928, Hitler had transformed the Nazi image: What had once been viewed as a dangerous paramilitary association was behaving like a regular political party, albeit one backed by a corps of storm troopers. The Nazis were ready to compete at the polls.

Hitler confers with party chieftains over coffee at an outdoor restaurant in Munich.

Einer allein von 2000 Millionen Menschen der Erde darf in Deutschland nicht reden!

A Nazi cartoon caption calls Hitler the only man not allowed to speak in Germany.

When their brown shirts were banned, SA storm troopers demonstrated bare-chested.

The brown-shirted bloc of newly elected Nazi deputies fills most of two sections on the left side of Berlin's Reichstag after the party's stunning gains in the 19

lections. Each Nazi answered roll call with a ringing "Present; Heil Hitler."

Hitler greets excited citizens while campaigning in Nuremberg in 1929.

"A NEW WEAPON FOR OUR STRUGGLE"

By the summer of 1930, the Nazis again had the hard times they needed to make dramatic gains: Germany's economic recovery had been undone by the Great Depression. Unemployment neared three million as the nation prepared to elect a new Reichstag.

"Working Germany, awake!" screamed Goebbels' *Der Angriff* newspaper. But Hitler had no intention of pitting class against class. Promising "bread and work for everyone," he launched into a frenzy of activity—shaking hands, kissing babies. He gave 20 major speeches in six weeks; all of them contained free-swinging attacks on the Communists, the international financiers and the inept government. Thousands of local leaders canvassed their districts, wards and blocks to get out the vote.

The election results surprised even the most optimistic Nazis. They had garnered more than six million votes, sending their delegate strength soaring from 12 to 107 seats out of a total 608 in the Reichstag.

The Nazis had now attained the balance of power and used it to paralyze the fragmented Reichstag, barring any Chancellor from governing. "We are a parliamentary party by compulsion," said Hitler. "The victory we have just won is nothing but a new weapon for our struggle."

THE POLITICS OF TURMOIL AND MURDER

In the chaotic early 1930s, Hitler played both sides of the political street. While he announced that he was standing "hard as granite on the ground of legality," his followers practiced Nazi *Realpolitik* as defined by Joseph Goebbels: "He who can conquer the street can also conquer the masses; he who has conquered the masses has thereby conquered the state."

Even as the legally elected Nazi deputies assumed their seats in the Reichstag, SA ruffians dressed in civilian clothes began vandalizing Jewish shops, cafés and department stores. Hardly a day passed without Nazis and Communists engaging in brawls and tit-for-tat murders.

Berlin was the bloodiest battleground. In one month alone, 99 men were killed, another 1,125 wounded in street brawls. The entire city, wrote an American journalist, "lay under an epidemic of infectious fear." There were "whispers of midnight arrests, of prisoners tortured in the SA barracks, made to spit on Lenin's picture, swallow castor oil, eat old socks."

In this lawless climate, democratic institutions disintegrated. The Weimar government was paralyzed. The people, exhausted, saw only one solution: to name Adolf Hitler Chancellor.

Shouting Nazi slogans, German university students fling "racially alien" books into a roaring bonfire in

h square in May 1933. The Nazis went on to purge German libraries and bookstores of unacceptable writings by Sigmund Freud, Thomas Mann and others.

Berliners study a campaign poster freshly pasted up by a Nazi slogan squad. It proclaims: "Hitler—Our Last Hope."

"We demand peace and equal rights," reads the slogan on a map of Germany made by miners scorning the League of Nations.

ELECTIONS TO LEGALIZE THE FÜHRER STATE

Shortly after his appointment as Chancellor, Hitler staged a series of carefully orchestrated plebiscites. By means of these democratic exercises, he intended to convince Germans that democracy was superfluous, that they should legally dispense with it and trust in his personal rule.

The first plebiscite was held on November 12, 1933, to ratify a move he had already made, withdrawing Germany from the League of Nations. The Nazis campaigned vigorously, with Hitler in the forefront as usual. He argued that the Reich could achieve equality with other nations only if all Germans held together "as one man." He offered himself as the rallying point. "Accept me as your Führer. I belong to no class or group. Only to you."

In a resounding endorsement of his policies, more than 95 per cent of the people voted "ja." Swept on this wave of popular sentiment, the Reich Cabinet immediately passed a law proposed by Hitler declaring the Nazi Party to be the official "representative of the German state." Thus Germany became a one-party nation.

Hitler sealed the Nazification of Germany on August 19, 1934. Barely two weeks before, President Paul von Hindenburg had died, and now the German people were being asked to ratify a hastily prepared law combining Hindenburg's vacated presidency with Hitler's chancellorship. The Nazis persuaded Hindenburg's son Oskar to address the nation by radio, urging all Germans "to vote in favor of handing my father's office to the Führer." The next day, 38 million Germans agreed.

Adolf Hitler, for 15 years the driving force of the Nazi Party, was now the heart and soul of the German state.

umping for the August 19, 1934, plebiscite, Hitler urges Hamburg shipyard workers to endorse the law making him President and Chancellor of the Reich.

49

1 *Adolf Hitler*
2 *Alfred Rosenberg, Commissioner for Education and Training*
3 *Max Amann, Nazi publisher*
4 *Walter Buch, leader of the Supreme Party Court*
5 *Heinrich Hoffmann, Hitler's personal photographer*
6 *Franz Xaver Schwarz, party treasurer*
7 *Hans Frank, minister without portfolio*
8 *Wilhelm Frick, Interior Minister*
9 *Martin Bormann, assistant to the Deputy Führer*
10 *Robert Ley, leader of the German Labor Front*
11 *Adolf Wagner, Gauleiter of Munich-Upper Bavaria*
12 *Otto Dietrich, Reich press chief*
13 *Joseph Goebbels, Propaganda Minister*

Under the paternal gaze of their Führer, officials of the triumphant
Nazi Party, identified above, assemble in the new Reich Chancellery to
pay homage to Adolf Hitler on his 50th birthday, April 20, 1939.
Berliners were treated to a pageant of Luftwaffe flyovers, marching bands
and goose-stepping troops that lasted throughout the day and climaxed
at midnight with a torchlight parade of Nazi Party members.

2

If Martin Bormann had written the scenario for his rise to power in the Nazi Party, he could hardly have conjured up better opportunities than those that came his way unbidden in May and June of 1941. It was pure luck that Deputy Führer Rudolf Hess had departed for England and left vital responsibilities that Bormann took over in his new post as chief of the Nazi Party Chancellery. Better still, Adolf Hitler was increasingly engrossed in final preparations for the invasion of the Soviet Union, which was scheduled to begin on June 22.

Hitler's preoccupation with military affairs gave Bormann a chance to play the leading role in the administration of the Reich. Bormann's purpose was, as ever, to serve his Führer efficiently. But to do so, he had to serve his own interests as well, establishing firm personal control over the whole apparatus of the party. For Bormann, duty and ambition were synonymous.

That Bormann had set his sights so high occurred to few of the top Nazi leaders. They tended to take him lightly because he had spent his 14 years as a party member in inconspicuous administrative posts, and it was his style to work quietly behind the scenes. Yet this drab bureaucrat had a mind of dazzling subtlety and boldness.

Soon after the Nazis took power in Germany, Bormann won Hitler's gratitude with an ingenious money-raising plan. He convinced the head of the postal service that Hitler had rights to a royalty for every postage stamp bearing his likeness. The revenue on each stamp was a tiny amount, but since most German stamps portrayed the Führer, the scheme raised millions of reichsmarks for his private use.

Bormann's biggest coup had been his creation of the Adolf Hitler-Spende, a private slush fund made up of enormous cash contributions from German industrialists whose companies had profited from Hitler's rearmament program, among them the I. G. Farben chemical cartel, the Krupp arms works and the Siemens electrical combine. Bormann used the fund for land purchases and lavish building programs to enlarge Hitler's retreat in the Bavarian Alps, the Berghof. In recognition of his general efficiency and all his personal services to Hitler, he was officially made a permanent member of Hitler's entourage in 1937.

No possibility for personal advancement was too small to escape Bormann's notice. One of his seemingly trivial

ALL THE "LITTLE HITLERS"

chores was to make room assignments in the hotel where Hitler stayed during the Nuremberg party rallies; Bormann capitalized on the task by awarding rooms near Hitler's suite to leaders from whom he wanted a favor. He pleased the party's "Old Fighters" by starting a compulsory aid plan for Nazi veterans injured in the early struggles. Since all Nazis had to subscribe, a huge surplus accrued, and the party coffers swelled with the extra receipts.

No less than Hitler himself, Bormann was a keen judge of men, and he used his judgment in ways just as unfathomable as the Führer's. For example, Alfred Rosenberg, the party's chief ideologue, had incurred Bormann's enmity by attempting to take over the post vacated by Hess. Yet in the days before the Soviet invasion, Bormann went about recommending Rosenberg for appointment as the party's principal representative in the territories to be conquered by the German armies. Bormann's tactic was not a simple effort to get Rosenberg out of his way; his schemes went deeper and further than that. He had long since pegged Rosenberg as a weak, ineffectual man, and he expected to manipulate him with ease in the Soviet post, which might otherwise fall to a more formidable rival.

Bormann's maneuvers were based on a principle universally recognized in the upper echelons of the party: that Hitler was the source of all power. But Bormann alone planned to monopolize that source of power—to make Hitler so dependent on him that he could deny rivals access to the Führer. Bormann was well on his way toward that goal even as three million German soldiers moved into attack positions along the Russian front.

Bormann had found the key to his success in Hitler's eccentric work habits. The Führer never sat quietly at his desk and studied papers in order to arrive at a decision; as Reich press chief Otto Dietrich put it, "Hitler could not concentrate sitting down and keeping silent—he had to be moving about and talking." While the Führer nervously paced to and fro, someone would explain the problem to him, and increasingly that someone was Martin Bormann. "He had the ability," said Walter Schellenberg, the chief of the SS foreign-intelligence service, "to simplify complicated matters, to present them concisely, and summarize the essential points in a few clear sentences. So cleverly did he do it that even his briefest reports contained an implicit solution."

Once the perambulating Führer had reached a decision, another problem arose. "Hitler did not issue orders in writing," Dietrich explained. "Instead he impulsively issued them orally to whoever happened to be standing near him." Visitors to Hitler would frequently extract some promise from him that they would then pass on independently as a *Führerbefel,* or Führer Order. Many a Führer Order was diametrically opposed to another Führer Order—producing numerous disagreements that brought important functions to a confused halt.

Bormann's knack of explaining problems to the Führer was matched by his uncanny ability to translate Hitler's rambling reactions into clearly understandable Führer Orders that could be released without fear of conflict with other orders. His proposals "are so exactly worked out," Hitler once told an aide, "that I only need to say 'yes' or 'no.' With him I dispatch in ten minutes a pile of papers over which other men take hours of my time."

Bormann was, in short, becoming Hitler's administrative alter ego. He basked in Hitler's growing trust, and in the lengthening periods they spent together he smoothly voiced the exact sentiments that the Führer wanted to hear. When they dined just two days before the start of the Soviet invasion, Hitler was nervous and fretful, haunted by last-minute doubts. But Bormann, Walter Schellenberg recalled, quickly put the Führer's mind at rest. "You are burdened with great worries just now," he said with respectful sympathy. "The successful conclusion of this great campaign depends on you alone. Providence has appointed you as her instrument for deciding the future of the whole world. No one knows better than I do that you have devoted the whole of yourself to this task, that you've studied every conceivable detail of this problem. I am convinced that you have planned everything thoroughly, and that your great mission will surely succeed."

As head of the Party Chancellery, Bormann was the chief administrative officer of the party and its eight million members. But to wield the power that went with the title, he had to install in numerous key posts men who were personally loyal to him. This called for complicated maneuvers to shift existing jurisdictions and personnel.

Bormann's immediate goal was to strengthen his control of the party's executive and policy-making body, the *Politsche Organisation* (Political Organization), or PO for short, which in turn controlled eight official divisions and numerous affiliated organizations. The official divisions included the potent SS, the Hitler Youth and such support groups as the National Socialist Motor Corps and the Fliers' Corps. The affiliates were special interest groups such as the Nazi Lawyers' Guild, the National Socialist Retailers' Association and the Reich Veterans' Association. The largest of the affiliates was the German Labor Front, the enormous Nazi-run labor union in which membership was compulsory for employers as well as employees.

The PO was itself a huge organization with a quarter of a million employees. It was directed by a staff of some 200 administrators established in the party's headquarters, the Brown House complex in Munich. The PO's influence and prestige had seriously declined under the lax administration of the otherworldly Rudolf Hess. Now Bormann proposed to turn this rusty apparatus into a well-oiled, efficient political machine.

At the top of the PO's sprawling hierarchy were the Reichsleiters and the gauleiters—politicians appointed by Hitler himself. There were 16 Reichsleiters, and they made up a sort of supreme party cabinet. Among the most well-known Reichsleiters, Joseph Goebbels was in charge of party propaganda, Alfred Rosenberg was the party's theoretician on foreign policy, Robert Ley was responsible for regulating the party organization and for running the German Labor Front, and Franz Xaver Schwarz held the party's purse strings as treasurer.

Other members of this Nazi cabinet had no special responsibility and very little power; their appointment to the rank of Reichsleiter was merely a reward for longtime loyalty or extraordinary service to the party during the 1920s and 1930s. In this category were Karl Fiehler, the Lord Mayor of Munich, and—until recently—a shadowy bureaucrat in Rudolf Hess's office named Martin Bormann.

In the official party pecking order, the Reichsleiters outranked their colleagues the gauleiters. Actually, though, the nominal subordinates were often more powerful than their superiors. While the Reichsleiters administered vaguely defined policies, the gauleiters were firmly in control of day-to-day party affairs within 42 clearly defined geographical

regions called gaus *(Gaue* in German). The gaus varied greatly in both size and population, ranging from a city such as Berlin with more than four million inhabitants to sparsely populated rural gaus such as Carinthia with only 450,000 people.

Each gau was divided into *Kreise,* or counties, with an average of 15 to 20 in each gau. A kreis, whose leader was called a *Kreisleiter,* was subdivided into districts or townships, each of which was headed by a local group leader. Below were the ward leaders, and below them the block wardens, who kept watch over four to eight houses or apartment buildings. At the bottom were the ordinary party members, mostly shopkeepers, small businessmen, craftsmen, schoolteachers, white-collar workers, veterans, industrial laborers and foremen.

The chief links in this long chain of command were the

Smiling ingratiatingly, Secretary to the Führer Martin Bormann enjoys some snapshots with Hitler. The corpulent Bormann went to extraordinary lengths to please his boss; on many occasions he even shared the Führer's vegetarian meals—but then retired furtively to his quarters to feast on his own favorites, Wiener schnitzel and pork chops.

60-odd Reichsleiters and gauleiters. They were a mixed bag. In their ranks were bankers, teachers, industrial managers and a few beer-hall brawlers and street-corner agitators. All were proudly and aggressively loyal to Adolf Hitler, and in return the Führer was willing to overlook the gauleiters' arrogance and independence.

Under Hitler's tolerant eye, the gauleiters had long since turned their territorial bases into more or less autonomous fiefdoms, where they reigned with the hauteur of feudal princes; one of them, Wilhelm Kube, Gauleiter of Ostmark, insisted that church bells be rung to announce his arrival anywhere in his domain. Several gauleiters had informed central party officials that they would obey only those orders coming directly from Hitler himself. For their outright defiance, Hitler nicknamed his cronies *Gaugrafen,* or gau counts, while frustrated party bureaucrats dubbed them "Little Hitlers."

Inevitably, the arrogant gauleiters caused trouble for their superiors. Adolf Wagner, the Gauleiter of Munich-Upper Bavaria, had enraged his many Catholic constituents by demanding that the Crucifix be removed from school classrooms and be replaced with the picture of Adolf Hitler. Even more bothersome was Julius Streicher, Gauleiter of Franconia and the publisher of the pornographic anti-Semitic journal *Der Stürmer.* Streicher's flagrant corruption, sexual aberrations and personal eccentricities—which included walking to work in bathing trunks when the spirit moved him—became a constant source of embarrassment to the party hierarchs.

In spite of these abuses, Hitler resisted suggestions that he fire his loyal old friends. Reluctantly he agreed to the suspension of Julius Streicher in 1940; Hitler allowed him to keep his title but never reinstated him. Yet the stiffest treatment he authorized was the banishment of the most corrupt gauleiters to administrative posts in the conquered territories. Two of these outcasts—Gauleiters Erich Koch and Wilhelm Kube—went on to win infamy as brutal Nazi rulers in the Soviet Union.

The intricate Nazi Party apparatus represented only one side of the dual bureaucracy that governed wartime Germany. At every level, the party offices paralleled or encroached on traditional bureaus of German government: the Reich Ministries of Economics, Labor, Foreign Policy and the Interior; the offices of provincial governors, city mayors and county executives; and the vast army of civil servants who handled the daily administration of a Germany that now included some 80 million citizens.

The Nazis had several reasons for preserving these pre-Nazi structures. The old forms of national and local government were familiar, respected and instinctively obeyed by most citizens. Then too, the Nazi Party had not attracted enough educated and experienced administrators to fill the tens of thousands of civil service positions. And the Nazi leaders much preferred to control the state from the outside. This arrangement left most of the onerous paper work to the state and relieved the party of such unpopular government tasks as collecting taxes and dispensing justice in the civil courts.

It was relatively easy for the party drones to dominate their hard-working government counterparts. For example, the kreisleiters controlled local governments by means of two convenient laws that the Nazis had railroaded through the Reichstag during the 1930s. One law had given the kreisleiters wide authority in the appointment of county executives and town mayors, and veto power over local budgets. The second law had extended the kreisleiters' sway by awarding them the power to make appointments and promotions throughout the civil service.

The kreisleiters made effective use of these laws and assumed any additional powers they needed to exercise absolute control over the lives and livelihoods of government officials and ordinary citizens in their districts. They gave direct orders to mayors and placed their friends in the best municipal and civil service positions. They maintained local discipline through their authority to approve or withhold marriage licenses and ration cards, applications for aid to dependent children, welfare benefits and such coveted civilian medals as the Gold Honor Cross, which was awarded for childbearing.

Kreisleiters assumed the roles of mediator in business disputes and enforcer of local ordinances. They protected small businesses owned by friends and enthusiastic Nazis against large diversified businesses, such as department stores. For example, one kreisleiter with a friend who owned a garden-equipment store forced the local variety store to stop selling gardening tools. Backsliding Nazis who failed to contribute money or worktime to the party could not count on preferential treatment.

At the outbreak of the War in 1939, the authority of the Nazi bureaucrats had been enhanced by their appointment as chiefs of the civilian war effort in their respective territories. The title of the gauleiters in this new post was Reich Defense Commissioner, and they were charged with an important duty. "Let no one report," Hitler had warned them, "that morale might be low in his gau. You are responsible for morale in your gau." It was an injunction that the gauleiters took seriously. To maintain morale—and their own popularity with the Führer—they worked hard to keep the local populace supplied with sufficient food, fuel and consumer goods. But in many ways their zeal worked against the war effort they were supposed to support.

To keep the people in their gaus happy, the gauleiters ran local industry with little or no regard for policy directives from either the government or the central party offices. They blocked efforts to put the Reich on a wartime footing so that local factories would keep churning out consumer goods—shoes, radios, cosmetics and vacuum cleaners. They lobbied to prevent the drafting of women or skilled factory workers for war service. When British bombers started pounding German towns and cities in May of 1940, some gauleiters were so anxious to prevent grumbling that they looted supply trains passing through their gaus and distributed the goods to local citizens.

The confusions caused by the gauleiters' plural offices were at least matched by the intermixed functions of the party and the government at the exalted Reichsleiter level. The party's Reichsleiters had as counterparts the government's Reich Ministers, and the Party Cabinet, or *Reichsleitung*, was duplicated by the Reich Cabinet. There were some instances in which the Reichsleiter and the Reich Minister were one and the same person. Joseph Goebbels, for example, was both the head of party propaganda and the Reich Minister of Popular Enlightenment and Propaganda—not to mention Gauleiter of Berlin.

Some Reich Ministers had more than one competing counterpart among the party Reichsleiters. Joachim von Ribbentrop, for example, was Reich Minister for Foreign Affairs, but Alfred Rosenberg held title as chief of the party's foreign-policy office and Ernst-Wilhelm Bohle headed the Foreign Organization of the National Socialist Party. Other Reich Ministers were Ministers in name only. In this unhappy category fell the Minister of Labor, Franz Seldte, whose power and influence had been usurped by the party's German Labor Front under Reichsleiter Robert Ley.

To compound the confusion still further, Hitler had also created such super-ministerial posts as the Plenipotentiary of the Four-Year Plan. This economic planning function was given to the Reich Air Minister, Hermann Göring, who thus superseded the Reich Minister of Economics, Walther Funk. Göring could and did issue orders that contravened directives from other Reich Ministers.

The Reich Ministers theoretically formed a Reich Cabinet to advise Hitler on decisions of government. But the Ministers were so torn by jealousy and personal rivalries that they could never agree on a chairman. Eventually Hitler lost patience with their bickering. After the outbreak of the War, he not only refused to call a single Cabinet meeting but actually forbade the Reich Ministers to meet as a group, even for a beer party.

To complete the array of parallel party and state authorities, the government machinery included a Reich Chancellery as well. The Reich Chancellery, the counterpart of Martin Bormann's Party Chancellery, consisted of a staff of 100 under lawyer Hans-Heinrich Lammers, a civil servant who performed for the state the same job that Bormann performed for the party—and just as capably. The difference was that the Reich Chancellery and its apparatus was virtually powerless.

This enormous nonsystem of overlapping offices and duplicated functionaries was expensive, wasteful and inefficient. It was a source of continual quarreling between the offices of the party and the state and also among party leaders themselves. It created what press chief Dietrich accurately described as "the greatest confusion that has ever existed in a civilized state."

And yet the monstrous, ungainly apparatus served certain purposes. Adolf Hitler had done all he could to create and encourage bureaucratic chaos, so that he alone stood above the confusion and feuding as the final arbiter of disputes. Hitler's own power could only be enhanced by the rivalries

Martin Bormann hovers in the background (right) as the Führer welcomes his Nazi Party gauleiters to a conference held in 1943. Bormann maneuvered tirelessly and cleverly to use these provincial leaders for his own purposes, flooding them with political assignments and directives.

among his subordinates and the conflicts between them and their opposite numbers in the state bureaucracy. The exhausting infighting left Hitler's lieutenants with neither the energy nor the inclination to mount any effective challenges to his own supreme authority as Führer.

The rivalries also had a constructive side. "Friction," Hitler once told an associate, "creates heat and heat is an excellent source of energy." With two or three subordinates competing in every important policy area, Hitler could be sure that his decisions were effectively, if not efficiently, executed. It was undeniably true, as Otto Dietrich said in retrospect, that Hitler "systematically disorganized the higher departments of government so that he could push the authority of his own will to the point of despotic tyranny." But it was no less true, as an official of the Interior Ministry said, that at the lower levels of the combative bureaucracy, "everyone does his work just to be sure that some other office doesn't grab it."

Hitler was perfectly satisfied by the administrative chaos he had created. But in 1941 his increasing involvement in military affairs made him an absentee landlord in Ger-

many's internal politics. "I've totally lost sight of the organizations of the party," Hitler told a group of dinner companions late in 1941. "When I find myself confronted by one or another of its achievements," I say to myself: 'By God, how that has developed.' " Whatever that development was, it was to a large degree the handiwork of the Führer's new deputy, Martin Bormann.

On May 15, 1941, only three days after his appointment to the Party Chancellery, Bormann dispatched a confidential memo to all Reichsleiters and gauleiters. It was a typical Bormann communiqué, combining a reassurance that business would continue as usual with a self-serving recapitulation of his own accomplishments as a loyal and hardworking functionary in Hitler's entourage. "Anyone who thinks otherwise," he advised, "should tell the Führer at once who he thinks could do my job better than I can."

As was to be expected, a number of Bormann's fellow Reichsleiters thought themselves better suited to head the Party Chancellery. Robert Ley posed the most serious threat from his two power bases.

Ley was Reich Organization Leader, in which capacity he

had broad but vaguely defined responsibilities for deploying the party's political workers and training promising young Nazis for party leadership posts. He was also boss of the German Labor Front and had at his disposal a large bureaucracy and an almost unlimited source of funds from 25 million members' dues. In both of his posts, Ley had ample opportunities to reshuffle personnel records and job assignments, and to influence promotions and the political training of future Nazi leaders.

Robert Ley had no shortage of either organizational ability or vaulting ambition. His main handicap was a pedantic mind: To him, political organization was an exacting science to be pursued with German thoroughness. Ley made order an end in itself, with little regard for the realities of wartime German politics. In his role as Organization Leader, for example, he codified every branch, office, rank, uniform and insignia of the Nazi Party in a massive 600-page manual that became the bible of every aspiring political worker. Ley's guidelines, known as *The Organization Book,* even specified the color of the heads of pins used to denote party leaders' houses on the maps in local offices.

Old party members sneered at such pernickety directives as "Ley's Fairy Tales." But if they had taken a close look at the manual's complex charts and job descriptions, they might have realized that Ley was subtly shifting more and more responsibility to his own office of Reich Organization Leader and head of the Labor Front.

Alfred Rosenberg was one of the earliest victims of Ley's elaborate pettifoggery. As the party's theoretician, Rosenberg was responsible for the ideological purity of all party training courses and materials. But in Ley's *Organization Book,* these responsibilities were transferred to his own office, leaving Rosenberg high and dry as the publisher of a dull monthly party magazine. Rosenberg awakened belatedly to find himself undone.

In the meantime, Ley was busily expanding his system of Nazi training establishments to every gau and kreis in Germany. Youngsters 12 to 18 years old could attend elite Adolf Hitler Schools, at which they combined the study of Nazi racial theories with intensive athletic activities; graduates of the Adolf Hitler Schools could receive advanced political and ideological indoctrination in Ley's *Ordensburgen,* or Order Castles—four-year finishing schools that took

Hitler appears in wartime uniform, wearing his World War I meda...

UNIFORMS TO INSPIRE THE PARTY LOYALISTS

In 1943, at the height of World War II, Germany was a nation in uniform. All told, about 12.5 million Germans, one out of every six, wore official dress. Most were members of regular military units and such organizations as the postal and railway services and local gendarmery. Millions more proudly wore Nazi uniforms.

As supreme soldier of the Reich as well as party chief, Adolf Hitler adopted a garb that served both functions: a Wehrmacht-gray outfit with the Nazi eagle instead of an armband. Except for the Führer's entourage, who usually wore field-gray uniforms similar to his, most party functionaries, such as the district political leader at right, wore trim brown uniforms with oak leaf-bedecked swastika armbands to show rank, and pistols at the waist. So striking was this dress that its wearers were known as "golden pheasants."

Members of the two major paramilitary organizations within the party also wore uniforms that distinguished them from the ranks of the regular Army. The kepi and brown uniform of the Sturmabteilung, or SA, was derived from the dress worn by the early Brownshirt battalions—Hitler's street-fighting storm troops of the 1920s. The grimly distinctive black regalia of the elite Schutzstaffel, or SS, and its Death's-head cap emblem perfectly symbolized its mission of destroying the party's political and racial enemies.

The Waffen-SS—the full-fledged military arm of the SS—fought alongside the Wehrmacht and dressed in the standard field-gray uniform of the Army. But the 800,000 members of the Waffen-SS could be distinguished from their comrades-in-arms by their Death's-head-emblazoned field cap, their SS rune insignia that resembled flashes of lightning and their belt buckle boldly inscribed with the slogan "Loyalty Is My Honor."

Even the nation's children were outfitted for their roles as aspiring party members. Boys between the ages of 10 and 18 in the Hitler Youth wore a short-pants version of the SA uniform. And girls between the ages of 10 and 21 in the League of German Girls wore the navy skirt and white blouse that marked them as the future mothers of the Greater German Reich.

Party District Leader

SA Master Sergeant

SS Technical Sergeant

Waffen-SS Corporal

Hitler Youth Member

League of German Girls Member

A GARISH PROFUSION OF NAZI EMBLEMS AND DECORATIONS

The Nazi Party showered its eight million members with a profusion of medals and insignia designed to enhance their self-esteem and sense of authority.

The commonest category simply identified the wearer as a party man or member of one of its many organs; in addition, the first 100,000 members of the Nazi Party were honored with the prestigious Golden Party Badge. There were scores of organizations, each with a pin of its own, from the Students' League and the Women's League to the Fliers

Corps. And when the uniformed men of the SS changed into mufti, they had a special pin to denote their status.

The Nazis struck medals to commemorate such celebrations as the 1931 party rally in Braunschweig and such milestones as the 1923 Munich Beer Hall Putsch. They also recognized service of every sort. Veterans of the SS were presented with a medal, as were loyal civilian party workers. Mothers were honored with a gold cross for presenting the Reich with eight or more children. The Nation-

al Prize for Art and Science was awarded to such artists and scientists as autobahn builder Fritz Todt and aircraft designer Willy Messerschmitt.

Naturally, the Nazi leaders reserved the supreme decorations for themselves. Perhaps the ultimate in ostentation was reached after the fall of France, when Hitler reinstated the Grand Cross of the Iron Cross for Luftwaffe chief Hermann Göring—and gave it to him in a leather case studded with a small fortune in topazes and diamonds.

Party Eagle Insignia

German University
Student League Pin

National Socialist Fliers
Corps Insignia

Beer Hall Putsch
Commemorative Badge

Golden Party Badge

German National Prize
for Art and Science

Women's League
Membership Pin

SS Civilian
Dress Insignia

Braunschweig Rally
Commemorative Badge

Twelve-Year
SS Service Medal

Gold Honor Cross
for the German Mother

Ten-Year Party Service Medal

Citation Case and Grand Cross of the Iron Cross

their name from the medieval fortresses of the order of Teutonic Knights.

But Ley's gains turned out to be empty ones. There was little demand for his crop of political soldiers; most of his *Ordensjunkers,* or Order Castle graduates, were so inept that no party leaders would employ them. The young graduates, said Albert Speer, "knew nothing about practical life, while on the other hand their arrogance and conceit about their own abilities was boundless." Ultimately, most *Ordensjunkers* were either drafted into the Wehrmacht or shipped off to serve in the occupied Eastern territories.

With Bormann's appointment to the Party Chancellery, Ley saw a new opportunity for gain. The Chancellery ran its own indoctrination program for political leaders, and Ley, seeing Bormann as a new and insecure leader, sought to transfer some of the Chancellery's functions to his own office. This time, however, Ley had made the mistake of underestimating his opponent. Bormann told Ley that his training proposal sounded fine, but that there was one procedural matter: Ley would first have to have his curriculum approved by Rosenberg, the party ideologue. Naturally, Ley refused to submit to his longtime enemy, Rosenberg. In that case, Bormann proposed, he would act as mediator and approve the plans himself. Ley gladly accepted this face-saving compromise, and Bormann at his leisure proceeded to strangle Ley's proposal in miles of red tape.

This was only one of many occasions when Bormann skillfully emulated Hitler's technique of exploiting the bitter rivalries of party officials. He encouraged a long-running three-cornered dispute between Rosenberg, Goebbels and Ley over National Socialist festivals—the pseudoreligious Nazi gatherings that paralleled traditional Christian holidays. He periodically threw fuel on the fiery feuds between Rosenberg and Ribbentrop over foreign policy. He assiduously exacerbated the disputes between Ribbentrop and Goebbels over propaganda in foreign countries.

In time, Ley rebounded from his first defeat at Bormann's hands and attacked from another direction. On this occasion, Ley used his position as keeper of the party's membership files in a transparent attempt to take control of the Chancellery's political organization. Since Hitler had assigned him the task of maintaining statistical information on political personnel, Ley wrote to Bormann, the analysis of personnel files and the preparation of recommendations for all promotions, appointments and dismissals also belonged in his area of responsibility.

Bormann went to Hitler himself for a decision, knowing full well that the Führer, now completely absorbed in moving armies like chess pieces in the Soviet Union, would be irked by the interruption. Hitler made it quite plain that he was not to be bothered with petty intraparty disputes and ordered that no changes be made in personnel policies. In triumph, Bormann replied to Ley: "The Führer orders me to inform you that personnel policy decisions will be referred to the Party Chancellery. The Führer stressed that processing proposals on personnel could be done properly only by someone constantly in his company."

After a few more defeats of this sort, Ley tried to regain some prestige by embarking on a speaking tour of German factories. Bormann encouraged this endeavor, since it gave Ley a new sense of self-importance while at the same time channeled his energies into an activity that presented no threat to the Party Chancellery. Ley misinterpreted or conveniently misconstrued Bormann's interest in his speaking tours. "There is a very curious relationship between Bormann and me," Ley told an associate. "I get the feeling he is jealous because I am always out making speeches while he sits in headquarters and scribbles. I offered to get him some audiences so he could be more in the public eye. But he said he couldn't do that, he was completely incapable of speaking before a group. That was for me to do—that was my big job in the War."

Even as Bormann turned aside Ley's inept challenges, he was working to quash other opposition before it surfaced. Pursuing his plan to monopolize the Führer, he carefully screened requests from party officials for an audience with Hitler. The party's Reichsleiters and gauleiters had to petition Bormann for appointments and explain the nature and purpose of their business with the Führer. Bormann soon made it clear that unless petitioners worked through him he would keep them waiting indefinitely.

In time, Bormann felt confident enough to refuse access to personal friends of Hitler's. In some cases, Bormann used his intimate knowledge of Hitler's eccentricities to turn him against old cronies. Upon deciding that Hitler's personal photographer and friend Heinrich Hoffmann took up too much of the Führer's valuable time, Bormann told Hitler, who was a hypochondriac, that Hoffmann had contracted a highly contagious disease. Hitler was alarmed, and for a while he stopped socializing with his photographer.

Bormann reportedly dared to exclude even the dangerous Reinhard Heydrich, a high-ranking deputy in the SS. On one occasion, when Heydrich flew in from Prague to present an important report to Hitler, Bormann kept him waiting outside Hitler's office for an entire day. At one point, Hitler and Bormann strode through the waiting room without even acknowledging Heydrich's presence. The next day, Bormann coolly informed Heydrich that Hitler had no need to see him.

Even those Nazi leaders who were lucky enough to be granted an audience with Hitler were not safe from Bormann's obstructive tactics. Walther Funk, Reich Minister of Economics, complained that it was "incredibly hard to have a reasonable conversation with the Führer because Bormann butts in all the time. He cuts me short and constantly interrupts."

After experiencing such humiliating treatment at Bormann's hands, most party and government leaders were glad to let Bormann present their problems and proposals to Hitler. Indeed some of them came to appreciate Bormann's bureaucratic efficiency, for they now received almost immediate responses to petitions that previously had gone unanswered for months.

Not all of the petitioners were grateful for Bormann's kind offices. Since Bormann was often the only person present when Hitler delivered his answers, the suspicion grew that Bormann was slanting or twisting the wording of Führer Orders to suit his own purpose. Some Nazi leaders went further, alleging that Bormann had authored certain orders without consulting Hitler at all.

By early 1942, Bormann had amassed such power that even the arrogant gauleiters feared him. Baldur von Schirach, Gauleiter of Vienna, later testified to Bormann's almost unassailable position: "When speaking to a leading party comrade, you would be very careful never to say anything negative about Bormann. You could risk it only with people who made no bones about where they stood, and openly criticized him. There weren't too many of those."

No one could think of a way of shaking Hitler's trust in his "most faithful party comrade." Before long, the Führer would not even tolerate criticism of Bormann. "To win this war I have need of Bormann," Hitler once said. "It's perfectly true that he is both ruthless and brutal, but the fact remains, everybody else has failed in their implicit obedience to my commands. But Bormann, never!"

Besides strictly managing audiences with Hitler, Bormann forged ahead with plans to bend the party to his will. His methods were numerous and varied, devious and crass. He used the Hitler slush fund to bribe allies and supporters. As head of the Party Chancellery, he catered to the status-conscious gauleiters by making sure that their salaries were much higher, and their expense accounts more generous, than those of their opposite numbers in the government. "This power to set the living standard of the Reichsleiters and gauleiters did not attract attention," said Albert Speer, "but it conferred on Bormann more power than many other positions in the hierarchy."

Bormann also exercised enormous influence over political workers of draft age—those between 18 and 29. Fully 20,500 of the PO's 85,000 full-time workers were susceptible to the draft but were officially exempted as critical workers on the home front. As Chancellery head, Bormann had the power to decide party members' draft status and generally he used it to protect them from the Wehrmacht's constant demands for more manpower. Nevertheless, the draft-age party workers knew that one word from Bormann could revoke their privileged status, and to forfend against the possibility of landing on the deadly Russian front, they did all they could to curry Bormann's favor.

These party workers served Bormann well as a private information-gathering force, enabling him to gauge public reaction to decisions in Berlin and events on the military fronts, and to take remedial action when needed. Each Friday, every kreis in Germany prepared a detailed report on the attitudes of local citizens during the preceding week. The reports included accounts of anti-Nazi jokes and rumors as well as the names of anyone who seemed to oppose the Nazi leaders or the war aims. The intelligence was gathered by the party's ward and block leaders as they made regular rounds collecting membership dues, selling raffle tickets for party-sponsored events or settling disputes between landlords and apartment dwellers. The information was then forwarded to the district leader's office, where it was organized into a comprehensive report for Bormann.

By late 1942, the weekly reports reaching Bormann's desk carried news of disturbing reactions among both party members and ordinary citizens to two shattering German defeats: Field Marshal Erwin Rommel's rout in North Africa and, even worse, the entrapment of General Friedrich Paulus' Sixth Army in Stalingrad. The debacle in Stalingrad changed things in Germany as nothing had since Hitler's rise to power. Many party members, the reports noted, no longer gave the traditional *"Heil Hitler!"* greeting, and some began appearing in public without their party badges. Subversive jokes were soon making the rounds. In Catholic Bavaria, where Allied bombers had recently destroyed a housing complex for Nazi leaders near Munich, it was said that the Virgin Mary had saved the city by guiding the bombers to the houses of party members on the outskirts. And cynics in Saxony were suggesting comparisons between the fighting in Russia and the Thirty Years' War. The War seemed to have reached a turning point—and not a good one for the Reich.

The Stalingrad defeat drove Hitler into solitude at the Wolf's Lair, his secret headquarters in a forest near Rastenburg, East Prussia. He was now brooding and embittered. His health was deteriorating; he suffered from gas, headaches, insomnia and a nervous tremor in his left arm and leg. Attended only by his doctor and his military aides—and Bormann—he plunged into plans for new military campaigns. He would emerge from isolation for only two public appearances and two party funerals during the remainder of the War.

The Stalingrad defeat also had the effect of relegating one of Bormann's leading rivals to disgrace and discard. As far back as 1939, Hermann Göring had failed to make good on his rash boast that not a single enemy bomber would ever reach the Ruhr. He had failed in his 1940 vow to obliterate the RAF in the Battle of Britain. Now Göring had broken his promise to the Führer that the Luftwaffe would air-drop enough supplies to sustain the surrounded Sixth Army. Stalingrad was one failure too many; it permanently lost for him the confidence of Hitler—and of the German people.

On a visit to a Berlin market in August 1943, the once-popular Luftwaffe chief was greeted with angry shouts from war-weary citizens: "What about the revenge you promised us? When will the air raids stop?" Göring withdrew to his sumptuous villa at Karinhall, where he found solace in hunting, morphine and his art collection.

For Joseph Goebbels, the Stalingrad disaster provided a golden opportunity to regain lost influence with the Führer, who had had little need for his talents while German armies were winning. Now, Goebbels knew, Hitler was in urgent need of his propaganda to counter the defeatism and war-weariness that were sweeping the Reich. Goebbels' morale-building campaign was more than a newspaper and radio blitzkrieg; he visited bombed cities, sympathized with the citizens in the streets and assumed responsibility for relief to the devastated areas—making himself the most popular Nazi leader in the bargain. If the Führer's reaction was any index, he was more than passingly successful in his efforts. Goebbels, said Hitler in 1943, "is one of the few who today know how to make something useful out of the War."

Under a banner proclaiming "Total War, Shortest War," thousands of Nazi Party members jam Berlin's Sports Palace on February 18, 1943, to hear Propaganda Minister Joseph Goebbels (at the podium) deliver a rousing appeal for drastic cutbacks in civilian living standards. Goebbels augmented the crowd's spontaneous enthusiasm by playing recorded applause over the loudspeaker and by calling forth well-organized chants of "German men, to your weapons!" and "German women, to work!"

Martin Bormann realized that Goebbels had become a formidable rival. But he was now prepared to face any threat. He had succeeded in reducing the power of the strutting corps of gauleiters by infiltrating their organizations with personally picked cronies who carried out his wishes right under their noses. He had pulled the teeth of the Reichsleiters by closing Hitler's door to them. He had undermined Robert Ley, who was drowning his failures in alcohol and was a public embarrassment to the party.

Bormann now used the Stalingrad crisis to expand his power into areas clearly outside his jurisdiction as party boss. He began to meddle actively in military affairs and to intervene in such governmental spheres as economic and judicial policy. To further these schemes, he allied himself with Hitler's chief military adviser, Field Marshal Wilhelm Keitel, and with the head of the Reich Chancellery, Hans-Heinrich Lammers, to form what became known as the Committee of Three. The idea was that the committee would steer the war effort in a more manageable and reasonable way, at the same time filtering all information destined for Hitler's action.

As might have been expected, the Committee of Three was quickly reduced to a committee of one. Keitel had already revealed himself as an irrelevant figurehead; he was bypassed by the chiefs of the Army, Navy and Luftwaffe, who had long despised him as Hitler's yes man and who had access to Hitler through their own adjutants. The pliant Lammers was easily disposed of; Bormann simply blocked his attempts to see Hitler, forcing Lammers to depend on him to present his point of view to the Führer. With the majority of government and party leaders effectively isolated from Hitler, Bormann could now run the internal affairs of the Reich as he wished.

Goebbels had no sooner returned to the Führer's favor than he challenged Bormann's stranglehold on domestic politics. It was outrageous, Goebbels asserted, that a mere party administrator like Bormann, who had "no qualifications for the real tasks of leadership," should manipulate the Committee of Three so that he could "establish a sort of kitchen cabinet and to erect a wall between the Führer and his ministers." Thus the stage was set for a ruthless power struggle between two of Hitler's most ambitious deputies.

In many ways, the two rivals were opposites. Bormann was uncultured and practically unknown to the German people. Goebbels was famous and sophisticated—a man who could demolish most rivals by the sheer force of his wit and biting sarcasm.

Goebbels had begun preparing for the clash as early as December 1942 by forming an alliance against Bormann. His allies were Albert Speer, now Armaments Minister; Walther Funk, the Minister of Economics; and Robert Ley, who was still Reich Organization Leader and head of the German Labor Front.

Goebbels had chosen his allies carefully. They were all bitter enemies of Bormann, who had thwarted each of them at one time or another. They were an intellectual minority within the Nazi Party, for they all had university training. And they were all of one mind on the measures needed to snap the country out of its post-Stalingrad depression and to regain the initiative on the battlefield.

The trouble was, Goebbels said, that Germany still had more than six million people producing consumer goods, that 1.5 million women were still employed as domestic servants, and that 100,000 restaurants and amusement centers still remained open as if it were peacetime. There had to be drastic cutbacks in living standards in order to release more manpower and material for the fighting fronts. Germans had to abandon the idea that they could not lose the War. "Of course we can lose the War," Goebbels told his department heads at the Propaganda Ministry in January 1943. "The War can be lost by people who will not exert themselves; it will be won by those who try the hardest."

Fired up with enthusiasm, Goebbels sent his proposals for full mobilization to Hitler—and Bormann let the papers go through. The campaign would be launched under Goebbels' slogan: "Total War." Hitler quickly endorsed the idea, but in a manner that bitterly disappointed Goebbels.

The Total War campaign, Hitler ordered, would be administered by Bormann's Committee of Three. Goebbels would serve as an adviser. It turned out that Bormann had not only appropriated Goebbels' idea but had convinced Hitler that Goebbels himself had suggested that the Committee of Three carry out his proposals.

Bormann's real interest in Total War was limited to thwarting Goebbels. If Total War won the day, Bormann might have to abandon his ambitious building program at the Berghof, where 5,000 foreign laborers were busy expanding Hitler's estate, and he had no intention of doing that. Besides, his friend Fritz Sauckel, a gauleiter who also served as Plenipotentiary for the Allocation of Labor, was firmly opposed to drafting factory workers and women so long as he could round up slave laborers in the occupied countries. And the gauleiters themselves, as Bormann knew well, would fight tooth and nail against any disruption of their local economies.

Nevertheless, Goebbels intended to fight for his plan. If Bormann, Sauckel and the gauleiters were going to sabotage his efforts for Total War, he would go over their heads with an appeal to Hitler himself. It would be delivered in a manner calculated to jolt the Führer: a rousing speech given before an enormous audience of party faithful in Berlin's Sports Palace.

On February 18, 1943, Goebbels stepped up to the speakers' podium of the Sports Palace to deliver the most important speech of his career. He had personally planned every detail of the stage setting and had carefully calculated the emotional effect of every sentence of his speech. Above his head stretched an enormous banner with the slogan "Total War, Shortest War" in huge bold letters. The audience of 15,000 had been brought by train, bus and plane from all over Germany.

In the front row sat the elite of party and state: the Reichsleiters, gauleiters, Reich Ministers and generals of the armed forces. Behind them Goebbels had placed representative groups from every segment of German society: artists, intellectuals, teachers, civil servants, engineers, office workers, tradesmen and ordinary soldiers. Around the stage he had carefully positioned wounded veterans from the Eastern Front; their bandaged wounds and the white-smocked Red Cross nurses attending them stood out in a sea of brown and gray uniforms. Microphones of the Greater German Radio Network stood at the ready to transmit the speech into every home in Germany.

The heart of Goebbels' speech consisted of 10 questions and answers, a format that made full use of his masterful oratory and built the audience up to an emotional pitch.

"I ask you," Goebbels' responsive reading began, "do you believe with the Führer and with the rest of us in the final total victory of the German people? Are you determined to follow the Führer through thick and thin in the struggle for victory and to put up even with the heaviest personal burdens?"

The Sports Palace echoed with roars of affirmation.

"I ask you," Goebbels continued, "are you and are the German people determined, when the Führer orders it, to work ten, twelve, or if necessary fourteen and sixteen hours a day and to give your utmost for victory?"

Thousands of voices shouted "Yes," and spontaneous demonstrations broke out in the giant arena, with flags and banners waving, and shouts of "Hail, the Führer" and "Leader, command, we follow!"

Arriving at the key question of the occasion, Goebbels demanded, "I ask you: Do you want Total War? Do you want it, if necessary more total and more radical than we can even imagine it today?"

By the time Goebbels had finished his 10 questions, the huge crowd was on its feet, applauding and cheering wildly. "I asked you," Goebbels told them, "and you gave me your answers. You are part of the German people and from your mouth the attitude of the German people has become manifest." Goebbels brought the event to its emotional climax with his electrifying conclusion: "Now, Nation, arise! Storm, break loose!"

A German journalist covering the meeting observed that if Goebbels had asked the crowd, "Do you wish to die?" they would have roared back, "Yes!" And the millions of Germans listening on the radio were equally intoxicated.

But if Goebbels hoped that Hitler would hand him control of the Total War campaign, or even push the campaign, he was in for a crushing second disappointment. The people were now geared up for Total War's sacrifices, but the Nazi leaders were not. Bormann moved quickly to make sure that no party workers would be caught up in a new mobilization drive. When Bormann's mother suggested that he release one of his housemaids for war work, he angrily told her to mind her own business, "since it is impossible for you to judge how many servant girls I need for keeping house in my official position."

Even Goebbels' personal efforts to set an example were thwarted by other Nazi leaders. His wife dutifully dismissed the family cook to work in a munitions factory, only to discover that she had been snapped up to cook for another high official. And when Goebbels used his powers as gauleiter of Berlin to close down the city's luxury restaurants, Hermann Göring roused himself from his lethargy to save his favorite dining spot, Horcher's. Tempers reached the boiling point when Goebbels responded by sending three men from his office to break the restaurant's windows. In the end, the Nazi leaders reached a face-saving compromise. Goebbels closed the restaurant, and Göring immediately reopened it as an exclusive Luftwaffe officers' club.

Goebbels seethed with frustration as the Total War campaign was sabotaged by party and government bureaucrats alike. In desperation, he summoned Speer, Ley and Funk to his home in Berlin to launch one last effort to mobilize the nation. "Things cannot go on this way," he told his allies. "Here we are sitting in Berlin. Hitler does not hear what we have to say about the situation. I cannot influence him politically, cannot even report the most urgent measures in my area. Everything goes through Bormann."

Touring bomb-ravaged Berlin in 1942, Joseph Goebbels commiserates with the homeless—one of many visits he made to increase his popularity and influence among the citizens of the Reich. For his solicitude, the people fondly called him "Jupp," the diminutive of Joseph, and prayed for his safety. Goebbels happily reported, "One can wrap these folks around his little finger with no more than a small gesture."

Speer proposed a daring plan. At the beginning of the War, Speer recalled, Göring had held enormous authority and power as chairman of a sort of war cabinet called the Council of Ministers for the Defense of the Reich. After a couple of meetings, Göring had lost interest and the council had lapsed into obscurity. But the council had never been abolished and Göring still held the power to issue orders without Hitler's approval. If Goebbels could now tap that power for the Total War effort, he could bypass Bormann entirely and even give direct orders to the obstructionist corps of gauleiters.

Speer's plan seemed to raise more problems than it could solve. Goebbels and Göring had been on bad terms ever since their battle over Horcher's restaurant. Göring was out of favor with Hitler, and the Führer's approval would be needed before the Council of Ministers was reactivated. Göring himself would have to clear his muddled head and behave like the energetic Göring of old.

Goebbels agreed to give the plan a try. And initially, everything went surprisingly well. Speer smoothed over the strained relationship between Goebbels and Göring and arranged for the two to meet at Göring's house. Göring, suddenly eager to avenge slanders by both Bormann and Lammers, heartily endorsed Goebbels' plan. "Depend on it, Herr Göring," said Goebbels, "we are going to open the Führer's eyes about Bormann and Lammers." Goebbels warned the impulsive Göring to do nothing rash; they would have to proceed slowly and carefully. As for the other members of the Council of Ministers, Goebbels said there "was no need for them to know that we intend to slowly spike the Committee of Three."

Next, Goebbels and Speer planned to sound out Hitler on their plans for the Council of Ministers. The only way to reach Hitler without going through Bormann was to contact Hitler's military adjutants, who handled appointments for the General Staff and the handful of civilians engaged in high-level military planning. Speer, as Minister of Armaments, now used this route to schedule a meeting with the Führer. Goebbels and Speer had supper with Hitler, and afterward the Führer invited them to join him around a roaring fire in his study. Goebbels entertained Hitler with reminiscences about the early days, or the "Era of Struggle" as they called it, and regaled his Führer with the latest gossip from the Berlin theater and film circles. Hitler enjoyed this distraction from his battle worries; he ordered wine for his guests and mineral water for himself.

With Hitler in such rare good spirits, Goebbels and Speer prepared to promote their plot against the Committee of Three. But just as they were about to bring the conversation around to the subject of the long-dormant Council of Ministers, an aide interrupted with a report of a heavy Allied air raid on Nuremberg.

Hitler furiously denounced Göring as an "incompetent Reich Marshal." Since Göring was too far away to reproach in person, Hitler ordered that the Luftwaffe chief's adjutant be hauled out of bed and brought before him to answer for Göring. Goebbels and Speer finally managed to calm Hitler, but it was clear that there was now no hope of resurrecting Göring. With Allied air raids increasing in number and destructiveness, it was unlikely that another chance would present itself in the near future.

In any event, Speer suggested, Göring could still play a major role in an indirect attack on the Committee of Three. Speer and the Nazi labor-allocation chief, Fritz Sauckel, had engaged in a long-running dispute over the number of workers Sauckel was supplying Speer's factories and armament works. The discrepancy between the number Sauckel claimed to have supplied and the number actually received came to several hundred thousand. It seemed certain that Sauckel, being a gauleiter and an ally of Bormann's, was faking the figures, but Speer had no proof. Göring, who still held broad economic powers as head of the Four-Year Plan, had the authority to challenge Sauckel's bookkeeping or even force him to change his labor-assignment policies. Göring readily agreed to Speer's plan and called a meeting in a conference room near the Berghof for April 12, 1943.

Each side realized the importance of the encounter and mustered all available support. Speer was backed by Goebbels, Funk, Ley, Göring and Field Marshal Erhard Milch, Göring's chief of aircraft production. Sauckel was supported by Bormann, Lammers and Keitel.

The meeting opened with two ominous surprises for Speer. Goebbels had had a sudden attack of kidney stones en route to the Berghof, and sent last-minute regrets that he could not attend. And Bormann's group included a guest: Heinrich Himmler, the owlish chief of the SS.

Speer nevertheless launched the attack, demanding that Sauckel produce the missing workers. Sauckel insisted that he had already delivered the labor in question. Speer said that Sauckel's statistics were totally wrong, and Sauckel flew into a rage at being called a liar. Speer held his temper in check, waiting for Göring, as Plenipotentiary of the Four-Year Plan, to intervene on his behalf and demand facts and figures from Sauckel.

Then, to Speer's utter consternation, Göring launched into a defense of Sauckel. Why, he demanded, was Speer's group stirring up trouble? Sauckel, said Göring, had already proven himself by his brilliant achievements, and was even now meeting Germany's labor requirements under the most difficult circumstances.

Stunned by this betrayal, Speer was speechless. "It was," he wrote later, "as though Göring had picked up the wrong phonograph record." The conference disintegrated when Himmler plausibly suggested that the missing hundreds of thousands of laborers might be dead.

The full story behind Göring's sudden switch of sides never came to light, but it seemed clear to Speer, at least, that Martin Bormann had engineered the betrayal. Bormann had probably conspired to form a temporary alliance with Himmler and then used the secret police's embarrassing information to blackmail Göring for his drug addiction and other indiscretions. Himmler revealed a certain partisanship when he later warned Speer that "it would be very unwise of you to try to activate the Reich Marshal again."

One thing was certain, however: Bormann had made a secret move to suborn Göring. Shortly before the April 12 conference, as Speer learned later, Bormann had given Göring a gift of six million reichsmarks (almost $2.5 million) from the Hitler slush fund. Because of this, Speer concluded, "our attempt to mobilize Göring against Bormann was probably doomed to failure from the start."

It was perhaps coincidental—and perhaps not—that on the very day of the conference, April 12, 1943, Hitler summoned Bormann to his study and handed him a sheet of paper bearing a letterhead reserved for momentous announcements. Beneath the gold-embossed words *Der Führer,* the message read:

"As my personal assistant, Reichsleiter Martin Bormann will bear the title 'Secretary to the Führer.' "

To an outsider, the new title was no more enlightening than Bormann's previous one, "Head of the Party Chancellery." But the announcement dismayed and angered Nazi insiders, who instantly grasped its real significance. As chief of the Party Chancellery, Bormann's power was officially limited to party matters. But as Secretary to the Führer, Bormann now had Hitler's official blessing to intervene in affairs of state and to give direct orders to Reich Ministers. "This new position," said Albert Speer, "now authorized him to act officially in any field he wished."

The significance of this new power was certainly not lost on Joseph Goebbels. With the collapse of his grand alliance against the Committee of Three, Goebbels sought an accommodation with Hitler's Secretary. If Bormann would use his influence to further Goebbels' projects with the Führer, Goebbels would agree to channel all his reports and directives to Hitler through Bormann's office.

For all practical purposes, Bormann now ruled the Reich in the name of his beloved Führer. But his power was primarily political, and he would have to be wary of a ruthless bureaucrat whose power rested in hundreds of thousands of armed men: Reichsführer-SS Heinrich Himmler.

THE FÜHRER'S PRIVATE WORLD

At the Berghof, an isolated retreat in the Bavarian Alps, Adolf Hitler enjoyed tranquil days with his mistress, Eva Braun, her friends and his close associates.

MASTER AND MISTRESS OF THE BERGHOF

When his duties permitted, Adolf Hitler disappeared from public view into a heavily curtained private life. In 1932, at the age of 43, he had taken a mistress: Eva Braun, a Munich clerk 23 years his junior. To avoid shocking the strait-laced German people, the Führer and Eva met at the Berghof, Hitler's secret retreat perched 3,300 feet above the village of Berchtesgaden near the Austrian border. Only here, Hitler said, could he "breathe and think—and live!" Here he spent "the finest hours of my life."

The Berghof grew as the Führer's affair with Eva matured. When she first started visiting the hideaway in 1932, it was just a small chalet he had bought with royalties from his book *Mein Kampf*. In 1935, with party funds turned over by his aide Martin Bormann, Hitler began expanding the chalet into a luxurious villa embellished with Carrara marble and fine woods. Soon thereafter, Eva began spending most of her time at the Berghof, and Hitler came more and more often, sometimes for a week or more. Eventually, the retreat became a 2.7-square-mile estate with guesthouses, farm buildings and barracks for Hitler's SS bodyguards.

"Staying at the Berghof," wrote Hitler's personal photographer, Heinrich Hoffmann, "was like living in a gilded cage." To ensure the Führer's privacy, the entire complex was fenced in and patrolled day and night by the SS. Hitler himself added to the regimentation, establishing stringent house rules for Eva, their guests and the permanent staff: no smoking, no whistling, no dancing, no heavy make-up or nail polish, no letter writing or diary keeping—and absolutely no political discussion.

Eva kept a diary and got away with it. She also put together a detailed and revealing pictorial account of her life with Hitler. She collected innumerable photographs, capturing events great and trivial; the pictures—a small sampling of which appears on these pages—eventually filled some 30 albums. The albums were so precious to Eva that when the Allies closed in on the Third Reich, she gave the books to an SS friend for safekeeping. Acting on a tip, American soldiers seized the albums in a house in central Austria.

The Führer's photographer, Heinrich Hoffmann, who introduced Hitler to Eva in 1930, watches as the lovers leaf through an album of photographs.

The Führer's mistress arrives at the Berghof's gates in one of his Mercedes touring cars. For appearance' sake, Eva usually rode with Hitler's secretaries.

Sitting on the terrace in Bavarian peasant costume, Eva savors the mountain air and Alpine scenery.

Eva shows off a gown—and bleached hair.

PORTRAIT OF A DICTATOR'S DARLING

Defying Hitler's orders, Eva powders her face.

Eva secretly indulges in a forbidden cigarette.

Athletic Eva exercises at nearby Königssee Lake.

Towed by a motorboat, Eva goes aquaplaning—no hands.

At lakeside with one of her Scotties, Eva embraces her best friend, Herta Schneider.

Press chief Otto Dietrich described Eva Braun as "a creature of pure emotion and *joie de vivre.*" She loved all sports and adored fashion, importing shoes by the dozen and changing clothes several times a day. "I never saw her wear the same outfit twice," Hitler's secretary said.

Eva was not unintelligent; her opinions in social and cultural matters influenced Hitler. But to the Führer one of her most endearing qualities was that she did not meddle in politics. "The great thing about Eva," he boasted, "is that she is no political bluestocking. The *chère amie* of a politician must be quietly discreet."

Eva relaxes in a deck chair while a waiter pours champagne.

Eva enjoys a pre-Lenten festival with her mother (center), her sisters and some friends.

Hitler and Eva rendezvous at a restaurant outside Munich in April 1935. On this occasion he was annoyed with her because she had gone to a dance.

In 1935 Eva wrote of her relationship with Hitler, "He needs me only for certain purposes." With that she put her finger on the bitter truth. To the Führer, Eva was—as Hoffmann observed—"just an attractive little thing in whom he found the type of relaxation and repose he sought." But to Eva, Hitler was the be-all and end-all. "You know that my whole life is loving you," she told him in a letter. The Führer's absences plunged her into deep despair, and twice, in 1932 and 1935, she attempted to commit suicide.

Eva's fondest hope was to become Hitler's wife. But the Führer, who publicly glorified marriage and censured irregular relations, wanted no part of wedlock for himself. "It is wiser to have a mistress than to be married," he told an associate. "Then there is no burden to carry and everything is a beautiful gift." But he hastened to add, "This, of course, only holds true in the case of an exceptional man."

Eva's bedroom at the Berghof adjoined Hitler's through a shared bathroom.

With playful gallantry, Hitler stoops to kiss the hand of his ladylove.

Hitler, Eva and the daughter of a friend pose as a make-believe family.

Eva and Adolf walk her Scotties and Hitler's German shepherd Blondi.

An avid amateur photographer, Eva snaps a picture of her favorite subject.

77

The late-rising master of the Berghof formally greets his guests at noon.

Hitler's sitting room was the place where he went to be alone.

Hitler leads his party down a narrow mountain path toward the teahouse.

En route to the teahouse, Hitler, Eva and their guests pause at an overlook.

At the teahouse, Hitler and Eva sample apple-peel tea, coffee and cake.

After the snack, the Führer dozes in his armchair—to Eva's amusement.

Life at the Berghof revolved around Hitler's unvarying daily routine. The Führer slept late, emerging from his room around 11 to review the morning's reports. Then he joined his guests at lunch—for him, a simple vegetarian repast.

Afterward, the party took a half-hour stroll to the so-called teahouse, a small pavilion on the property. Here Hitler would treat his guests to long monologues on the arts, his travels, raising dogs, astrology, and the evils of hunting and consuming meat, which he called "corpse-eating."

At about 6 p.m., the group returned by car to the Berghof. Now Hitler conferred with aides and visiting dignitaries. The talks usually lasted two hours—by which time dinner was ready. After dinner, movies were shown in the main salon.

Hitler could not bear to be alone at night, so he kept everyone up until he felt sleepy. When the guests finally retired in the wee hours of the morning, they knew that they would face more of the same on the morrow. "After a few days of this," recalled Albert Speer, Hitler's favorite architect, "I felt exhausted and vacant from the constant waste of time."

A fastidious host, Hitler inspects the table settings with two SS waiters.

In a rare moment of levity, Hitler enjoys a hearty laugh with his guests.

Heinrich Hoffmann gives an art book to his boss at a Hitler birthday fete.

The Führer and guests admire a painting he received for his birthday.

PARTYTIME AT THE BERGHOF

Hitler wears a lugubrious expression at a wedding party for Eva's friend Marion Schönemann.

Hitler's bucolic stays at the Berghof were enlivened by elegant parties celebrating holidays, birthdays and the weddings of Eva's friends. The Führer was a lavish host. He often served up mounds of caviar and cases of champagne. At formal dinners, the guests ate their way through the many courses with solid-gold utensils.

The most elaborate galas took place on New Year's Eve. Hitler and Eva would invite about 30 guests and regale them with a grand banquet, a fireworks display and hours of band music.

To climax the festivities, the superstitious Führer would attempt to foretell the future through an ancient divining method (right), pouring molten lead into a bowl of water and interpreting the metal blobs that took shape. At the party to usher in 1939, Hitler saw evil omens for the year ahead (which actually turned out to be a good one). "He sat down in an armchair," Eva's sister Ilse recalled, "gazing dejectedly at the fire, and hardly spoke for the remainder of the evening."

The Führer's despondent mood cast a pall over the party. But, said Ilse, "when Hitler and Eva had taken their leave, the atmosphere relaxed."

Preparing to divine the future in a traditional lead-pouring ceremony, Hitler melts a spoonful of lead over a candle at a party to ring in the year 1939.

Every year during the late 1930s and early 1940s, at special sites scattered through the Reich, thousands of young men in black uniforms came together at midnight on April 20. It was the date of Adolf Hitler's birthday and the hour for a solemn rite of initiation. All of the men had been carefully screened to make certain that their ancestry was impeccable, free of any Jewish taint back to the 18th Century. All had proved to be superior physical specimens, proud of bearing, sound in morals and ideals, with the mental toughness they would need to execute certain distasteful assignments. In short, they were worthy of becoming members of Heinrich Himmler's elite Schutzstaffel, or protection squad, better known—and feared—by the initials SS, which appeared on their uniforms in a stylized emblem resembling twin lightning flashes.

The ceremony unfolded in torchlighted settings adorned with runic symbols. At the climax, the black-clad young men chanted an oath they would never be permitted to breach in the smallest detail:

> I swear to thee Adolf Hitler,
> As Führer and Chancellor of the German Reich,
> Loyalty and Bravery.
> I vow to thee and to the superiors
> whom thou shalt appoint
> Obedience unto death,
> So help me God.

No one present could be less than impressed by the spectacle of massed men dedicating their lives to service, binding themselves to a mystical brotherhood much like the monkish order of Teutonic Knights. Said one of the few outsiders privileged to witness the ceremony: "Tears came to my eyes when, by the light of the torches, thousands of voices repeated the oath in chorus. It was like a prayer."

This annual ceremony poured thousands upon thousands of prime young men into the ranks of the SS—a vast independent state whose inner workings were a closely guarded secret. Through its dozens of departments, bureaus and agencies the SS permeated the lives of the Germans and of the peoples they conquered, maintaining the Nazi regime with constant intimidation and the unsparing use of force.

The SS was far-flung and multifarious. Its most famous and fearsome bureau was the Gestapo, which had 45,000

3

Vows of loyalty in a midnight ceremony
"A man from another planet"
A dangerous recruit named Reinhard Heydrich
Blood bath on the Night of the Long Knives
A grab for power that created the Gestapo
"Protective custody" for enemies of the state
Himmler's Knights of the Round Table
Patriotic candidates for "biological marriage"
Kidnapping "Nordic" children
The killer squads behind the lines
Drumhead justice in Prague

THE DARK EMPIRE OF THE SS

members by 1944, and was responsible for suppressing opposition to the Third Reich. The SS also included a security service known as the SD, whose staff and 100,000 informers engaged in counterintelligence at home and abroad. The SS issued orders to hundreds of forces of uniformed policemen in states, cities and towns throughout Germany and the conquered lands. About 40,000 SS guards ran the labor camps and concentration camps as money-making enterprises, feeding profits into the coffers of the SS main office in Berlin. The SS was the parent of the immense Waffen-SS (armed SS), whose 600,000 troopers fought in 38 divisions alongside regular Army units.

Other SS bureaus did genealogical research to upgrade the German racial quality; issued marriage licenses to approved SS applicants; operated free maternity homes in the interest of breeding a master race; owned and managed hundreds of industries, from stone quarries to porcelain factories and bread bakeries; published the organization's own newspapers and ran a network of law courts that alone could mete out justice to SS men suspected of offenses.

Because it was ubiquitous, the SS appeared to be monolithic, but quite the opposite was true. Like the Nazi Party itself, the SS was a loose collection of semiautonomous departments whose rival chieftains accorded Himmler the same sort of fealty he rendered to Hitler. Yet for all that, Himmler's bureaus functioned with ruthless efficiency. He was not ashamed to say that "many people in Germany shrink when they see our black tunic." And he declared triumphantly, "Without pity, we shall wield a merciless sword of justice. We assemble and march according to inalterable laws as a National Socialist military order of Nordic men, and as a sworn community on our way into a far future."

Himmler the man was an enigma. To many Nazis he seemed inhuman. Some compared him to a robot; one associate called him "a man from another planet." But in fact, as his closest comrades knew, the enigma was more apparent than real. Himmler had created the SS—and re-created himself—in Hitler's image, and the organization revealed all of his strengths, weaknesses and lurid, muddled dreams.

In 1922, at the age of 22, Heinrich Himmler was a follower without a leader, a lonely seeker, a frustrated former cadet who had been denied a chance to fight in the Great War by his youth. Then he found a leader—not Hitler, but Captain Ernst Röhm, war hero, homosexual and right-wing commander of one of the many bands of rootless veterans that roamed Germany in the chaotic aftermath of World War I.

The next year, Röhm and his band joined forces with the fledgling National Socialist Party in Adolf Hitler's Munich Beer Hall Putsch. Himmler took part in that abortive uprising, but he played such a minor role that he escaped arrest. The Röhm-Hitler alliance survived the putsch, and Röhm's 1,500-man band grew into the Sturmabteilung, the SA, Hitler's brown-shirted private army. Hitler recruited a handful of men to act as his bodyguards and protect him from Communist toughs, other rivals, and even the SA if it got out of hand. This tiny group was the embryonic SS.

In 1925, Himmler formally joined the SS, becoming member No. 168. He, who had never been very good at anything, immediately discovered a kind of work at which he could excel: business administration. In his hometown of Landshut, Bavaria, he became district organizer for the SS in Lower Bavaria and managed a group of local SS men who solicited subscriptions and advertisements for the party newspaper, *Völkischer Beobachter*. He was correct, ambitious and preoccupied with the details of the job. But he was so prim and colorless that few of the early Nazis paid him serious attention. One who did, Joseph Goebbels, described him as "a good fellow and very intelligent."

In the next few years, Himmler changed radically. The transformation began with what amounted to a religious experience: He took as his god Adolf Hitler. Here was a man who seized destiny by the throat—a true leader, bold, charismatic, the prophet of a dazzling new world dominated by the great German people. Himmler dedicated his life to serving his god and, perhaps, to rising in his service.

In every spare moment, Himmler studied Hitler's speeches and the works of party ideologues Alfred Rosenberg and Walter Darré, which led him to fascinating books on Germanic lore, mysticism and secret societies. Though he had not been particularly anti-Semitic, Himmler spoke more and more in hate-the-Jew jargon.

He saw another bête noire in what had formerly been his guiding light: Roman Catholicism. Himmler never lost his early interest in the Church's intellectual elite, the Jesuit order, but now he began to develop an anti-Catholic bias that would eventually lead him to advocate the public execution of the Pope and to compel many of his Catholic SS men to leave the Church.

Previously, Himmler had shunned sex, believing that it deprived men of their will power, and he had primly deplored extramarital relations. However, in 1928 he married an East Prussian landowner's daughter, Margarete Boden, with whom he had a daughter, Gudrun. He later took a mistress, Hedwig Potthast, who would bear him two more daughters. He then began urging the abolition of marriage, which he described with Hitlerian self-assurance as "the Church's satanic achievement."

In 1929, Hitler named the new Himmler as commander of the SS, which was still a relatively unimportant organization of only 280 members within Röhm's SA. To the Nazis who bothered to note the appointment, Himmler made an unlikely Reichsführer-SS, but Hitler was a keen judge of men. Himmler, he knew, was a meticulous office manager—the sort of paper-work expert he needed to ensure efficient behind-the-scenes operations. Furthermore, Himmler was incorruptible; he lived frugally on his salary while other party chieftains appropriated huge sums of money to support sybaritic lives. And most important, Himmler worshipped Hitler; during their infrequent meetings, he hung in awe on Hitler's every word and then hurried off to do his bidding—and more. Whatever Himmler might do to compete for power with Hitler's lieutenants, he would never pose a threat to the Führer himself.

During the early 1930s, Himmler was increasingly occupied with an assignment that really gave birth to the SS: Hitler had ordered him to form an "elite troop of the party, a troop dependable in every circumstance." The chief reason for this order was that the SA, which had never been particularly well-behaved, was proving undependable and worse. Röhm's force, about 100,000 strong in 1930 and growing fast on a torrential influx of men left jobless by Germany's recent economic collapse, was engaging in brawls that alarmed the Army and the powerful industrialists whom Hitler was wooing for financial support. Hitler still hoped to bring the SA into line as a "disciplined marching column," but at the same time he was cautiously trying to dissociate himself from the Brownshirts.

This policy was a boon to Himmler and his SS. Late in 1930, Hitler cut the organizational cord that bound the SS to the SA, declaring that henceforth "no SA commander is entitled to give orders to the SS." To stress their independence, Himmler dressed his men in a new uniform conspicuously different from the SA's light brown—all black with silver trim to denote rank and unit. This smart, dramatic outfit had great appeal to uniform-loving Germans.

Another attraction of the SS was its elite mystique, which Himmler laboriously evolved from his esoteric reading. For a creed, he took Darré's "blood and soil" cult, with its romantic proclamations of the sacredness of the German people and their ancestral lands. For his SS oaths, symbols and rituals, Himmler drew upon Germanic tribal tradition and Nordic lore, and to some extent he imitated the structure and strict discipline of the Jesuit order (which prompted Hitler to call Himmler "our own Ignatius Loyola"). In sum, the Reichsführer-SS conjured up a secret society of modern pagan knights, tough as tempered steel, dedicated selflessly to the energetic and efficient execution of their leader's will.

To Nazi pragmatists, the fanciful aspects of Himmler's elite dogma were so much nonsense. But the elitism itself worked. Himmler showed just how well it worked one night in a recruitment speech before an upper-class gathering in Munich. The German upper class had been repeatedly vilified by the Nazis and was suspicious of the party and all its works. Himmler set out to change all that. Summing up all his thoughts in purposely vague generalities, he declared that the SS could succeed only if "its members brought to the social requirements of the present day the genuine military tradition, the distinctive outlook, bearing and breeding of the German nobility, and the creative efficiency of the industrialist, on the basis of racial selection."

This message was so reassuring—so surprisingly different from the Nazis' usual rantings against the upper classes—that nearly everyone in the audience joined the SS. And with good cause. Himmler's invocation of order, respectability and old values came at a turbulent time when even peaceable men considered it wise to join some militant group for self-protection.

Elite volunteers streamed into the SS. First came the restless sons of the gentry, men who were born to the German military tradition but who had grown up too late to serve in

Reichsführer-SS Heinrich Himmler, seated (center) in his Berlin headquarters, confers with SS security chief Reinhard Heydrich (second from left) and other aides. A compulsive worker, Himmler spent his spare time studying secret dossiers full of evidence against everyone of consequence. The files of several Reich leaders even revealed that they listened to the forbidden music of Jewish composer Felix Mendelssohn.

the Great War; they would form the backbone of Himmler's officer corps. Then came men of the educated middle classes—the lawyers who would help legitimize Hitler's rule, and the economists, engineers, agronomists and other specialists who would staff the proliferating SS bureaus. To enlist outstanding young men from the lower classes, Himmler set up an SS academy that offered the possibility of a commission without the education required by the regular Army. As a result of Himmler's vigorous recruitment, the SS membership leaped from about 2,000 in 1931 to perhaps 30,000 the next year.

Himmler acquired his most valuable—and most dangerous—recruit in 1931. To detect any plots against the Nazi leaders, he decided to set up an SS counterintelligence branch, and he discreetly passed the word that he needed a clever man to serve as his deputy. A trustworthy aristocrat who had left the SA to join the SS recommended a 27-year-old former Navy lieutenant whose elegant name would, in time, strike fear into nearly everyone's heart, including Himmler's. The man was Reinhard Tristan Eugen Heydrich.

Himmler called for Heydrich's Navy dossier, which made him out to be everything that Himmler wished to be: brilliant and arrogant; tall, handsome and typically Nordic; an expert fencer, skier and horseman. Also a compulsive womanizer, he had recently been cashiered from the Navy for seducing the daughter of an important industrialist and then refusing to marry her—a position Himmler now found convenient to forgive or to ignore.

Heydrich arrived for his interview on June 4 and revealed two flaws: His long torso was mounted on hips of almost feminine width and his voice was disturbingly high-pitched for so Nordic a six-footer. But no matter. Heydrich was respectful and tough-minded, and he seemed to take it for granted that he could do anything required of him. Himmler handled the interview poorly; he always was uneasy in the presence of men who he sensed were his superiors. In turn, Heydrich saw in Himmler a weak man who could help him grasp the only thing he desired: power.

Himmler, ever the schoolmaster, gave Heydrich a 20-minute test, asking him to sketch out his plan for setting up a counterintelligence corps. Heydrich, with little relevant experience, set down a lot of brazen platitudes—e.g., "Security is just as important as espionage." Himmler hired him on the spot—at 180 reichsmarks a month (then approximately $40)—to start a new SS department: the Sicherheitsdienst, or security and intelligence service, abbreviated SD.

Heydrich and a small staff set up headquarters not far from Himmler's office in Munich. Heydrich quickly built up a tight network of spies and informers, and with the information they developed he started a secret file that eventually included a dossier on countless Germans. Heydrich's object, of course, was to find some scrap of scandal that could be used to break a man or to blackmail him into obedience. With no difficulty whatever, Heydrich collected reams of useful evidence on Röhm and several of his top SA associates, who were flaunting their homosexual affairs. To reward Heydrich for his enterprise, Himmler in 1932 made him head of the SD and promoted him to colonel.

In 1933, after the Nazi Party had taken power in Germany, increasing trouble with the SA made a showdown inevitable. As German Chancellor, the Führer could no longer afford to tolerate the disruptive Brownshirts; under the ambitious Röhm, the SA had grown to be an organization of three million men, and its unpredictable activities prevented Hitler from consolidating his shaky control of the Reich. He had to dispose of the SA to hold the support of his industrial backers, to satisfy party leaders jealous of the SA's power, and most important, to win the allegiance of the conser-

vative Army generals. Under pressure from all sides, and enraged by an SA plot against him that Heydrich had conveniently uncovered, Hitler turned the SS loose to purge its parent organization.

To lead the purge, Hitler selected his trusty comrade Josef "Sepp" Dietrich, commander of his SS bodyguard regiment. Dietrich, a crude and callous man, formed a task force of 220 like-minded SS comrades. Meanwhile, Himmler's and Heydrich's spies had established the whereabouts and daily routines of the marked SA leaders, and on June 30, 1934— the Night of the Long Knives—SS killer squads struck. Hitler himself led an early-morning raid that took Röhm and several others by surprise in their boardinghouse headquarters in Bad Wiessee. The Führer could not bring himself to murder his old comrade. Röhm and his associates were taken to a local jail, where SS assassins shot them down.

The killings went on for two days and nights and took a toll of perhaps 200 "enemies of the state." It was quite enough to reduce the SA to impotence, and it brought the Führer immediate returns. The dying President of the Reich, Field Marshal Paul von Hindenburg, congratulated Hitler on crushing the troublesome SA, and the Army generals—

SS troopers of Hitler's personal bodyguard, the Leibstandarte-SS Adolf Hitler, stand at rigid attention outside the Führer's study in the Berlin Chancellery (left). This elite unit, numbering only 120 men in 1933, expanded vigorously and reached regimental strength of 3,100 by 1937, when it marched en masse through the streets of the capital (right) to celebrate the fourth anniversary of the Nazi seizure of power.

concluding that Hitler was now their pawn—swore personal loyalty to him.

Himmler and Heydrich were meanwhile playing a leading role in consolidating Nazi power—and their own. Shortly before Hitler became Chancellor, they set as their goal the take-over of all the German police forces. Their first target was the most important and the most dangerous one: the political-police forces—tight-knit organizations staffed by just the type of tough professional officers that Himmler needed to make his security services truly efficient. Since there was no national administration controlling or coordinating the political police, Himmler and Heydrich would have to take over the 16 state forces one by one, coercing the veteran—and often anti-Nazi—officers to serve as loyal followers. Heydrich was confident that as these forces succumbed, Germany's state and local organizations of ordinary uniformed policemen would fall into line without much resistance.

Himmler and Heydrich struck first at the political police in Bavaria, their SS power base. The Bavarian officers knew that an SS take-over was inevitable and feared reprisals for all the Nazi skulls they had cracked during demonstrations and street fights. At the very least, they expected to be fired.

Heydrich gave them time to nurture their fears. Then, with some SD men, he occupied the Munich headquarters of the political police. In a long series of closed-door sessions, he subjected each officer to a grueling interrogation on his methods and policies. Then Heydrich let the officers sweat some more. Finally, at his leisure, he called the officers back and told them one at a time that they would retain their jobs—as members of the SD. The officers were vastly relieved. In a rush of enthusiasm for the Nazi cause, they assured Heydrich that they were ready to serve without reservation. In one move, he had converted them from enemies to allies.

Himmler and Heydrich barely paused to enjoy their victory in Bavaria; one by one they extended SS sway over 14 of the remaining 15 state political-police forces. By the end of 1933 they were ready to take on the last holdout, the massive Prussian force, which Hermann Göring had commandeered by similar tactics.

It was not much of a contest. Göring, his heart set on becoming head of the entire German military, had already lost interest in the control of his police, and he offered only spo-

radic resistance as Heydrich's men infiltrated his force. Before long, Heydrich wielded all the power, leaving Göring a somewhat embarrassed nominal leader. But Himmler graciously gave Göring an opportunity to save face. On April 20, 1934, Göring assembled his men in the presence of Himmler and Heydrich and commanded them to support his new deputy, the Reichsführer-SS, against all enemies of the state. Himmler seemed to be deeply touched by Göring's trust and told him, ''I shall forever remain loyal to you. Never will you have anything to fear from me.''

Himmler now combined all of Germany's political-police forces into a nationwide organization under the name Gestapo and appointed Heydrich its chief. To justify this move, Himmler had informed Hitler that a Communist plot to assassinate Göring had been afoot and that he had been obliged to make certain impromptu arrests. Under the circumstances, Himmler said, it was desirable to place all the police in the Reich under a unified command. Hitler endorsed the *fait accompli*.

Not long afterward, on June 17, 1936, Hitler named Himmler chief of the German police. In this role Himmler was nominally responsible to Dr. Wilhelm Frick, the Minister of the Interior. But as Reichsführer-SS, Himmler was responsible to no one but Hitler—and as a result all his police forces were independent of any governmental restraint.

On June 26, only nine days after his appointment, Himmler ordered a fundamental reorganization of the police into two branches. One was the Ordnungspolizei (Orpo), or regular police, comprising the uniformed national, rural and municipal police, to be headed by Police General Kurt Daluege. As chief of the German cop-on-the-beat, Daluege remained efficiently and unglamorously important.

The second branch, under Heydrich's leadership, was the Sicherheitspolizei (Sipo). It included the Gestapo and the Kriminalpolizei (Kripo), or criminal police, whose plainclothes detective forces had belonged to the regular police before Heydrich appropriated them for his own. In a later move, Himmler merged Sipo with Heydrich's SD, a party organization, forming the powerful Reichssicherheitshauptamt (RSHA), or Main Office of Reich Security. With the creation of the RSHA, the Nazi police state came of age.

In the course of securing national police power, Himmler established a detention camp similar to others that were springing up in Germany to hold political prisoners. There were many of these institutions, known as concentration camps, but Himmler's was by far the most important, since it would serve as a model for dozens more. He set up his camp 12 miles northwest of Munich. It came to be known by the name of a nearby village—Dachau.

Neither Dachau nor the other concentration camps were explicitly authorized by Hitler, but the Führer had legalized the arrest of more than enough prisoners to fill them all. In February 1933, he had decreed that, ''in the interests of public security and order,'' anyone could be taken into ''protective custody'' and detained indefinitely, on mere ''suspicion of activities inimical to the state.'' Himmler began to interpret the edict more and more freely; soon the Reichsführer-SS was detaining in Dachau not only Communists but Social Democrats, Freemasons, leaders of Jewish and Catholic fraternal organizations, union organizers, opposition journalists—and even Nazis if they departed from the party line.

Himmler installed as commandant at Dachau, Theodor Eicke, a former Army officer who was known to have trustworthy views on racial matters. To attract volunteers to the dull job of guard at Dachau, the Reichsführer-SS created Death's-head units whose members wore the distinctive collar insignia of a silver skull and crossbones. The little emblem became so popular that Himmler later vouchsafed it

to other bureaus and branches, most notably the Waffen-SS.

Unfortunately, Dachau had accommodations for only 5,000 prisoners, and Heydrich was unearthing many more real and potential enemies of the Reich. So Himmler soon organized three more concentration camps—Buchenwald, Sachsenhausen and Lichtenburg. Eicke's service at Dachau proved so commendable that Himmler put him in charge of all the camps.

While Himmler endorsed Eicke's enthusiasm, he was concerned about rumors that the Death's-head men were expediting the interrogation of prisoners with torture. It was not so much the torture that bothered him as the stories that were going around. So Himmler helped Eicke frame a statement announcing strict limitations on physical punishment dealt out at Dachau. The document said that Eicke would not go much beyond flogging. However, it would be proper to hang anyone who, "for the purpose of supplying the propaganda of the opposition with atrocity stories, collects true or false information about the concentration camp." These and other punishments were illegal at the time, but SS lawyers worked out the justifying laws and had them approved by Hitler a few years later.

By 1936 Himmler, with the invaluable help of Heydrich, had laid the foundations for his rise to even greater heights. Now, for the first time, all of the Nazi leaders regarded Himmler with respect, and they began coining ugly names

for Heydrich, such as "the blond beast" and "Himmler's evil genius." The two men were free to multiply, expand and embellish their operations.

After 1936, when the upheavals of Nazification were largely over in the Reich, Heydrich took an ever stronger role in running the police and intelligence operations of the SS. Heydrich concocted new plans to extend SS hegemony; he would work out a scheme and present it to Himmler in a staccato, high-pitched soliloquy. "I had the impression that after one of these expositions Himmler was quite overwhelmed," wrote Felix Kersten, Himmler's masseur, in whom the Reichsführer-SS confided in the way men confide in their barbers. Himmler acknowledged his admiration for Heydrich: "He saw the ways that men would take with a clarity that was absolutely amazing. His colleagues hardly dared lie to him."

Though the Reichsführer-SS was well aware of Heydrich's insatiable appetite for power, he felt that he held a whip over his man. He had heard a rumor that Heydrich had a Jewish grandparent, and Himmler felt sure that Heydrich would remain obedient to him for fear of being revealed as a Jew and dismissed. The fact of the matter was that the party's top genealogist had conducted a careful investigation of Heydrich's family background and found no trace of a Jewish forebear. But the rumor persisted, and per-

Reichsführer-SS Heinrich Himmler marks the 1,000th anniversary of the death of King Heinrich I by laying a wreath on the Saxon monarch's tomb in Quedlingburg Cathedral on July 2, 1936. Heinrich I was known as the "Conqueror of the Slavs" for his campaign against the Eastern peoples, and Himmler, with similar ambitions, came to fancy himself a reincarnation of the medieval King.

At an archeological site in Bavaria, SS chief Himmler inspects ancient runic inscriptions, which possessed mystical significance for Germanic tribesmen. Himmler used several runes in secret SS rituals, and one—a double zigzag—served to represent the initials of his organization: SS, for Schutzstaffel.

haps because of it Heydrich continued to treat Himmler with slavish deference; he knew better than most men that Nazi policy decided what was true or false.

In any case, the Reichsführer-SS was grateful to Heydrich for relieving him of many onerous operational concerns; this gave him time to concentrate on matters of greater interest to him—race, genetics and his cult of the SS elite. Himmler busied himself contentedly with Nordic lore and the establishment of SS rituals. He created pagan SS holidays, among them a midsummer substitute for Christmas, and made a special observance of November 9, the anniversary of the 1923 Putsch, at which time SS trainees received their daggers. He improved SS training techniques, indoctrinating potential leaders with a grotesque caricature of the Catholic catechism. For example:

Question: "Why do we believe in Germany and the Führer?"

Answer: "Because we believe in God, we believe in Germany, which He created in His world, and in the Führer, Adolf Hitler, whom He has sent us."

For the most promising SS officers, Himmler took over the enormous castle of Wewelsburg near Paderborn in Westphalia and turned it into a combination monastery and knightly playground. His favorite officers, for whom he ordered coats of arms devised, dined at a great round table, as in the King Arthur legend, and engaged in proper pursuits, such as fencing and chess. Beneath the dining hall, which measured 145 feet by 100 feet, Himmler built a shrine where the holiest ceremonies of his mystical order took place amid urns containing the ashes of the heroic SS dead.

Himmler heartily endorsed the dueling code, declaring that "every SS man has the right and the duty to defend his honor by force of arms." However, he preferred not to lose good men in duels to the death, so he made sure that the offending party had ample opportunity to apologize honorably—that is, to give "clarification." He also extended an honorable escape from shame for SS offenders who had been condemned to death by SS courts: The man was given a cocked revolver with one round in the cylinder and six hours to expiate his crime. After his suicide, the SS made certain that the widow and her family had adequate funds, just as if the deceased had fallen in action.

To ensure the racial purity of the Reich in general and the SS in particular, Himmler devoted endless energy to his Ahnenerbe, or Ancestral Heritage Bureau, which was charged with the study of the German people's racial origins. SS officers were pledged not to marry until the SS Race and Resettlement Office had investigated the prospective bride and vouched for her unadulterated Germanic background. Of course the Reichsführer-SS was hostile to the "hypocrisy" of monogamy, but he continued to tolerate conventional marriage. Himmler realized that even the cream of his elite might need some time to accept fully his radical secular faith, and in the meantime, babies and more babies were what the Reich needed.

With an application for a marriage license, the SS man was required to submit a photograph of his would-be bride, preferably wearing a bathing suit. With idealized German-Nordic measurements in mind, Himmler himself often studied the photographs, paying special attention to the shape of the skull and forehead, the distance between the eyes, the curvature of the nose, the breadth of the hips. He put every woman into one of three categories: "in complete accordance with SS selection principles; average; not suitable." If Himmler's verdict and the genealogical investigation concurred, a marriage license would be issued.

In his early years as Reichsführer-SS, Himmler had started the *Sippenbuch*, a sort of SS stud book, and he often pored through the genealogical register with the scholarly discrimination of a professional horse breeder. He also studied

the census statistics and was distressed to discover that the birth rate of SS families was only fractionally higher than the national birth rate. Indeed, the Germany of 1885, though only half as populous as Nazi Germany, had produced as many children. To bring the population of the Reich up to the quality and quantity Hitler desired (120 million Aryans by 1980), Himmler decided that it was the patriotic duty of every SS man to sire at least four children. Six would be better: The Reichsführer-SS liked to point out that Richard Wagner was a sixth child and that without his glorious music Germany would be impoverished.

Himmler's concern over population growth led him to conceive a new program, the Lebensborn, or Fountain of Life, and also to form a new bureau to run the enterprise under his close supervision. "My first aim in setting up the Lebensborn," he later explained, "was to meet a crying need and give unmarried women who were racially pure a chance to have children free of cost."

Toward this end, the bureau established a network of SS "homes," many of them in houses and hospitals that had been confiscated from the Jews. (Cynical Germans called the homes breeding farms and SS officers' clubs.) SS men would send their pregnant women friends there to have their children. And if the mother considered her offspring an encumbrance, the Lebensborn staff would go to great lengths to place the child with foster parents whose status and means resembled the natural father's or mother's.

Himmler and the Lebensborn executives worked in concert with state ministries and party leaders to persuade young German women that they were "racially valuable" and should have offspring out of wedlock—a "biological marriage," it was called—in order to satisfy the Reich's "urgent need for the victory of the German child."

Simultaneously, the Reichsführer-SS campaigned vigorously against any practice that contravened a higher birth rate: contraception, abortion, the possession of pets ("Those who give a dog the place to which a child is entitled commit a crime against our people") and that darkest crime against Germanhood, homosexuality. Himmler was so adamant about homosexuals that he had his own errant nephew—an SS officer to boot—put to death in Dachau. He denied promotion to childless SS officers and enthusiastically backed a new law in 1938 that made a childless marriage grounds for divorce. (It apparently never occurred to Himmler that the SS man, rather than his woman, might be infertile.)

Himmler was appalled to think of the damage that a war would do to Germany's genetic pool; warriors, the best breeding stock, might die in such numbers as to jeopardize the future of the German race. The flower of one generation had been destroyed in the Great War and now another generation was threatened. So when World War II came in 1939, he took extraordinary measures to prevent a disaster. He ordered SS men to get their wives with child—and if possible to serve as "conception assistants" to childless

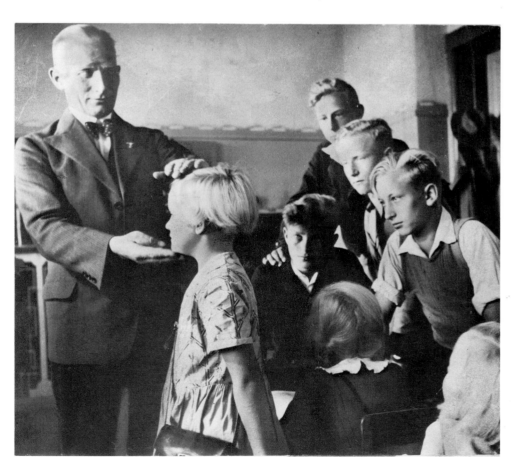

SS doctors examine a group of kidnapped Polish children who have been judged "racially valuable" for adoption by German foster parents. Children in the occupied territories learned to flee SS squads roaming the towns and villages in automobiles, so the Nazis turned to specially trained women who were less conspicuous as kidnappers.

A German teacher singles out a child with striking "Nordic" features for special praise in class. Through the use of such examples, German school children were encouraged to judge one another from a racial point of view.

women of 30 or older—before they put themselves in mortal peril. He gave the men generous leaves in which to perform their patriotic procreative duty. He urged idealistic German women to consummate biological marriages—"not in frivolity but in deep moral earnestness." He had an insatiable curiosity about his men's connubial relations and was delighted to learn from one commander of his unit's "pleasingly large number of illegitimate children."

After the invasion of Poland, Himmler greatly expanded his Lebensborn program. Although the Poles, as a Slavic people, were racial mongrels to the Nazis, the sight of many blond, blue-eyed Polish children persuaded Himmler to make an "assumption of Nordic parentage" on their behalf. Thus, in 1940 he proposed to Hitler—and the Führer approved—that all such children between the ages of six and 10 be brought to the Reich and raised as Germans.

More than 200,000 Polish children were removed and Germanized. Most of them were orphans, or the children of Polish soldiers killed during the invasion, or the illegitimate offspring of Polish women and German conquerors. Himmler hoped that this and other "fetching home" operations would increase the Reich's "Nordic" population by another 30 million by 1980. But to Himmler's dismay, the Lebensborn program had no measurable effect on the Reich's wartime population. All the SS babies and the kidnapped Slavic children could not begin to make up for Germany's military

and civilian casualties, which would pass the six million mark before the end of the War.

Concurrent with the invasion of Poland, Himmler organized several special units of SS men to carry out the "negative" aspect of the Reich's racial policy in the conquered East, reducing the Slavs to a permanent slave population. These were the *Einsatzgruppen,* or task groups—extermination squads of 500 to 1,000 men each that trailed the German armies eastward for the express purpose of liquidating Jews, gypsies, Communists, priests, aristocrats, the professional class—anyone and everyone who could conceivably be defined as subhuman or dangerous in the Nazi lexicon.

The men of the *Einsatzgruppen* were recruited from the dregs of the SS, from German police forces and from dubious foreign auxiliaries. They somewhat debased the elite standards of the SS, but their hard work helped spread SS power through the Eastern provinces.

The SS service that Himmler loved best—"as if it were his own child," said an associate—made its official debut at division strength in May of 1940 as part of the German armies thrusting into Holland, Belgium and France. Combat units of the Waffen-SS went into action against retreating British forces around the port of Dunkirk, and if their role was small it was nonetheless significant.

The name Waffen-SS was still unknown to the German

Reinhard Heydrich (right), chief of the SS security and intelligence service, dines with Admiral Wilhelm Canaris, head of the Abwehr (military intelligence), in Berlin in 1936. Despite their convivial meetings, they were constantly conspiring to outdo and undermine each other's network of agents.

people, but the organization had been evolving since the dawn of the Nazi era. The original personnel came from three SS sources: the Führer's personal bodyguard, known as the Leibstandarte-SS Adolf Hitler; the Death's-head battalions that Himmler had formed to guard the concentration camps; and the SS training schools, commanded by an elegant former Army general named Paul Hausser. Applicants were judged by strict elitist standards. The men in the Leibstandarte had to be at least 5 feet 11 inches tall, and up to 1936 an otherwise impressive volunteer would be turned down if, as Himmler noted with pride, "he had even one filled tooth." It was Himmler's dream that such magnificent specimens would one day fill the ranks of his very own independent armed force, passionately loyal to the Führer, which would serve the Reich on a basis of parity with the Army, the Luftwaffe and the Navy.

By 1937, Hausser was graduating 400 SS officers a year, and the military units grew slowly but steadily thereafter, the regiments expanding into brigades and brigades into divisions. The growth rate was not nearly fast enough to suit Himmler. Part of the trouble was that he had to compete for men and equipment with the regular Army, whose High Command was anxious to protect its military monopoly and represented to Hitler that the SS troopers were policemen, parade martinets and "asphalt soldiers," who were inadequately trained for combat. Himmler remonstrated with the Führer, but to no great avail.

As it happened, Hitler was not completely unsympathetic to Himmler's protests. His own relations with the top Army generals had always been difficult. But he wanted to keep the SS a small elite force—not another bloated monster like the SA. Besides, he needed the generals' cooperation, and to mollify them he kept a low ceiling on SS combat forces—about 25,000 men in 1939. Moreover, he ordered that when Himmler's units were in the field they were to serve as auxiliaries under Army command.

Thus, in virtual anonymity, Himmler's units joined the Army in its 1938 stroll into the Czech Sudetenland. The following year, the units received their baptism of fire in the blitzkrieg against Poland; they suffered proportionally higher casualties than the regulars. Himmler called this gallantry; the Army blamed it on sketchy training and on unnecessary recklessness. The generals also complained that the SS troopers were "frigid if not hostile" to their Army comrades.

Another special SS trait manifested itself in 1940, when the Waffen-SS—then consisting of about 125,000 men in three divisions and one reinforced regiment—began operations in the West. In two incidents, both of them carefully withheld from the newspapers, SS troopers went considerably beyond the accepted rules of warfare. Captain Fritz Knochlein of the Death's-head division ordered 100 British prisoners taken into a meadow near the tiny French village of Paradis and shot; two men, buried under their comrades' corpses, played dead and survived. The next day, farther north along the perimeter, Sepp Dietrich's Leibstandarte-SS Adolf Hitler dealt death to another group of about 100 British prisoners. Dietrich's men murdered some of their prisoners by firing squad, others by automatic-weapons fire, most by hand grenades. In the confusion 15 prisoners managed to escape with their lives.

The brutal indiscipline of these two incidents genuinely appalled the Army generals. SS headquarters chose not to punish Knochlein. As for Dietrich, Hitler's former bodyguard was well on his way to achieving command of an entire SS panzer army.

Though the Army had yet to give a morsel of credit to the Waffen-SS, Himmler's units had proved their mettle by the time France capitulated in June 1940. The SS divisions were effective partly because they were larger than their regular Army counterparts by about 5,000 men, partly because their infantry was fully motorized, and partly because the troopers fought with a death-defying zeal that fairly pleaded for the adjective "fanatic." For all this, Hitler in his July speech to the Reichstag praised "the valiant divisions and regiments of the Waffen-SS" and gave thanks to "Party Comrade Himmler, who organized the entire security system of our Reich as well as the Waffen-SS."

After the Hitler speech, the Army generals could no longer ignore the Waffen-SS, but they still insisted that Himmler be limited to a 3 per cent share of the available German manpower. However, the Reichsführer-SS found ways to circumvent the restrictions. He juggled his unit designations to free men from service under Army aegis. He expanded his practice, begun in 1938, of recruiting non-Germans of "Nordic blood" who lived in such advanced and racially acceptable Western nations as Norway, Denmark and Holland. Ultimately 125,000 Western foreigners would serve with distinction in the Waffen-SS. But these outlanders lowered the statistical perfection of the force. To his chagrin, Himmler was obliged to accept shorter, less-perfect specimens—provided, of course, that they could prove themselves free of the Jewish taint.

Himmler's troubles with the Army continued—and got worse. During the conquest of Yugoslavia and Greece in 1941, Army officers found that inexperienced SS units were retarding their progress along narrow mountain trails. On one occasion, when an Army convoy attempted to pass some SS trucks and a hot argument ensued, the SS officer in charge turned on the Army commander and shouted, "If you drive on without my permission, I will order my men to fire on your column!" Another such incident brought Himmler a formal complaint from the Army Commander in Chief, Field Marshal Walther von Brauchitsch.

All the same, the Waffen-SS was making headway. The Führer allowed it to raise another division in preparation for the momentous 1941 invasion of the Soviet Union; and its strength stood at more than 160,000 when the blitzkrieg was launched on June 22.

But then disaster struck. The SS units took heavy casualties, and in a battle at Salla near the Finnish border, the troopers in one newly organized SS outfit threw away their weapons and fled in panic. Slowly and with difficulty, Himmler faced up to facts. The Army commanders had not been entirely wrong in saying that the Waffen-SS lacked sufficient military training and experience. He also admitted that the Russians, inferior though they were, fought on "like some prehistoric monster caught in a net." But experience—and SS victories—came as the armies plunged deep into the Soviet Union.

It was Dietrich's division that first made the Army commanders own up to the Waffen-SS's sterling fighting qualities. On December 26, 1941, the commander of the 3rd Panzer Corps, General Eberhard von Mackensen, wrote

Himmler an unsolicited letter in which he declared that "the Leibstandarte enjoys an outstanding reputation not only among its superiors, but also among its Army comrades. Its inner discipline, its cool daredeviltry, its cheerful enterprise, its unshakable firmness, its camaraderie (which deserves special praise)—all these are outstanding and cannot be surpassed." The Waffen-SS had arrived. Before long, crack SS divisions were generally recognized as the Reich's finest ground units.

In the spring of 1942, Himmler was handed a great victory over the Army. Hitler, enraged at winter reversals on the Russian front, had taken direct personal command of the Army and now authorized Himmler to form an entire SS corps, free of Army control. Henceforth, the Waffen-SS would double in size annually.

But this new growth was not an unmixed blessing. The combination of high SS losses and a prolonged two-front war forced Himmler to rely more and more on less and less reliable foreign recruits—many of whom were forced into service. In February 1943 the Führer ordered the creation of an SS unit of Balkan Muslims, and the ranks of the proudly Germanic Waffen-SS soon opened to all manner of racial inferiors from the East. Eventually some 200,000 Ukranians, Albanians, Croatians—even Russian Cossacks—served in

Reinhard Heydrich (center), newly arrived in Prague as Reich Protector of Bohemia and Moravia, confers with aides in September 1941. Heydrich quickly informed his staff of his policy toward the Czechs. He intended to deport or eliminate those of "inferior race with hostile intentions." Czechs who were "of good race and well-intentioned" would be sent to Germany to work and to be Germanized. "If that doesn't work," Heydrich said, "we will finally put them against the wall."

the Waffen-SS. Himmler was obliged to swallow his racial pride and trim his ideology to fit the different groups: Slavic units, for example, were excused from official instruction in the inferiority of Slavs.

Himmler never reconciled himself to all those dark little men—five feet five inches became an acceptable minimum height—walking about wearing the proud Death's-head insignia on their field-gray uniforms. In the end, his pride and joy rested in a dozen or so SS panzer and panzer-grenadier divisions composed mostly of ethnic Germans. These units were better equipped and armed than regular Army forces, and would become the Third Reich's "fire brigade," rushing from front to front to put out fires, always attacking, always feared by the enemy.

Himmler and the SS reached their political pinnacle in 1943, thanks to a remarkable succession of conspiratorial events. It all began in September of 1941. Heydrich, in recognition of his ruthless efficiency, was appointed Reich Protector of Bohemia and Moravia and dispatched to Czechoslovakia to suppress the restless Czechs. Heydrich blamed the troubles on the head of the puppet government in Prague, General Alois Elias, and rigged a plot to get him convicted of high treason. He enlisted the aid of Dr. Otto Thierack, President of the People's Court, who aspired to become Reich Minister of Justice. Heydrich then had Elias arrested on trumped-up evidence and Thierack held a show trial that ended with a sentence of death.

In reward for his service to the state, Hitler in August 1942 appointed Thierack Reich Minister of Justice. Thierack then repaid the SS by officially ceding it a whole string of judiciary rights and privileges that virtually empowered Himmler to make his own laws. One of these prerogatives was a free judicial hand with the Poles and Jews in the Eastern territories.

Hitler then ratified the autonomy of the SS by removing the only government official who had even nominal authority over it, the Minister of the Interior, Wilhelm Frick. On August 25, 1943, the Führer awarded the vacated post to his "ever-true" Heinrich Himmler.

By law as well as by might, the SS was now supreme in the Nazi establishment—a largely independent state within the Reich. In its new guise it was all-pervasive. It infiltrated every branch of the party and the government, and it cast a heavy blanket of oppression over Germany and over every country that had fallen to the armies of the Reich.

The Gestapo rooted out political enemies at home, abducting and liquidating suspects at will, without accounting to any other authority. In the occupied countries Gestapo agents tortured saboteurs into betraying their comrades, and whipped and drove hordes of puppet police in cross-country sweeps for labor-draft evaders and armed resisters.

The SD, Heydrich's creation, spied on five continents—in foreign embassies, in enemy war plants, in fashionable brothels wired for sound.

At the midpoint of the War, the *Einsatzgruppen* on the Eastern Front were carrying out mass executions of Jews and other undesirables.

The Waffen-SS, now possessing one fourth of Germany's armored divisions and one third of the mechanized divisions and still growing fast, was heavily engaged on the 1,800-mile Russian front, in Finland, and against the resistance in France and Yugoslavia.

The WVHA—the SS Economic and Administrative Main Office—ran an industrial empire that stretched from the English Channel to the Caucasus Mountains in the Soviet Union. Among many other things, it owned 313 brickworks, produced 75 per cent of Germany's mineral water, manufactured armaments for the SS in its own war plants and operated slave-labor industries in a constellation of more than 150 concentration camps sprinkled through Europe from eastern Poland to southern France.

By the summer of 1943 the only person in the Greater German Reich who was safe from the SS was the man to whom every black-clad recruit had vowed "obedience unto death": Adolf Hitler.

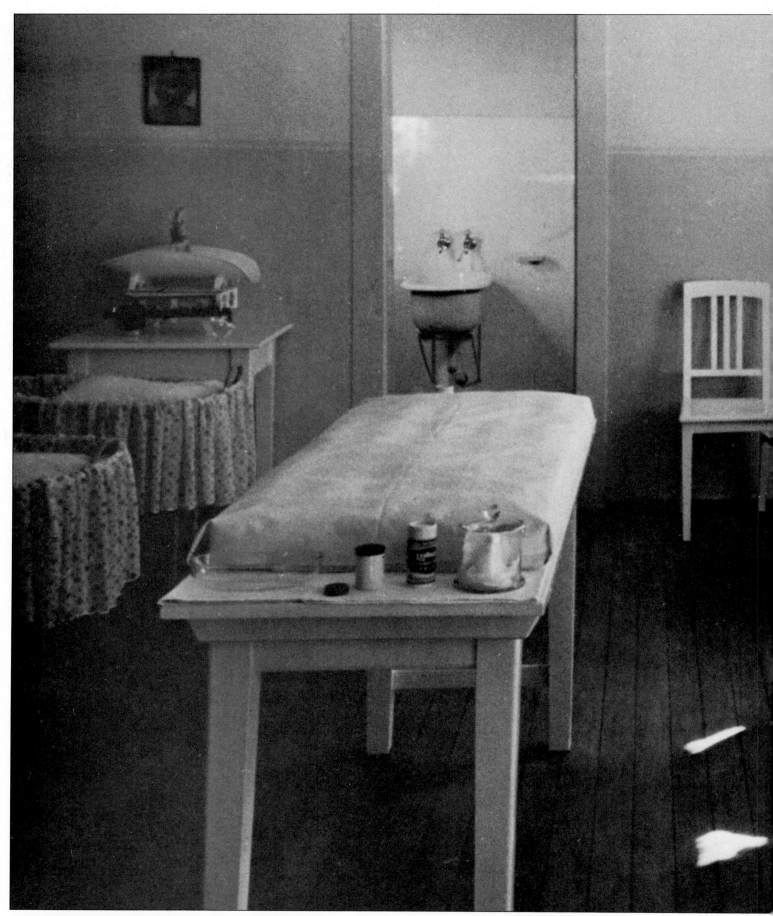

BREEDING THE "MASTER RACE"

Sunlight streams into the cheery nursery of an SS maternity home in Bavaria. There, children were born and nurtured in an SS program of planned propagation.

THE CHILDREN OF HIMMLER

On December 12, 1935, at the order of Reichsführer-SS Heinrich Himmler, the SS Race and Resettlement Office set up a program known as the Lebensborn, or Fountain of Life. It was dedicated to producing a master race whose swelling numbers would provide the Reich, said the program's medical chief, with "600 extra regiments in 30 years' time."

To meet their goal, the Lebensborn authorities set up a chain of maternity homes throughout the Greater German Reich and encouraged all women—married or single—to produce children as a "sacred duty" to the Führer. Specifically, "racially valuable" young women were urged to mate with SS men, whose "Aryan" or "Nordic" pedigree had already been ascertained and who themselves had been exhorted "to maintain stable conjugal relations with one or more women." They did not have to get married; the children of such unions were considered legitimate.

The SS men responded patriotically. "Nowadays there is no shame in having an illegitimate child," an SS trooper wrote to his girl friend. "On the contrary it is the greatest happiness of a German mother." Said one thoroughly indoctrinated woman: "We shall abandon ourselves to the rich emotional experience of procreating in the company of healthy young men without troubling about marriage."

Women who conceived a child by a "racially unobjectionable" young man, or better yet an SS officer, were entitled to give birth at one of the luxurious Lebensborn centers, many of which were resort hotels, health spas or villas confiscated from Jews. It was said that patriotic women often waived anesthesia during delivery, preferring instead to gaze at a portrait of the Führer.

If the mother took the "parcel"—i.e., baby—with her, she was entitled to be called "Mrs.," even if she was a "Miss." If she did not want the child, the Lebensborn authorities placed it with a suitable family. Often, recalled a woman official, the natural father adopted the baby. Thus, she said, "he both produced a child in accordance with the Reichsführer's wishes and increased the size of his family, which gave the Reichsführer additional pleasure."

An SS officer displays the perfect features of an "Aryan" sire: "tall, long head, narrow face, narrow nose, fair hair, light eyes and pink white skin."

A Nazi propaganda photograph idealizes a German mother who seems to be doing a magnificent job of bringing up her "Nordic" brood all by herself.

SS men welcome visiting members of the League of German Girls, who had been thoroughly indoctrinated in their duty to bear children for the Reich, in or out of wedlock. Such meetings took place in sports camps, social centers and, on a large scale, at the annual rallies in Nuremberg. The 1936 rally produced nearly 1,000 patriotic pregnancies.

A bride and groom descend through an arch of Nazi salutes following their wedding at an SS social center. Every SS couple was presented with a cellar of salt, symbolic of purity, and a bread dish inscribed, "Be worthy of the bread of your own soil, then your kin will live forever."

COURTSHIP AND MARRIAGE SS STYLE

As the fountainhead of a future racial elite, the men of the SS were given every encouragement and opportunity to sire children in great numbers.

Social events were arranged to bring SS men together with young women of several Nazi organizations. The get-acquainted sessions were casual and quite proper. One meeting frequently led to another and then to a pre- or extra-marital relationship, but everything was discreet and in good taste. In fact, the relationships seemed to be dutiful rather than emotional. The correspondence of Lebensborn mothers seldom revealed a feeling of love or even affection for the father.

Nonetheless, for whatever reason, many couples felt a need to solemnize their relationship. Every SS man who wanted to marry had to forward the woman's genealogy to SS headquarters, which alone could endorse her as "biologically flawless" and therefore eligible for an SS marriage.

If an old-fashioned couple insisted, they might be married in a civil ceremony. But they—and everyone else—had their relationship consecrated in the SS "marriage-vow ceremony," one of the neopagan rituals devised by Himmler to replace Christian sacraments.

This rite, presided over by the groom's commanding officer, usually took place in settings that evoked the Germanic tribal past: under a tree or in an SS hall festooned with fir twigs, sunflowers and SS totemic runes. Before an altar topped with an eternal flame, the couple exchanged rings and vows.

LIFE IN THE LEBENSBORN HOMES

"It was a marvelous time, the best time of my life," said a woman of her stay at a Lebensborn home, and many others agreed.

Throughout the war years, even when German soldiers went hungry, the expectant mothers were provided with fresh fruit and vegetables, chocolate and real coffee. They had no duties except to keep their pleasant rooms neat and to ensure the health of their unborn babies. Since light exercise was conducive to good health, the women were permitted to take strolls through the broad lawns and gardens that surrounded many of the country homes.

For the most part, the only unpleasantness at the homes was caused by the staff's insistence on secrecy to protect the privacy of the mothers, not to mention the reputation of the program. Many new patients would be brought in furtively in curtained Mercedes to avoid the local gossips, who made snide remarks as, "Look, there are some new cows for our stud bulls."

To scotch rumors that the homes were brothels or "SS officers' clubs," fathers were denied visiting privileges, and the grounds were patrolled day and night by SS guards with police dogs.

The Steinhoring maternity center in Upper Bavaria was the model for the Lebensborn homes. It was surrounded by high walls to shield the residents from the world outside.

Two student nurses bottle feed infants at one home. Most mothers preferred to breast feed for as long as they could to prolong their confinements at the comfortable Lebensborns.

Beneath an SS banner, a student nurse, or "little blond sister" as they were known, wheels a pram into the sunlight. Student nurses were carefully screened, for they too had to "fulfill a lofty duty to the nation."

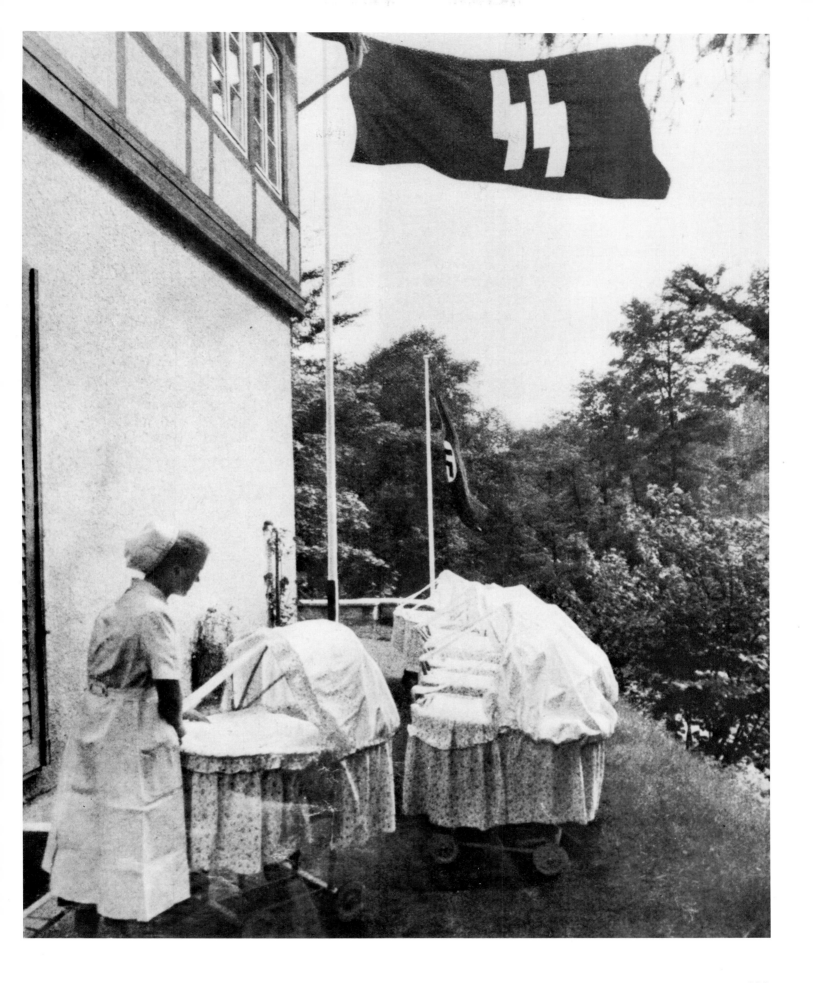

BESTOWING A NAME ON THE SS INFANT

In place of Christian baptism, Lebensborn mothers had their babies "christened" in the secular SS "name-giving ceremony," which could be performed by an SS officer. In a churchlike setting, the infant—swaddled in a rough wool shawl embroidered with swastikas and SS runes—was set down before an altar. The parents laid their hands on the infant's head and solemnly intoned his given name. Thousands of parents chose the name Heinrich in honor of Himmler, who took pride in becoming a "godfather" so many times over.

Every SS child was given a silver beaker and silver spoon, and a blue silk shawl—all manufactured at an SS-owned factory near Munich. For every fourth child that they produced, SS mothers were presented with a silver candlestick engraved with the legend "You are only a link in the clan's endless chain."

And the SS did not forget the Lebensborn children. On every birthday, each child received an SS gift of the appropriate number of candles, which were manufactured at no cost by prisoners at Dachau.

An SS infant is named before an altar topped by Hitler's portrait. Some Lebensborn children grew up so steeped in Nazi pagan dogma that they believed Hitler was God, a misconception the SS did not try to correct.

4

Adolf Hitler considered himself at once a visionary and a realist. The qualities, in his judgment, were complementary: Great men dream great dreams; these may be brought to life by a transcendent leader making hard, often unpleasant, workaday decisions. Hitler frequently gave free flight to his imagination—and, for history's sake, called in his secretaries to write down his thoughts about the future of the Germanic empire.

In the Soviet Union, entire regions of which were to be annexed to the Greater German Reich, a colonial system would be established and millions of German ethnics from the fatherland, and from Scandinavia and the Low Countries would be sent in as permanent settlers. These pioneers, or "peasant-soldiers" in the Führer's phrase, would probably find themselves in a more or less permanent state of war with the *Untermenschen*—the subhuman Slavs—on their eastern borders. But even that would bring positive benefit: This conflict, by a Darwinian process of selectivity, reasoned Hitler, would create of the colonists "a sound race of men, and will prevent us from relapsing into the softness of a Europe falling back on itself."

As for the despised *Untermenschen* living within the new boundaries, they would be prohibited from propagating and would be given only as much schooling as was necessary for them to understand German orders and "to learn the meaning of traffic signs."

From the Ukraine and the Volga basin, Hitler foresaw wondrous bounties for the taking. "Where is there a region capable of supplying iron of the quality of Ukrainian iron? Where can one find more nickel, more coal, more manganese, more molybdenum? And on top of that, so many other possibilities: the vegetable oils, the rubber plantations to be organized!" In return for stripping the Ukraine of its natural resources, Hitler offered long-range esthetics: "In 300 years, the country will be one of the loveliest gardens in the world."

The Crimea would also bloom for the Greater German Reich, furnishing citrus fruits and cotton. The Black Sea, Hitler said, "will be for us a sea whose wealth our fishermen will never exhaust." And the same for the rest of the country. "This Russian desert," said Hitler, "we shall populate it. We will give this country a past. We will take away its character of an Asiatic steppe. We will Europeanize it."

A RULE OF PLUNDER

Poland? That benighted nation was barely worthy of Hitler's personal attention. He scarcely mentioned it during his musings. But Poland had a place in the Nazi scheme of things, and Heinrich Himmler, aping his leader as a visionary, had set a 10-year goal of 100 settlers of German blood origins per square kilometer of Polish soil. Those on the farms would set an example of Aryan pastoral industry to the world; they would also devote much of their time to folk dancing, music and handicrafts. To this idyllic life was added the assurance of a bath and shower for every farmhouse.

In the West, the New Order of Europe would take more mundane form. It was Hitler's belief, bolstered by Nazi geneticists, that the people of Norway, Denmark, Finland, Holland and Flemish Belgium were racially related to the Germans and, once undesirable political and blood types had been eliminated, could become part of the Reich. In addition, Hitler had examined maps of northern France and found a good many places with "German" names—Rethel, Hirson, Phalsbourg, Cherbourg. It naturally followed that northern France could safely be re-Germanized.

Hitler understood of course that his grand design would be years in the making, and he said, somewhat wistfully: "I shall no longer be here to see all that." In the meantime, there was the business at hand. Thus on July 16, 1941, the Führer had met with German leaders, including Hermann Göring, Alfred Rosenberg and Martin Bormann, at his Rastenburg headquarters. And there, succinctly and with devastating clarity, he had set forth the policy by which he meant Europe to be governed:

"We now have to face the task of cutting up the cake according to our needs in order to be able: first, to dominate it; second, to administer it; third, to exploit it."

By then, the domination phase was almost completed—or so Hitler thought. France was divided into two harmless entities: the German-occupied north and the nominally free south, which was administered by the collaborationist Vichy government of Marshal Henri Philippe Pétain. Five other Western nations—Norway, Denmark, Holland, Belgium and Luxembourg—had been vanquished and occupied. In the East, Poland, Czechoslovakia, Yugoslavia and Greece had been seized. Finally, and crucially, the German invasion of the Soviet Union, which had begun less than a month before, was swiftly driving the Russians eastward.

At their Führer's bidding, the Nazi leaders enthusiastically went about administering and exploiting the conquered lands. The two actions were perfectly complementary, one existing for the other, as a glove clothes a hand. In their methods of government, the Nazis established a wide range of apparatus tailored to their special needs and opportunities in the occupied territories. Some were military regimes; others were civilian in nature. All were designed with one primary purpose in mind: to facilitate by whatever means necessary the exploitation of the conquered lands and the subjugated peoples.

Hermann Göring, in a rare burst of candor, scorned even the word "exploitation." It was, in his view, a foolish euphemism. "It used to be called plundering," he told an audience of Nazi Occupation commissioners. "But today things have become more humane. In spite of that, I intend to plunder, and to do it thoroughly." In the name of the Third Reich, on behalf of the German war machine and in the naked course of personal aggrandizement, businesses and entire industries were taken over, vast sums of money were extorted or stolen, nations were stripped of their national resources, art treasures were looted and millions of humans were driven to labor as slaves.

The six conquered Western European nations were mature, productive, largely Aryan countries, and therefore candidates for incorporation into the Greater German Reich. In the hope of winning the peoples' cooperation, Hitler allowed puppets to rule in some countries and tried not to disturb the existing order any more than was necessary.

Just as the Nazis had consolidated their power within Germany, so they sought to control existing government institutions with a network of their own supervisors. The SS, for example, took charge of the local police, and Göring's Four-Year Plan, a superagency originally set up to mobilize the German war effort, sent administrators to run the local economies. The advantage, if the system could be made to work, was clear: Since effective domination could presumably be maintained by small German cadres, the bulk of the Third Reich's administrative bureaucracy would not be diverted from normal duties.

The idea worked remarkably well in Denmark and Norway. The Danes, realizing the futility of contesting the inva-

TERRITORY TO BE ANNEXED
TO HITLER'S GREATER GERMAN EMPIRE

MAXIMUM EXTENT OF
GERMAN RULE OR DOMINATION

0   100   200   300   400   500
Scale of Miles

Barents Sea

North Sea

Ireland

England

Denmark

Netherlands

Belgium

Luxembourg

France

Switzerland

Spain

Sweden

Norway

Finland

Estonia

Latvia

Lithuania

East
Prussia

Germany

Poland

Czechoslovakia

Austria

Hungary

Rumania

Yugoslavia

Italy

Albania

Bulgaria

Greece

Union   of   Soviet   Socialist   Republics

Caspian
Sea

Black Sea

Turkey

Iran

Syria

Iraq

Mediterranean Sea

Tunisia

Algeria

Libya

Palestine—

Trans-
Jordan

Egypt

Saudi Arabia

sion, had accepted Germany's lenient Occupation terms. King Christian X, his cabinet and the Danish parliament went about their business almost as before. The German military commander confined his activities to defending the occupied country against attack. A German plenipotentiary, appointed by the Foreign Ministry and reporting to Joachim von Ribbentrop, submitted German "requests" to the Danish government, which gave reasonable cooperation. For nearly two years, Denmark was governed without serious difficulty by Cecil von Renthe-Fink, a career diplomat with the rank of minister and a staff of fewer than 100 Germans.

For Norway, Hitler had an almost identical arrangement in mind. But Norway's King Haakon VII inconvenienced him by escaping to England with members of his government, and Norwegian forces stubbornly kept on fighting in the north. A Norwegian Nazi, Vidkun Quisling, appointed himself the head of a puppet government, but neither the Norwegians nor the Germans paid much attention to him. The real power was wielded by Reich Commissioner Josef Terboven, a former bank official and an effective executive who was soon directing Norwegian civil servants with the help of only about 300 Germans.

Holland also was favored with civilian rule, and the Nazi selected for the top job was perhaps the most experienced and most accomplished bureaucrat among all the Occupation chiefs. Arthur Seyss-Inquart, an Austrian who had played a large part in turning his native land over to the Reich in 1938, was elated when Hitler appointed him Reich Commissioner of Holland in May of 1940. "Trude," he said on the telephone to his wife, "the Führer wants me to go and plant tulips."

Seyss-Inquart tended his garden skillfully. German staffers, he told the Dutch, would be "placed next to the central Dutch governmental bodies. It is the Dutch duty to look after the interests of the occupying power according to the needs of the moment. In other words: The people of the Netherlands are governed by their own authorities and civil servants." Seyss-Inquart made a particular point of permitting political freedom—within reason—to Dutch civil servants. "It is immaterial," he said, "what political views the individual has so long as he fulfills his duties in his particular profession." Of course all the German ministries, bureaus and agencies poured into the Netherlands to get their

share of the action and—if possible—considerably more.

In Belgium, General Baron Alexander von Falkenhausen and his deputy for administration, Lieut. General Eggert Reeder, coolly and efficiently set about using the established bureaucracy. As an anti-Nazi himself (he would end the War in a concentration camp for his part in a conspiracy against Hitler), Falkenhausen was uninhibited by the political views or even the racial strain of the civil servants he used. Moreover, even before the invasion Reeder had drawn up guidelines for occupying Belgium. In World War I, Reeder reported, the Germans had used more than 10,000 of their own bureaucrats to run the country. He and Falkenhausen would not repeat that experience. By the middle of 1941, after more than a year of occupation, only 200 or so Germans were needed to oversee the Belgian civil service; most of Belgium's bureaucrats stayed at their posts throughout the War.

In occupied France, Hitler invested the military governor—who, like Falkenhausen, reported directly to the Army Chief of Staff—with "supreme executive power." But owing to the peculiarities of the 1940 Armistice, the Germans had to pay lip service to French freedom of action. In the day-to-day running of the country, such a situation served the Germans well. They ran the country while the French collaborationist government in Vichy did most of the paper work.

"The German advisers are in contact only with the higher ups," wrote Thomas Kernan, an American magazine editor in Paris. "As far as the French workman is concerned, he is working for the same French foreman, at the same wages. If a foreman, he works with the same French department superintendent as before." Thus did the French keep the railroads running, the highways repaired, the telephone and postal services and other institutions of daily life functioning—all for the benefit of the Nazis, whose economic assault on the occupied nation was every bit as fierce as their military blitzkrieg had been.

There was a vast difference of style, however. The military conquest of France had been a smoothly coordinated thrust, with all forces working together. But the economic exploitation of the country involved a bewildering assortment of German bureaus and bureaucrats clamoring and competing for the loot Adolf Hitler had set before them.

At the peak of his power, Hitler held sway over most of continental Europe. The Führer either ruled the striped territories on this map directly or dominated them through alliances. At war's end, he intended to effect his grand dream of empire by annexing to the Reich the tinted areas on the map, including parts of the conquered Western nations and great tracts of the Eastern Lebensraum territory overrun by the Wehrmacht.

In 1940 an organization called the Franco-German Armistice Commission set up a special agency, the Waffenstillstandsdelegation für Wirtschaft, or Armistice Delegation for Economic Affairs, to coordinate the exploitation of the French economy. Its members were to allocate priorities and centralize German demands. In practice, the German economic exploitation resembled nothing so much as a pack of jackals at a carcass—all snarling and snapping at one another while nevertheless devouring the victim in amazingly swift time.

The scavengers included representatives of Ribbentrop's Foreign Ministry, of Göring's Four-Year Plan, and of the Wehrmacht and the military government. There were functionaries for the Reich Ministries of Finance, Economics, Commerce, and Armaments and Munitions; also on hand were administrators for Organization Todt, which was responsible for building roads and military installations, and operatives of Alfred Rosenberg's *Einsatzstab,* or special group, which confiscated Jewish and other "enemy" property. The recruiters of Fritz Sauckel, Plenipotentiary for the Allocation of Labor, were everywhere in evidence, as were the agents of numerous German private businesses, and the black-uniformed SS officers of Heinrich Himmler, whose economic tentacles were every bit as far-reaching as his political ones.

Those plunderers were all over France—and each other. A Four-Year Plan representative sent in to examine a French firm's books might find himself shoulder to shoulder with someone from the Reich Ministry of Finance's commission on French banking, or someone from the Ministry of Commerce's commission on French industry, or a representative from Fritz Sauckel's commission on French labor, or an accountant from one of the large German firms such as I. G. Farben or Krupp.

Every agency sent Hitler bitter complaints against its rivals; he ignored most of them. Just as in Germany, the Führer tolerated—even encouraged—vicious fighting among his followers. It kept them on their toes, it prevented any one man or organization from growing more powerful than Hitler intended, and yet it did not seem to affect unduly the conduct of business. For all its weaknesses, this dog-eat-dog arrangement made possible the exploitation of occupied Europe on a scale hitherto unimagined by any conqueror.

Some of the occupied countries were required to pay for support of the exploiters. Thus, the French were charged up to 400 million French francs (approximately nine million dollars) a day to defray the cost of the German Occupation. In the Netherlands, Reich Commissioner Seyss-Inquart ordered the Dutch to make "a voluntary contribution" of 50 million gulden ($26 million) a month, beginning in April 1942, not for the Occupation but to defray costs of the German invasion of the Soviet Union—and he made the payments retroactive to July of the previous year.

The total haul from such assessments levied throughout occupied Western Europe was put at a staggering 60 billion reichsmarks ($15 billion) according to war's end estimates by Count Schwerin von Krosigk, Germany's Minister of Finance. Not included in that figure was the value of businesses confiscated by the Germans. In France, companies belonging to Jews and to refugees who had fled the country were considered "enemy" property and could legally be confiscated.

When agents of the Four-Year Plan wanted to take control of other French firms that interested them, they resorted to a different method of legal chicanery. "As soon as they moved in, a German commissioner was placed in each French bank," observed Thomas Kernan. "He went through

The coarse and brutal face of the "subhuman" Slav glowers menacingly from the cover of this 1942 propaganda pamphlet issued to German troops in Russia. According to the text, the Slav "is only a rough copy of a human being, displaying human-like facial traits but nonetheless ranking lower in morality and mentality than any animal."

the books and noted demand loans outstanding of certain interesting companies. As is common practice everywhere, a number of large industrial plants had call loans, which, by mutual consent, the banks had no intention of calling without ample warning.

"The German commissioners calmly told the French bankers that this loan, and that one, and the other, should be called in at once. The anxious officers of the companies appeared at the bank to plead for time, and were informed by the bankers that this was impossible. Well, it was impossible to pay, too. What was to be done?"

The German commissioners, said Kernan, instructed the bank directors to advise the debtor companies to float new stock to pay the debts. But as there was, in fact, no stock market still operating, the bankers should offer to arrange for financial assistance from sources with which they had contacts—meaning the Occupation authorities. The Germans would then come forward to purchase the new stock, either with confiscated French francs or with reichsmarks, whose prewar value—14 French francs to one reichsmark—had arbitrarily been raised to 20 francs.

In spite of this disadvantage, some French companies were financially strong enough to withstand the Germans, notably the Compagnie de Batignolles, which manufac-

tured locomotives, and the Peugeot automobile company. But many other firms were transferred to German hands through stock "purchases."

When it came to exploiting natural resources, the Germans wasted little time on legalities. They simply commandeered what they wanted. France's bauxite ore was converted into aluminum for the German war machine. By the summer of 1941, Belgium and the two French departments Nord and Pas-de-Calais were supplying almost 45 per cent as much coal as the Ruhr. Norway, however, was a disappointment. Its one great natural asset was hydroelectric power, and Hitler briefly envisioned the country as the power-generating center of Europe. "In that way," he said, "the Norwegians will at last find a European mission to fulfill." But transporting hydroelectric equipment to Norway proved both difficult and costly, and by the end of 1942 the giant project had been largely forgotten.

By the end of 1941, the Germans had begun to suffer reverses in the Soviet Union and North Africa, and they seized more and more goods and resources for the German military, causing frightful shortages and rampant inflation in the occupied countries. In France, the Germans confiscated so much of everything that prices doubled and trebled. Roy P. Porter, an American correspondent stationed in Paris until the United States entered the War, reported: "Soap, at 3 francs (6 cents) a bar normally, was 25 francs (55 cents) if it could be found, wine was four times its original selling price. A suit of clothes worth 1,500 francs ($33) was worth 4,000 ($88) on the black market."

Inevitably, the black market burgeoned throughout occupied Europe—and though the Germans officially outlawed it, they also used it to their own advantage as a way of sopping up still more goods from the occupied countries. Göring, as head of the Four-Year Plan, ordered the formation of clandestine companies to traffic in scarce commodities. In the Netherlands, for example, the Germans set up the Roges Company—directed by one J. Veltjens, a Luftwaffe colonel undoubtedly chosen for his Dutch name—to centralize black-market purchasing so the Germans would not bid against themselves. By 1943 the company had managed to buy more than 73 million reichsmarks' ($29 million) worth of food, metals, furniture, diamonds and assorted luxury

A German woman and a Polish man accused of "racial disgrace" are bound to a stake in Germany's Eisenach district. The woman was lucky: To punish her "blood sin" of intimacy with an "inferior" male, the Nazis shaved her head and then forced her to carry a sign confessing her "crime." The standard punishment for her companion was death.

items on the Dutch black market. The goods were paid for with money extorted from the Dutch.

One observer privy to a black-market transaction in France noted that the Germans used "new thousand-franc notes taken from bags sealed with lead seals bearing the stamp of the Bank of France." Whether this was money paid by France as "Occupation costs" or whether the Nazis had simply helped themselves to the Bank of France's vaults was immaterial. In all, of roughly one billion reichsmarks ($400 million) in goods bought by the Germans on the French black market, an estimated 90 per cent was in fact paid for by the French.

German officialdom sometimes dispensed with such manipulations in favor of confiscating goods as openly as they commandeered raw materials. In Holland, special "removal commandos" scoured the country in search of anything worth sending home. Fifty trolley cars from Amsterdam ended up in Germany, as did more than 100,000 Dutch bicycles. In late 1942, Seyss-Inquart subjected the Dutch to the so-called Christmas Action, a campaign to supply German civilians with Christmas gifts. In all, more than 2,300 boxcars of toys, clothing, cosmetics and other items were shipped to the Reich that yuletide. Even Anton Mussert, the sycophantic leader of the Dutch Nazi Party, protested that the "voluntary" campaign was in fact out-and-out robbery.

Of all the plundering projects, by far the most pleasing to certain high Nazis was what Alfred Rosenberg called "the biggest art operation in history." As head of the *Einsatzstab* charged with confiscating "enemy" property, Rosenberg found himself a fascinated observer at a museum-looting contest between Hermann Göring and his master in all other matters, Adolf Hitler.

Hitler the Visionary had in his mind's eye a gigantic Führer Museum to be built at his Linz, Austria, birthplace. Within would repose a collection without equal in world history, easily surpassing Paris' Louvre, London's Tate and New York's Metropolitan. Architect Albert Speer toiled on blueprints for the project; as fast as they were submitted, Hitler rejected them as falling short of his dream. But if his magnificent edifice was slow in taking shape, his treasures could at least be gathered and placed in storage awaiting the day.

For his part, Göring fancied himself a connoisseur of greater artistic sensibilities than Hitler. Göring also contemplated a museum, but one that would be smaller and much more tasteful than the colossus-to-be at Linz. Göring's plan was that on his 60th birthday—January 12, 1953—he would bequeath to the Reich his museum, which was to be erected at his Karinhall estate in the Schorfheide forests 45 miles north of Berlin.

Thus the two inadvertently became rivals for the stolen art of Europe, with Alfred Rosenberg zealously trying to please both collectors. Rosenberg took up headquarters in the Jeu de Paume museum in Paris' Tuileries Gardens, to which his agents brought their art finds for cataloguing before shipment to Germany. Göring himself drew up the order of preference for acquisition: Hitler had first choice, Göring came next, other Nazi leaders followed, and anything left over would go to German museums. Then, having received Hitler's approval, Göring set about making certain that, in practice, he headed the list. What Hitler did not know could hardly hurt him; the Führer, moreover, was in Germany, preoccupied with waging war, while Göring made frequent visits to the Jeu de Paume.

But Hitler became suspicious. In February 1941, probably at Martin Bormann's urging, the Führer ordered that each art work arriving at the Jeu de Paume be photographed for his viewing before distribution. It was now Göring's move. He saw to it that his agents were in charge of the picture taking—and though Hitler received a multitude of photographs, they rarely included works of the 17th Century Dutch masters whom Göring so greatly admired.

And so, between October 1940 and July 1944, countless works and *objets d'art* were pillaged and transported to Germany. Among them were priceless paintings of Rembrandt, Rubens, Goya, Velázquez, Watteau and Reynolds—as well as various sculptures and tapestries, and porcelains and coins of every kind.

Göring missed one find that resided, in a manner of speaking, beneath his very nose. The Luftwaffe in Paris had taken over a mansion at 23 Avenue de Morigny formerly owned by important Jews—the Rothschild banking family. Inside the house, in a secret room behind a bookcase, were concealed some of the most valuable pieces from the Rothschilds' fabulous art collection—a fact of which Göring remained entirely unaware as he paced only a few feet away.

The Nazi theft of Europe's currency, of its business, of its possessions great and small could scarcely compare to the enslavement of its workers. This was a campaign of the highest priority and greatest magnitude for all involved—and in the end it led the Nazis into brutalities hitherto reserved for Jews, gypsies and other *Untermenschen*.

Every German agency from the Todt construction corps to the SS made its claim on the conquered populations. In the West, the master dealer in people was Fritz Sauckel, Gauleiter of Thuringia, a crude former sailor and factory worker whom Göring had installed as Plenipotentiary for the Allocation of Labor under the umbrella of the Four-Year Plan. Of the millions of people he rounded up to toil for the German war effort, Sauckel later admitted that "not even 200,000 came voluntarily."

In Holland, Sauckel began his recruitment drive by promising good working conditions, good pay and paid vacations—promises that he soon broke, threatening workers with confiscation of their ration coupons if they refused to go to Germany. In any event the results fell short of expectations, and by 1942 the Germans had resorted to mass arrest and streetside conscription, the so-called Sauckel Actions. In a single day in Rotterdam, 50,000 men were corralled for forced labor; eventually, between 400,000 and 500,000 Dutchmen were laboring for the Germans, most of them unwillingly.

In France by early 1942 nearly 900,000 people were working for the Germans, constructing the Atlantic Wall fortifications along the Channel coast and laboring in plants turning out arms and ammunition. In Germany itself, another million Frenchmen—most of them prisoners of war—were slaving in factories and on farms.

The Germans were insatiable. In June of 1942, Hitler ordered Sauckel to recruit yet another 250,000 Frenchmen to work in Germany. The Germans offered each volunteer a thousand-franc bonus and "superior accommodations," and Sauckel privately told Vichy Prime Minister Pierre Laval that if promises failed to attract enough labor he would use whatever force was required to meet Hitler's quota.

Laval replied to Sauckel—whom he once described as "the greatest brute I have ever met"—that force would not be needed, that he could get plenty of volunteers by appealing to every Frenchman's patriotic nature. Thus was born *la relève*, a program under which the Germans promised to repatriate one French prisoner of war for every three French volunteer workers. By September, however, only slightly more than 50,000 Frenchmen had volunteered to work in Germany. The Germans reneged on a one-for-three exchange; the ratio actually worked out to something like four or five workers for every prisoner of war.

Those who did labor in Germany soon had cause to regret it bitterly. Dr. Wilhelm Jäger, a physician for the Krupp factories, described housing for one group of French workers at a work camp near Essen. "Its inhabitants were kept for nearly a half a year in dog kennels, urinals and in old baking houses," he recalled. "The dog kennels were three feet high, nine feet long, six feet wide. Five men slept in each of them. The prisoners had to crawl into these kennels on all fours. There was no water in the camp."

As German losses mounted in the War and more and

The ranking Nazi occupiers of Holland solemnly attend a 1943 military ceremony for German war dead held in Grebbeberg, where German panzer units first smashed into the country. Hitler's viceroy, Reich Commissioner Arthur Seyss-Inquart (second from right), ruled with such a bloody hand that he was known as the "Butcher of Holland."

more men were called to Army duty, the Germans in early 1943 enacted the Service du Travail Obligatoire, or Compulsory Labor Service, to draft French workers to man the Reich's factories. The families of men who refused to report were threatened with the loss of their food ration cards. By the middle of 1942, as in the Netherlands earlier, the Germans began to round up people in streets, in movie theaters and in their homes.

The French soon began to resist. At Montluçon, a group of women stood on railroad tracks to block a train that was to carry 160 French workers to Germany. As the women sang the "Marseillaise," the workers stole away. The French police, complained a German officer who witnessed the incident, stood around and did nothing. By the time German military units were called in, only 20 out of the 160 workers remained. Hundreds of such incidents took place all over France, and thousands of people fled into the countryside rather than work for the Germans—and this naturally fueled the already spreading resistance movement.

The Nazi occupiers were increasingly bedeviled by the French Resistance. Actually every occupied country—even tiny Luxembourg—had a resistance, but the French Resistance was the biggest and most effective in Western Europe, sabotaging plants and transport, rescuing Allied airmen and laying deadly ambushes for lone or ill-protected Germans. Whenever a German soldier or civilian was killed in France, hostages selected from the population were to be shot at publicly proclaimed ratios ranging up to 100 to 1.

The German reprisal killings escalated in October 1941, with Field Marshal Wilhelm Keitel, the Army staff chief in Hitler's headquarters, specifying that the victims "should include well-known personalities or members of their families." On the 21st of October, 1941, a French newspaper ran a notice signed by Keitel: "Cowardly criminals in the pay of England and Moscow killed the field commandant of Nantes on the morning of October 20. As expiation for this crime, I have ordered that 50 hostages be shot. Fifty more hostages will be shot in case the guilty should not be arrested between now and October 23." The assassins were not found, and the hostages were executed. Wrote a French witness to the shooting, "The horror overwhelms us."

The ultimate Nazi weapon against disobedience and resistance was the *Nacht und Nebel Erlass,* the Night and Fog Decree. On December 7, 1941, Hitler ordered that persons

Czech agents Josef Gabčík and Jan Kubiš (top) studied commando techniques while training in Scotland for the assassination of Reinhard Heydrich, the SS overlord of their homeland. They parachuted in and neatly accomplished their mission on May 27, 1942. Heydrich's wrecked car, blasted by a grenade, lies empty (bottom) in a Prague suburb.

114

"endangering German security" were to be seized by SD agents and dragged off into the night and fog, never to be seen or heard of again.

Five days later, Keitel amplified Hitler's decree. "Efficient intimidation," he asserted, "can only be achieved either by capital punishment or by measures by which the relatives of the criminal and the population do not know his fate." Even the burial places of the victims were to be kept secret. And though SD files captured after the War bulged with orders dealing with the decree, the number of people who were abducted and murdered was never established.

In February of 1942, General Otto von Stülpnagel, military governor of occupied France, protested to Keitel that "I can no longer commit mass shootings with a clear conscience nor can I justify them to posterity." Keitel replied that Stülpnagel should stop interfering with political matters and "just be a soldier."

Instead, Stülpnagel chose to retire. He was replaced by his cousin, General Karl-Heinrich von Stülpnagel, then head of the Armistice Commission. The second Stülpnagel also opposed hostage shootings, and when he became military governor he demanded "a clear division of his military duties from all political matters." What this meant was that the SS was now openly to take over the responsibility for the hostage system, and the SS was rigorous in the exercise of its responsibilities. The number of hostages executed in France was to total nearly 30,000; another 40,000 died or disappeared in French prisons. The executions, far from curbing resistance, provoked more and more of it.

Thus, by 1944, the Nazi Occupation of Western Europe, which Hitler had once envisioned as an orderly process in which civilized peoples peaceably—even if unwillingly—contributed to the German Reich, had degenerated into open warfare between the conqueror and the conquered.

For all its ultimate brutality, the German Occupation of Western Europe at least commenced under a cloak of moderation. In the East, there was little dissembling and no attempt to explain away the enslavement and slaughter of millions of people. "In view of the vast size of the conquered territory in the East," said Hitler, "the forces available for establishing security in these areas will be sufficient only if, instead of punishing resistance in a court of law, the occupying forces spread such terror as to crush every will among the population."

For the fourth time in its sorrowful history, Poland was partitioned: Its western provinces were annexed by the Reich, and the eastern provinces—ruled as a protectorate under a governor general—were designated as a dumping ground for racial and political undesirables from all parts of Europe. Named as protector and supreme civil authority was Hans Frank, who had served as the Nazi Party's lawyer during its rise to power.

On October 3, 1939, Frank enunciated the policies by which he intended to rule eastern Poland. Poland, he said, was to be administered "through means of ruthless exploitation, deportation of all supplies, raw materials, machines, factory installations, etc., which are important for the German war economy. Poland shall be treated as a colony. The Poles shall be the slaves of the Greater German Reich."

SS guards survey the corpses of the men of Lidice, massacred on June 10, 1942, in reprisal for the assassination of Heydrich. Jewish prisoners from Terezin concentration camp were brought in to dig a mass grave and to strip the bodies of valuables before burial. In the weeks that followed, 84,000 square yards of rubble were removed from the bulldozed village, and the entire area was planted with grain to obliterate every trace of habitation.

Ensconced in his castle in Cracow, the crown city of the Polish Kings, Frank dwelt in a style that caused a German Army officer to describe him as a "megalomaniac pasha." Before he was done, he had provided himself with a Rembrandt landscape and a da Vinci portrait, both stolen from the Cracow Czartoryski Museum, a 14th Century *Madonna and Child* from the Cracow National Museum, a gilded chalice and an ivory chest from the Cracow cathedral, and an ornamental vestment festooned with pearls. In starving Poland, the governor general and his retinue gorged themselves on fresh beef, geese and butter—and 1,000 eggs a month found their way to Frank's festive table. Both Frank and his wife dealt extensively with Jews in the Warsaw ghetto, where furs and jewels were to be had for little or, in most cases, nothing.

For all Frank's tough talk and imperial life style, he had a good deal less power than his counterparts in the West. The Army paid him little heed and took any actions it wanted to in the name of military security. Frank's budget was controlled and approved by the Reich Ministry of Finance; Poland's railroads, or what was left of them, were under the control of the German Reichsbahn, the state-owned railway system. Through the Four-Year Plan, Hermann Göring claimed jurisdiction over all economic exploitation. Heinrich Himmler was armed with a decree enabling him "to combat acts of violence"—which he interpreted as a mandate to do whatever he pleased. And most ominous of all, Himmler and Martin Bormann were conspiring to circumvent Frank entirely.

Frank's worst fears were realized on March 5, 1942, when he was summoned to a meeting on Himmler's private train. There, before Himmler, Bormann and his henchman Hans-Heinrich Lammers, the head of the Reich Chancellery, Frank was told that some very serious charges had been leveled against him.

He was accused of corruption and nepotism. The SS had files to prove that his brother-in-law had dared to renounce German citizenship to become a Swedish national, and his sister-in-law had been caught dealing with Jews. No mention was made of Frank's own grand larceny in the ghettos, which only heightened his anxiety.

The Führer did not have to be disturbed with such trifling matters, said Lammers, if Frank would agree to the installa-tion of SS man Friedrich-Wilhelm Krüger as state secretary for security and would agree not to interfere with him. Frank had no choice but to acquiesce. From that day on, he later recalled, Krüger never obeyed any of his orders or even bothered submitting any SS orders to him for review.

The same competition for power was just as savage in occupied Soviet territory. On July 17, 1941, after German armies had advanced about 300 miles to Smolensk, Hitler named Alfred Rosenberg to head a giant administrative body, the Ostministerium, or Ministry of the East. Rosenberg was supposed to have complete authority over all civil administration in the Soviet Union. But his decrees carried no weight when they ran counter to plans of the Plenipotentiary of the Four-Year Plan for confiscating economic resources, or when they displeased the Reichsführer-SS, whose duty it was to maintain security and order. Rosenberg also learned that regional military commanders and provincial civilian commissioners were both issuing their own decrees, and he discovered that he was powerless to prevent them. The results fully justified a nickname that the waspish Joseph Goebbels coined for the Ostministerium: the Chaostministerium.

Chaos or no, the looting went forward with great vigor in both Poland and the occupied Soviet territory. Göring began by appropriating private and state property in the annexed areas of Poland and placing it in the hands of his Four-Year Plan administrators. This territory included 22 million acres in the provinces of West Prussia and Posen as well as Kattowitz and Zichenau. Homes, shops and factories were confiscated. The Polish owners had to leave behind everything except what they could fit into one small bag and 50 to 100 reichsmarks in cash.

In the part of Poland under Frank's nominal governorship, many large and small plants were dismantled and shipped to the Reich; in the case of seven electric generating plants in Warsaw, it took 4,500 freight cars to ship all the equipment. Polish banks were forced to turn over their currency to the Germans in exchange for German bonds, which were nonredeemable and therefore valueless. Goods were purchased by various German agencies and private firms, also in exchange for these worthless bonds.

For the economic exploitation of conquered Soviet territories, Göring had created his most grandiose plans. Huge German monopolies under the central direction of Göring would control vital sectors of the economy. Thus, the Central Trading Company East would supervise agricultural production and distribution; the Continental Oil Company would be responsible for all petroleum operations; other corporations would be responsible for iron and steel, mining, textiles, leather goods, etc.

But the Soviet dictator, Josef Stalin, had ruined everything: What the German military forces did not destroy in their advance, the Soviet armies razed while retreating. "The whole centralized system of trade and distribution is disrupted," reported an observer who followed behind the Army. "Supplies have been burned, evacuated or looted. Factories and enterprises have been destroyed in part or in their entirety, their machinery wrecked. Spare parts cannot be located or have been willfully mixed up. All rosters of parts and machinery have been destroyed."

To Göring, the prospects were bleak. Under wartime conditions, complete reconstruction of the wrecked industries was clearly impossible. But as the War dragged on it became increasingly evident that the Wehrmacht would be busy in the U.S.S.R. for a distressingly long while and would require Soviet production even to stay in the field. The Plenipotentiary for the Four-Year Plan was compelled to rebuild what he could.

The enormous job was begun in tiny ways. Laborers were collected and put to work in a shop repairing Wehrmacht horse carts; a small shoe factory was refurbished to mend footgear for German troops. Slowly, with anguishing delays, major industries began to operate. The iron ore mines at Krivoi Rog, in the southern Ukraine, had been put out of action by the Soviets; by the end of 1942 the mines were producing 5,000 tons a day—still far short of the German goal of 15,000 tons. The manganese ore mines at Nikopol yielded a meager 36,000 tons per month during the summer of 1942; a superhuman effort brought production to nearly 123,000 tons—exceeding the Soviet prewar output of 100,000—by early 1943. Of 178 coal mines in the Donets Basin, the Russians had left only 25 operable; with the enforced help of 60,000 Russian prisoners of war, production rose from 2,500 daily tons in June 1942 to 10,000 by the year's end.

The Germans arrived in the rich Ukraine with elaborate agricultural plans. To appeal to the Ukrainians, many of whom were anti-Communists and ardent separatists, they announced plans to abolish Soviet collective farms and return the lands to private ownership. But German administrators took much of the best land for their estates, and because the Reich was in such desperate need of foodstuffs, they retained the collective-farm system in most areas. At least it was a system.

To make the farms work, administrators had to ship in vast amounts of machinery and breeding stock from the rest of occupied Europe and from the Reich itself. All in all, some 15,000 freight cars of machinery—including 7,000 tractors, 250,000 plows and three million scythe blades as well as thousands of bulls, cows, pigs and horses—were sent to rejuvenate Soviet agriculture.

The return, although statistically impressive, fell far short of Hitler's dream that the Ukraine alone would serve as the granary of the Greater German Reich. Through 1943 the Germans were getting enough provender from Soviet farms to feed the Occupation army without bringing food from the Reich. By March 1944 the Germans estimated they had delivered to the Reich 13,000 tons of potatoes, 67,000 tons of meat, 1,161,000 tons of bread grains. During the entire War, Soviet farm lands produced for the Germans only about one billion dollars' worth of agricultural goods—somewhat less than Germany received in normal prewar trade with the U.S.S.R.

By 1942, Heinrich Himmler had thrust himself to the fore as the most powerful of the German exploiters in the East. Nobody, not even Hermann Göring at his best, could compare with Himmler in his masterful use of the two commodities that the East possessed in endless supply: real estate and human beings.

In his capacity as Reich Commissioner for the Consolidation of the German People, Himmler had concocted a fantastical scheme for rearranging the demography of Eastern Europe. Its goal was to separate the ethnic Germans and thereby save them from contamination by Poles of "undesirable" blood, or by Jews, gypsies and other "trash." These would be uprooted from their homes and transported to Hans Frank's Polish protectorate.

The confiscated lands would be turned over to half a million so-called ethnic Germans from the Baltic States, Bessarabia, Czechoslovakia and Bulgaria, whom Hitler had ordered to settle in the annexed provinces.

There was one major problem: No test existed by which ethnic Germans could with any degree of certainty be distinguished from lesser mortals. Himmler experimented with several solutions, including racial questionnaires disguised as routine health surveys. The results were sometimes embarrassing. For example, one racial inventory indicated that 45 per cent of the population of Slavic Bohemia and Moravia was predominantly "Germanic"; in the neighboring Sudetenland, on behalf of whose ethnic Germans Hitler had annexed Czechoslovakia, only 25 per cent met the desired standard. But no matter. Himmler kept trying.

Himmler decreed that it was not necessary to deport valueless Eastern Europeans in order to make room for the chosen German ethnics; the subhumans might be shot. Between October of 1939 and April of the following year, SS units directed by Reinhard Heydrich murdered some 10,000 Poles in Piasnica Forest near the city of Danzig. The hapless refugees were told, as the Germans loaded them onto railway coaches, that they were being resettled. But when the coaches reached their destination, the Poles were loaded onto buses and trucks, and then driven off into the forest and executed.

"There were people of all ages, from small children to old people, men and women of various social classes," recalled a railroad employee who had helped to transport the victims. "Outside Wejherowo Station, these people were taken onto buses or trucks, the men separated from the women and children. I heard how the women lamented as their children were being taken away. Those who resisted were beaten up with rifle butts by the SS men."

Once in the forest, the men and women were shot; most of the children were seized by their legs, and their heads were bashed into tree trunks to kill them.

This and other methods of racial purification occupied much of Heinrich Himmler's time but did not prevent him from feathering the SS nest. Expropriations in Poland provided the SS knights of commerce with hundreds of cement works, lime kilns and woodworking plants to add to their building-materials industry. Shale-oil deposits, mines, timberlands and country estates came under their management. No factory or industry was too small or too large for their management, and there were uniformed SS men running textile mills, refineries, canneries, iron foundries, printing presses, shoe factories, and even nightclubs.

As the Germans pillaged the East, they exploited the people, dooming millions in their relentless roundup of slave laborers for the fields and factories of the New Order.

At first the Germans were comparatively easygoing in their enlistment of Eastern workers, or *Ostarbeiter;* in one typical roundup, in the Ukrainian city of Uman, Count Hans Erwin Spretti, one of the German labor recruiters, announced a meeting at the local cinema. When the curious residents showed up at the theater, Spretti made his appeal for volunteers. "I want you people of Uman to go voluntarily to Germany to help the German Army," he announced. "If you don't want to go, you will be politely requested to go all the same."

As resistance increased, so did the brutality of German methods—to the extent that one German officer in the Polish protectorate actually complained to Hans Frank.

"The wild and ruthless manhunt, as exercised everywhere in towns and country, in streets, squares, stations, even in churches, at night in homes, has badly shaken the security of the inhabitants," the official reported. "Everybody is exposed to the danger of being seized anywhere and at any time, suddenly and unexpectedly, and of being sent to an assembly camp. None of his relatives knows what is happening to him."

Once taken, the hapless victims were jammed into freight cars and sent to Germany, usually without food, water or toilet facilities during their journey. It was a sample of what was in store for them once they went to work in Germany. If conditions were bad for French workers in German factories, they were appalling for the *Untermenschen* shipped in from the East.

One physician for the Krupp munitions conglomerate provided an account of conditions at a slave-labor camp populated by Poles and Russians:

"They worked and slept in the same clothing in which they had arrived from the East. Virtually all of them had no overcoats and were compelled to use their blankets as coats in cold and rainy weather. Many were forced to go to work

Guards check the identity papers of women coming into the Jewish ghetto in Munkacs, Hungary, for centuries the home of a thriving Hasidic community. Hundreds of thousands of Jews were confined in Hungarian ghettos, and millions more were behind walls in Poland, Yugoslavia, Czechoslovakia and Russia. Wrote one despairing ghetto dweller: "We are segregated from the world, driven from the human race."

in their bare feet, even in winter. Sanitary conditions were atrocious. At one of Krupp's slave-labor camps, Krämerplatz, only 10 toilets were available for 1,200 inhabitants.''

On an average day, the workers in a slave-labor camp would get up at five in the morning and, without food, work until about two in the afternoon. Then they would be fed a few spoonfuls of boiled turnip and a slice of sawdust-laden bread and work another four hours until dinner, which might consist of three or four small baked potatoes and a cup of ersatz coffee.

On their one day off, the foreign workers typically would be put to work unloading railroad cars. For seven days' work, an *Ostarbeiter* might receive one reichsmark, 20 reichspfennigs (48 cents). (They also had expenses, such as the 50 reichspfennigs they had to pay to wear the "Ost" badge—a blue shield with white lettering—that set them off as Slavic *Ostarbeiters*.)

All told, during the War the Germans imported more than four million Russian, Polish and other Slavic civilians to work in the Reich. Uncounted numbers of them died there.

In the ordeal of the East, Czechoslovakia was a special case. Its Slavic inhabitants were, in Hitler's eyes, undeniably *Untermenschen*—but they were also skilled workers, and they were required to man the factories upon whose production the Germans depended heavily, particularly the huge Škoda arms works. Thus, during the Occupation, the Czechs were treated with greater consideration than any other Eastern people—until an event over which they had no control brought down upon them a terrible vengeance.

Hitler's first administrator of the Czech provinces of Bohemia and Moravia was Konstantin von Neurath, a diplomat of the Old Guard who had been Foreign Minister until his place was usurped by Ribbentrop. When radical Nazis protested the appointment, Hitler explained: "People will see in it my decision not to deprive the Czechs of their racial and national life.''

And so, for a while, the Czechs—from top-ranking government officials to rubbish collectors—stayed on their jobs. Of course, there was a certain amount of coercion. "Everyone is to remain at his post and continue to work," said an Occupation decree. "Cessation of work will be regarded as sabotage.''

Still, for the East it was a soft policy, and Hitler was never comfortable with it. Despite his pronouncements of leniency and his undeniable need for Czech skills, he could not abide a nation of Slavs within the Reich. Increasingly, he came to refer to the Czechs as "a foreign body in the Ger-

man community" that had to be eliminated, not coddled. Finally, the Führer's patience gave out—and Reinhard Heydrich was named to replace Neurath as the Reich Protector of Bohemia and Moravia.

Heydrich immediately earned himself the title "Butcher of Prague" by executing 394 Czech resisters whom he accused of high treason. A month later, however, Heydrich surprised and pleased the country by announcing an increase in the fat and other food rations for Czech workers. It was a demonstration of what he called his "whip and sugar" policy; the little extras would discourage resistance, and the implicit threat of lowering the ration again would inspire the workers to increase their production. Heydrich continued his two-edged dealings with the Czechs; his policy was, he told Martin Bormann, "to pretend there is autonomy but simultaneously to liquidate this autonomy from within."

The British government and the Czech government-in-exile viewed Heydrich's apparent success with vast alarm, and decided upon a desperate measure: They would send an assassination team to take the life of Reinhard Heydrich. The London Czechs understood that this act would bring the most awful reprisals down upon their hapless countrymen, but they judged that the benefit would be worth the sacrifice. "It will warn the slave masters and give the people hope," said one of the organizers of the plot, and he added: "We have to become monsters to destroy monsters."

On the night of December 28, 1941, two men dropped by parachute from a British Halifax bomber, flying low over Czechoslovakia. Code-named "Anthropoid" for some curious reason, Jan Kubiš and Josef Gabčík were Czech operatives specially trained in England to seek out and murder Heydrich. Landing 10 miles north of Prague, the assassins linked up with Czech partisans who eventually hid them near the tiny village of Panenské Březany, where Heydrich occupied a baronial manor house confiscated from a Jewish family.

There Kubiš and Gabčík waited for a signal from London to carry out their lethal assignment. For unknown causes, the signal did not come for months, and they did not resume work on their plot until May 23, 1942. The date for the assassination attempt was set for May 27, when Heydrich was scheduled to travel to Berlin for conferences with Hitler and Himmler.

By fateful and freakish chance, Kubiš and Gabčík had come into possession of Heydrich's precise itinerary for May 27. An antique clock in Heydrich's office at Hradcany Castle in Prague required repair, and Joseph Novotny, a clockmaker—and a member of the Resistance—was called in for the job. While he was taking the clock apart, Novotny spied on Heydrich's desk a piece of paper with the protector's May 27 schedule. Novotny quickly balled it up and threw it in a nearby wastebasket.

A few minutes later, having repaired the clock, Novotny left. Later in the day, Marie Rasnerova, one of the maids employed at the castle, removed the paper from the wastebasket and took it to Gabčík and Kubiš. During their long wait, the assassins had become familiar with the Prague suburbs; they decided to attack Heydrich at a hairpin turn near where the Dresden-Prague road merged with a road leading to the Troja Bridge. There, Heydrich's driver would be forced to slow down and present a better target.

At half past nine on the morning of May 27, Gabčík waited at the turn, a raincoat draped over his Sten gun. Kubiš loitered nearby, carrying two grenades in his jacket pockets. Two hundred yards away, Jan Valčík, a member of the Czech Resistance, waited to signal that Heydrich's green Mercedes was approaching.

At 10:25, Valčík took a mirror out of his pocket and flashed the signal. Seconds later, Heydrich's car, driven by his personal bodyguard, an SS lieutenant named Klein, came within the assassins' view. Heydrich, his head down, was concentrating on paper work. As Klein shifted gears to make the turn, Gabčík dropped his coat, took aim and pressed the trigger.

But the Sten was jammed. As Gabčík tried desperately to clear the weapon, Klein saw him and, instead of speeding away from the trap, elected to stop and leap from the car, shooting wildly at Gabčík. Gabčík ran. Klein dashed after him—and Kubiš hurled a grenade into Heydrich's car.

His stomach riddled by grenade fragments, Reinhard Heydrich lurched from the car, raised his pistol, pointed it at Kubiš—and collapsed before he could pull the trigger. Kubiš escaped. Meanwhile, Gabčík had turned on the pursuing Klein and severely wounded him with a pistol he had been carrying as a spare weapon. Then Gabčík also fled.

Reinhard Heydrich, Reich Protector of Bohemia and Moravia and one of the most sinister figures of the Nazi era, was taken to a nearby hospital in a delivery van. There, one week after the attack upon his life, he died.

The manhunt was already under way. Karl Hermann Frank, chief of the protectorate police forces, halted all public transportation, blocked every road leading into Prague, closed virtually every public place—except the Škoda armaments complex—and brought SS reinforcements in from all over Europe to press the hunt for the assailants and to round up hostages. In a black fury of revenge, Adolf Hitler ordered the execution of 10,000 Czechs. The Germans went about the task with vigor, and within five days they had killed 1,300 Czechs.

As Reinhard Heydrich's corpse, clad in the somber black and silver of the SS, lay in state in a gun-metal coffin in Berlin, Adolf Hitler and Heinrich Himmler planned a further revenge. Receiving tips that members of the Resistance were being sheltered at Lidice and other villages, they decided to obliterate those places.

In the meantime, the search for Heydrich's killers was making headway. The SS got a lead on a family that had helped Kubiš and Gabčík. The family was arrested and taken to the basement of a headquarters in Prague. While the father and a 19-year-old son were being interrogated, the mother, presumably fearing that she would talk under torture, went to the bathroom and committed suicide. The son, who knew the whereabouts of the two assassins, was tortured unmercifully but did not break down—until he was presented with the severed head of his mother. He revealed the hide-out of the Czech agents.

Working on the young man's information, the Gestapo surrounded an Orthodox church in Prague, then burst in with machine pistols and grenades. Kubiš was killed in a grenade blast. Gabčík and some partisan companions held out in a crypt. They saved their last bullets for themselves and were later found dead.

But the SS had not waited for the death of Heydrich's assassins to execute Hitler's revenge on Lidice. On the night of June 9, hours after Heydrich's Berlin funeral, 10 trucks carrying SS security police under the command of Captain Max Rostock surrounded the village of Lidice. Houses were combed and their occupants herded into the village square. As the men returned from the nearby coal and iron mines, they were shoved and kicked into barns.

Next day, the men were brought out in groups of 10, lined up against the wall of the village tavern and shot by a firing squad in full view of their families. After 173 men had been killed, Rostock decided the killings were taking too long. The remaining 26 men were marched into a barn and burned to death.

Of the 195 women of Lidice, seven were sent to the Theresienstadt prison north of Prague. Four were pregnant and were transported to the Bulovka Hospital, the same hospital in which Heydrich had died; they were aborted and then were shipped off to various concentration camps in Germany. The remaining 184 women were carted off to the Ravensbrück concentration camp in Germany, where 41 of them later perished. Of the 98 children of Lidice, 90 were sent to the Gneisenau concentration camp in Poland; eight were adopted by German families. Of all the children only 16 were ever heard of again. Of Lidice's 492 citizens, only 159 survived.

The village of Lidice was burned to the ground and bulldozed over. Its death was, in the scale of things, a small event, but it was to stand as a paradigm of the holocaust the Germans were unleashing all over their European empire.

THE CAMPAIGN OF HATE

Urging a nationwide boycott of all Jewish-run businesses in 1933, four placard-bearing storm troopers form a picket line outside a warehouse in Berlin.

"JEWS ARE TO BLAME FOR EVERYTHING"

Considered by many to be the sole intellectual among the Third Reich's most powerful officials, Minister of Popular Enlightenment and Propaganda Joseph Goebbels offers a steely stare in this 1933 portrait.

In 1933, when the Nazi Party took control of Germany, less than 1 per cent of the 66 million population was Jewish. And yet, to hear the Nazis, Germany was at the mercy of the Jews; they were to be found behind every wicked scheme. The Jews had helped engineer the humiliating German capitulation that ended World War I. The Jews controlled the international financial networks that kept Germany in desperate poverty. The Jews, said the Nazis, were physically repulsive—and obscenely oversexed. The Jews were a lower form of life, yet they somehow held beloved Germany in thrall. "Jewish parasites plundered the nation without pity," Hitler declared to the Reichstag; "for this race, the misfortune of our people became an end in itself." Joseph Goebbels put it most succinctly: "The Jews are to blame for everything."

To combat the Jews, the Nazis turned to one of their most formidable weapons: the Ministry of Propaganda. Under Goebbels, the ministry burgeoned from five divisions in 1933 to 17 in 1942; its annual expenditures meanwhile increased more than tenfold, to 187 million reichsmarks. Goebbels was the absolute czar of the press, radio, motion pictures and the arts. Through these media and others—even children's books, posters and handbills—the insistent message was carried: Whatever the problem, the Jew is the culprit.

There was nothing subtle about Goebbels' campaign. "The rank and file are usually much more primitive than we imagine," he once declared. "Propaganda must therefore be essentially simple and repetitious." Every trace of Jewish achievement vanished from the national scene; even the physics of Albert Einstein was discredited.

Ultimately, anti-Semitic propaganda attempted to create an emotional climate in which the killing of Jews would become permissible. The film *Jud Suss (The Jew Suss)*, a pet project of Goebbels', concluded with the public execution of a swindling, lascivious Jew. Released in September 1940, *Jud Suss* enjoyed an extraordinary success in Germany; by Christmas it was playing at 66 theaters in Berlin alone.

In a widely distributed poster, the German people pull back a curtain of conspiracy to find "the Jew: purveyor of war, prolonger of war."

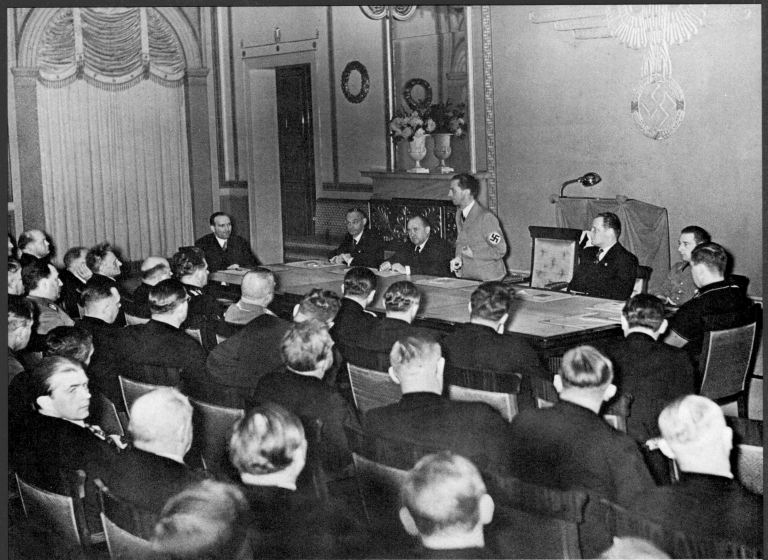

In the auditorium of the Propaganda Ministry, Goebbels delivers an address at a November 1936 meeting of his top-level deputies for the press and the arts.

HARNESSING THE POWER OF THE NATIONAL PRESS

"A National Socialist editor never is a journalist exclusively," advised a German newsman in 1935, "but always and foremost a propagandist." In that spirit, Berlin correspondents from papers throughout the Reich, and editors of newspapers in the capital, gathered each day at the Propaganda Ministry to be told what to print.

With the ascension of Hitler, many respected newspapers that took an anti-Nazi slant were forced out of business. Soon, newsstands were stocked with publications that reserved much of their editorial space for savage denunciations of Jews. In 1933, Jewish editors and writers were barred from the newspaper business. By the early 1940s, the Reich Press Chamber, headed by veteran Nazi Max Amann, ran 70 per cent of the press.

Anti-Semitic caricatures cover the pages of Der Stürmer, a Nuremberg-based Nazi Party publication.

Preis 20 Pf. | *HEUERT* | Berlin, 17. VII. 1935 — Folge 22

DER JUDENKENNER

Ende der Judenlüge von Deutscher Kriegsschuld

Frankfurter Rabbi-Tagung, 1897

F∴ M∴ Fabrikmarken

Todesfahrt Kitcheners mit der „Hamshire"

Das Geheimnis Jahveh's

Die Pandorabüchse des Weltjuden

In einer merkwürdigen Schrift, die im Jahre 1836 in England erschien (wieder abgedruckt durch die „Theosophisal Publishing Society 1888) wird der

„Wandernde Jude"

als Künder jüdischer Weisheit dargestellt. Bei der Zerstörung Jerusalems nahm er den Talisman der Juden, das Zeichen Salomons, vom Tempel an sich. Durch die Kraft dieses Zeichens bewirkte er für sein Volk den Aufstieg zur Macht in allen Ländern der Erde bis zur vollkommenen Unterwerfung der Völker, ihrer Könige und Regierenden. Die Mittel dazu sind in den Protokollen der sogenannten Weisen von Zion, die gerade jetzt wieder zum Leidwesen der Hebräer durch das Gutachten des gerichtlichen Sachverständigen Fleischhauer in das Licht der geschichtlichen Wahrheit gerückt worden sind, meisterhaft dargestellt.

Das Ziel läßt sich in zwei Sätzen ausdrücken. Erst das Chaos, dann die Weltherrschaft des Juden.

Wie das Chaos aussehen wird und wie sich die Juden wie in einer Arche Noah darüber unversehrt hinwegbringen werden, erleben wir seit 1918 in Rußland. Die Totenopfer, die diese „Entwicklung" dort gefordert hat, übertreffen die gesamten Opfer des Weltkrieges, von der Schändung des großen russischen Volkes durch die vom Weltjudenstaat aufgestellte Weltrevolutionsmaschine — Sowjet genannt — ganz zu schweigen.

Alle okkulten Bünde sind mit an der Arbeit, die Weltherrschaft des Juden herbeizuführen.

Babylon, die Mutter aller verderbten, ungesunden und geheimen Kulte, feiert Triumphe. Ihr liebster Sohn, der Jude, schüttet die Pandora-Büchse über die Völker aus. Krieg, Revolution, Unzucht, Lüge, Gift, Bolschewismus, alle schmählichen Laster, die den Menschen je geschändet haben, steigen heraus.

Dieser Jude, wie wir ihn nebenan abgebildet haben, ist die menschliche Gestalt seines Herrn Zebaoth und das Sinnbild der gegen alle Völker gerichteten zerstörenden Kräfte.

Die 4 K's

Betrachten wir die Frage statt vom Standpunkt der Judenherrschaft mit einem Blick auf die Kirche, dann kommen wir zu folgenden Erwägungen:

Der Vatikan, also die Stelle, durch die der Papst als Oberhaupt der Kirche seine politischen Maßnahmen trifft, hat in den Jahren 1918 bis 1933 (nach nur äußerlicher Neutralität im Krieg) durch das politische Bündnis (Zentrum) mit den Marxisten und anderen gegen den Bestand des Reiches und das Leben des deutschen Volkes gerichteten Bestrebungen (Separatismus) die deutsche Volkskraft zu schwächen, ja zu vernichten versucht.

Ohne Hitler wäre dieser Plan, zu dem sich die Kirche durch den Jesuiten mit der Weltfreimaurerei und dem Judentum verbunden hatte, gelungen. Dieses Bündnis wurde am 28. Juni 1928 in Aachen erneuert und verewigt.

Es handelte sich hier nicht um eine vorübergehende politische Auffassung, sondern um den uralten Kampf des die Oberherrschaft beanspruchenden Priestertums gegen jedes eine Oberherrschaft nicht anerkennendes, ja es verabscheuendes freies Volk.

With a wicked grin, an outsized Jew opens Pandora's box to turn loose all the evils of the world in this cartoon from a 1935 Berlin paper.

A PRIMER OF PREJUDICE FOR GERMAN CHILDREN

Public education in the Third Reich quickly became a weapon in the campaign of hate. Every schoolteacher in Germany was forced to become a member of the National Socialist Teachers' League and to swear an oath of loyalty to Hitler. Courses in "racial sciences" were introduced into the curricula, and textbooks were hastily produced to lend to Nazi ideology a scholarly legitimacy.

In the society that was depicted in party-approved children's books, Germans were strong, blond and happy; Jews were bloated, swarthy and malevolent, "the greatest scoundrels in the whole Reich," as one of the books put it. Charts illustrating desirable Aryan facial features were displayed in classrooms.

While German primary schools were vilifying the Jews, they were deifying Hitler. The students were taught to sing, "Our Hitler is our Lord, who rules a brave new world." One of the lessons explained how "Jesus and Hitler were persecuted, but while Jesus was crucified, Hitler rose to the Chancellorship."

Seventh-grade students in the town of Bad Wilsnack study the Völkischer Beobachter, the Nazi Party's official daily newspaper, as part of their 1939 current-events class.

Illustrations from children's books of the Nazi era show alleged physical and character traits of the Jew. At right, a pupil informs his classmates that the Jewish nose is shaped like the numeral six. In the same book, *The Poison Mushroom*, a Jewish child-molester (below) tempts his victims with sweets. The lecher draping his arm over an Aryan maiden is "The Jew from Mussbach," who uses his important position in a metal-goods factory to seduce a girl who works there. "It is disgraceful," says the accompanying text, "to witness this German officer's daughter letting herself be led around by this Jew."

„Die Judennaſe iſt an ihrer Spitze gebogen. Sie ſieht aus wie ein Sechſer..."

„Hier, Kleiner, haſt du etwas ganz Süßes! Aber dafür müßt ihr beide mit mir gehen..."

Joseph Goebbels, the Nazis' leading anti-Semitic speaker, addresses the Reich in a July 1938 broadcast from Breslau. The Minister of Propaganda greatly

People's radio receivers are given out to 500 Berliners to mark Goebbels' 41st birthday on October 29, 1938.

BRINGING THE MESSAGE TO MILLIONS AT ONCE

From the first, the Nazi Party had great hopes for the magic of radio. The state-run broadcasting network, one Reich radio official noted approvingly, engineered "a fantastic wave of political manipulation, agitation and propaganda in every form."

Goebbels spearheaded the anti-Semitic radio campaign. Among other things, he held German Jews responsible for the actions of foreign Jews after World War I. "If they announce today," he proclaimed in one broadcast, "that they could do nothing when their kin in England and America dragged the German national regime in the mud, then we can do nothing when the German people take it out on them."

Goebbels did not stop with putting the message of hate on the air. He made certain that Germans heard it by ordering full-speed production of the *Volksempfänger*, a simple "people's radio receiver" that cost only 76 reichsmarks, or about $12, less than it took to buy a cheap suit of clothes. By 1939, there were close to 15.5 million radio sets in Germany and radios could be found in 70 per cent of Germany's households—a higher ratio than in any other country save the U.S.

enjoyed carrying the anti-Jewish message, fancying himself "a preacher, an apostle, a crier of battle."

Germans hear Hitler boast in 1937 that "removing the Jews" had led to "a vast flowering" of culture.

Goebbels and Hitler personally appraise a new German movie. When the Führer complained that films espousing the Nazi line were too scarce, Goebbels rushed a pair of anti-Semitic pictures into production.

In one segment of a Nazi "instructional" film (right), the genetic heritage of the Jew is purportedly traced to Oriental, Negro, Near Asian and Hamitic peoples. Hence, the film concludes, "the Jew is a bastard." Below, the villainous title character of Jud Suss, a violently anti-Semitic melodrama, spins schemes with his crony, Rabbi Loew.

MOVIES HINTING AT HORRORS TO COME

To Joseph Goebbels, films were "one of the most modern and scientific means of influencing the masses." Though the German film industry remained largely in private hands, every movie needed the imprimatur of the Propaganda Ministry before it reached the screen, and Goebbels became notorious for meddling with scripts, directors and actors. In 1938, he set movie studios to work producing anti-Jewish films.

In addition, a special team was assembled at the ministry itself to undertake a project called *The Eternal Jew*. The result, a virulent 45-minute harangue billed as a documentary, was shown to audiences throughout Europe. The film featured a lingering look at kosher animal slaughter, imputing sadism and bloodthirstiness to the "Jewish race." Jews were likened to rats and other vermin: "They carry disease," warned the narration.

Such films, which depicted the Jews as a plague to be eradicated, hinted darkly at the real-life horrors to come.

Vorderasiaten

Hamiten

Bastard

5

In January 1942, there were an estimated 11 million Jews in Europe. By the end of the War in May 1945, six million Jews were dead, victims of a Nazi program of systematic annihilation. The Nazi leaders called the program the Final Solution. The survivors called it the Holocaust.

Thousands of Jews had been killed on Nazi orders before the summer of 1941, when Hitler and his inner circle adopted genocide as national policy. All the same, the idea of exterminating an entire people presented problems of staggering technical, legal and logistical complexity, and the Nazi leaders did not institutionalize the program without long and careful consideration.

In July 1941, Hermann Göring, acting on the Führer's instruction in his capacity as Reich Marshal, nominally the highest official in the government after Hitler, ordered SS security chief Reinhard Heydrich to draft "an overall plan of the organizational, functional and material measures to be taken in preparing for the implementation of the Final Solution of the Jewish question." Heydrich was instructed to involve all other departments that had any sort of jurisdiction in the proposed project.

Heydrich sent a copy of Göring's order to 14 of the most powerful Nazi bureaucrats and invited them to discuss the matter at a conference in the Berlin suburb of Wannsee on the 20th of January, 1942. The selected officials—representing the Nazi Party, the Ministry of the Interior, the Foreign Ministry, the Ministry of Justice and the administrators of the occupied territories—came armed with pertinent documents and a number of proposals for their departments' contributions to the effort.

At noon that day, Heydrich formally opened the proceedings. He announced that his own SS security department, known by its German initials RSHA, would direct the Final Solution in all aspects and jurisdictions. He said that Hitler's policy was to evacuate all Jews to the Eastern occupied territories. He explained that the evacuees were to be organized into huge slave-labor battalions, that many would "fall away through natural reduction," but that the remainder, "which doubtless constitutes the toughest element," would "have to be dealt with appropriately" so it could not become the "germ cell of a new Jewish development."

The task that Heydrich outlined was a colossal one. According to a detailed RSHA tabulation, 131,800 Jews still

THE "FINAL SOLUTION"

lingered in the territory of the prewar Reich, and 43,700 hung on in Austria. Fully five million Jews would have to be evacuated from the Soviet Union, 865,000 from France, 160,000 from the Netherlands and 58,000 from Italy; smaller Jewish populations would come from Norway, Denmark and Belgium. Germany's Balkan allies would send several hundred thousand Jews, and Hungary would contribute 742,800. The RSHA report also listed Jews who would have to be dealt with at a later date: 330,000 in England, 4,000 in Ireland and 6,000 in Spain.

Heydrich went on to explain that the Jews would be combed out of Europe from west to east. They would be collected first in ghettos or conveniently located holding camps. Then, country by country, they would be transported to selected terminals in Poland. Clearly, the underdeveloped areas of Poland would permit more efficient operations than the populous West.

One by one, the delegates presented the proposals that they had worked up for the conference. Their suggestions dovetailed neatly with Heydrich's overall plan. Martin Luther, the crude and ambitious assistant secretary of the Foreign Ministry, suggested a deportation schedule, complete with the order in which countries might best be cleared of Jews. Josef Bühler, Deputy Governor General of Poland, said that his territory should be cleared first, since "no problems of transport existed"; the local Jews would have only a short journey to their final destination. Otto Hofmann, chief of the SS Race and Resettlement Office, urged the use of sterilization to solve "complicated legal questions" as to the treatment of those troublesome people who had one Jewish parent or grandparent, or Jews who had intermarried with Aryans. Wilhelm Stuckart, Undersecretary of the Interior, declared that sterilization should be made compulsory in all such cases.

The formal meeting lasted about an hour, then cocktails and lunch were served. As butlers passed through the commodious room with food and drink, the delegates gathered in small groups to debate liquidation timetables and the relative efficiency of mass killings by gunfire versus carbon monoxide fumes.

Heydrich assured his colleagues that "even now practical experiences are being gathered," but he added no specifics to what some delegates knew in a general way. For exam-

ple, he did not dwell on the energetic work of the SS killer squads, which for several months had been liquidating large numbers of Jews in Latvia, Lithuania and the Ukraine. Nor did he discuss the six production-line extermination camps —Auschwitz, Chelmno, Belzec, Sobibor, Majdanek, Treblinka—that were already under construction in Poland.

When the Wannsee conference broke up, Heydrich was greatly reassured by all he had seen and heard. The proceedings had laid to rest his concern that the many contentious government departments would not pull together in the interest of their common goal. He was pleased by the enthusiasm of the delegates and felt sure that the necessary bureaucratic machinery would work smoothly. He was confident that the delegates realized that the Final Solution was as important as the War. In fact, they would sometimes give it even higher priority in the competition for manpower, transportation and matériel.

The delegates at the Wannsee conference had seen nothing odd about their business-like discussion of mass murder. Killing was a standard Nazi method of problem solving. Violence against Jews had been a force in German history for centuries, and it had played a key role in Hitler's rise to power. In the view of these hardened Nazi bureaucrats, they had merely set in motion the most practical means of disposing of the Jews once and for all.

When Hitler began preaching anti-Semitism, he might have taken his text from the 16th Century German theologian Martin Luther, who in railing against many groups that opposed his new church declared that the Jews were "like a plague, pestilence, pure misfortune." Luther charged: "They let us work in the sweat of our noses, to earn money and property for them, while they sit behind the oven, lazy, let off gas, bake pears, eat, drink, live softly and well from our wealth."

Actually, Martin Luther's anti-Semitism—and German anti-Semitism for generations after him—differed little in kind from anti-Semitism anywhere else in Europe. But the ancient prejudice seemed to grow stronger in Germany in the early 19th Century with the rise of nationalism; in fact, in Germany the two often intermeshed.

The philosopher Johann Gottlieb Fichte was perhaps the first to link the two ideas. In the face of Napoleon's devastat-

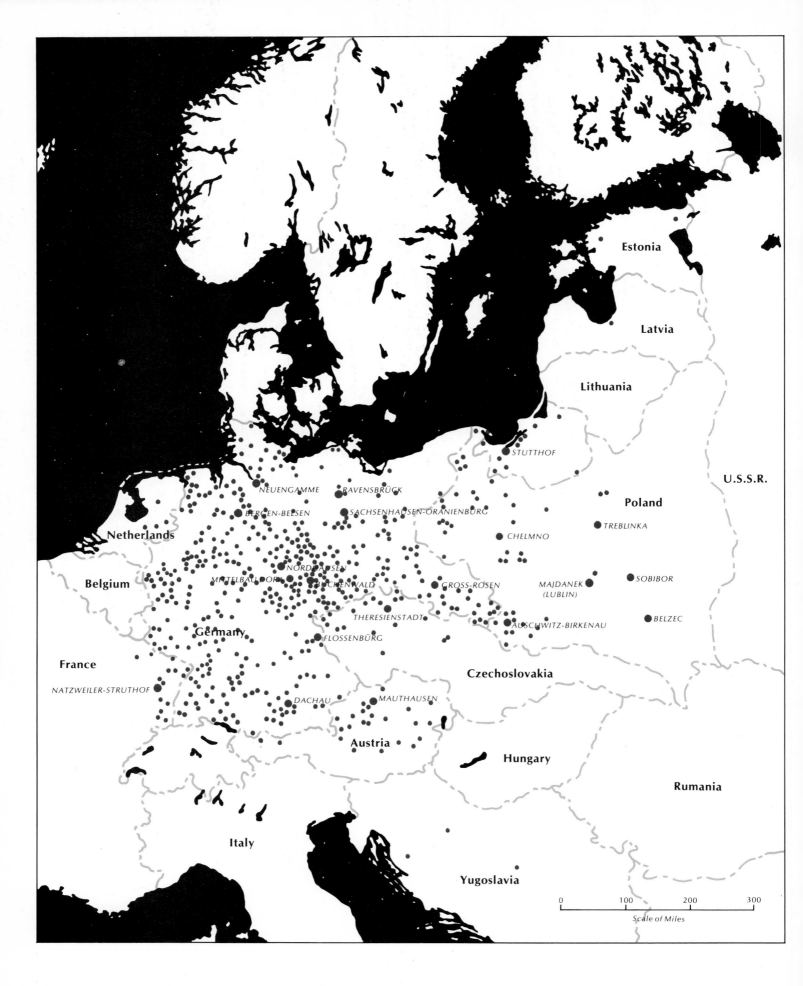

Estonia

Latvia

Lithuania

U.S.S.R.

STUTTHOF

NEUENGAMME   *RAVENSBRÜCK*

BERGEN-BELSEN   *SACHSENHAUSEN-ORANIENBURG*

Poland

Netherlands

TREBLINKA

CHELMNO

Belgium

NORDHAUSEN

MITTELBAU-DORA   *BUCHENWALD*   *GROSS-ROSEN*   *MAJDANEK (LUBLIN)*   *SOBIBOR*

THERESIENSTADT   *AUSCHWITZ-BIRKENAU*   *BELZEC*

Germany

FLOSSENBÜRG

France   Czechoslovakia

NATZWEILER-STRUTHOF

DACHAU   *MAUTHAUSEN*

Austria   Hungary

Rumania

Italy

Yugoslavia

0   100   200   300
Scale of Miles

ing occupation, which began in 1805, Fichte solaced his countrymen with a messianic vision of the German mission on earth: "It is you in whom the seed of human perfection most decidedly lies. If you perish in this your essential nature, then there perishes every hope of the whole human race for salvation." To Fichte, the Jews were the primal enemies of the German nation. Before he would grant rights to Jews, he would have "to cut off all their heads in one night, and set new ones on their shoulders, which should contain not a single Jewish idea."

Following the withdrawal of the French in 1813, the civil rights of Jews were severely restricted in many German duchies. Peasants and burghers in Bavaria, Württemberg and elsewhere rioted against the Jews and scourged them with pogroms. Out of Würzburg spread the nationalist Hep! Hep! movement, named for its battle cry: "Hep! Hep! Hep! Death and destruction to all the Jews!" Respected academicians such as J. F. Fries and Friedrich Rühs argued that Jews could never be a full-fledged part of the German nation.

In the 1840s, a new German constitution proposed expanded rights for all, including Jews. After it was drafted, peasants in the Rhineland rioted and looted Jewish properties, and in Bavaria anti-Semites collected 80,000 signatures on petitions opposing Jewish rights. The constitution was roundly rejected.

In the 1850s, scientists lent another rationale to anti-Semitism. Some scientists advanced new anthropological theories that classed Jews—who merely practiced a religion—as a "race apart." Christian Lassen, a respected professor at the University of Bonn, asserted that "Semites do not possess the harmony of psychic forces that distinguishes the Aryans." Semites instead were "selfish and exclusive." Many German anti-Semites embraced the tenets of a widely published French count, Joseph Arthur de Gobineau, who made a cult of racial purity and anathematized any dilution of the Aryan stock by Jews or anyone else.

Everywhere in Germany, Gobineau societies were organized, and Houston Stewart Chamberlain, an eccentric Englishman who had settled in Germany and married composer Richard Wagner's daughter, expanded upon the French count's ideas. The Jews, according to Chamberlain, were a "negative" race, a "bastardy." Nordic peoples, on the other hand, especially the Germans, were the "Master Race," re-

sponsible for everything that was great and good in history.

With the unification of Germany in 1871, the Jews made some gains. Otto von Bismarck, in his drive to form the Second Reich, conceded full civil and political rights to the Jews and everyone else. But the worldwide economic crisis of 1873 plunged Germany into a six-year depression, and Jewish bankers and financiers, who had played a major role in amassing the investment capital needed by the new nation, bore the brunt of the blame, with many people embracing the stereotype of the Jew as a manipulator of international finance. The Reichstag passed a "law against the pernicious pursuits of Social Democracy"; the law abolished freedom of the press, speech and assembly.

The appeal of anti-Semitism was convincingly demonstrated in 1892 when an obscure schoolteacher named Hermann Ahlwardt, running for the Reichstag without any party endorsement or funds, won an easy victory over the Conservative opponent by his shrill baiting of the Jews. Partly as a result of Ahlwardt's victory, conservatives all over Germany noted that anti-Semitism was now too powerful a political weapon to be left to splinter groups. One of the nation's most prestigious parties—the Conservative Party—adopted it as a platform plank.

For two decades thereafter, power seesawed between the liberals and conservatives; the Jews, for a time, were largely left alone. The Great War came and passed with little effect on the status of Jews.

But after World War I and the establishment of the Weimar Republic in 1919, anti-Semitic orators again took to the hustings. During the early 1920s, Adolf Hitler and other Nazis blamed Jewish bankers and industrialists for Germany's humiliating defeat. In the winter of 1916-1917, Hitler later charged, "nearly the whole production was under the control of Jewish finance. The spider was slowly beginning to suck the blood out of the people's pores."

Campaigning on anti-Semitism and a host of populist causes, the Nazis in 1923 garnered nearly one million votes. Hard times and the Weimar Republic's unpopularity added to their appeal. In the 1930 elections, 6.4 million Germans voted Nazi, and two years later, in the last free election of the Republic, the total was 13.7 million. The noose around the neck of European Jewry began to tighten.

To implement Hitler's decision to annihilate the Jews, the SS built or adapted more than 100 major installations, located on the map with red dots. Many of these facilities were local detention camps and Gestapo prisons, but those indicated by large dots were the biggest concentration camps where Jews were sent to be slave laborers. Auschwitz, Belzec, Chelmno, Majdanek, Sobibor and Treblinka were specialized death camps in Poland where large-scale extermination began early in 1942.

In April 1933, just one month after the Reichstag voted Hitler unlimited executive powers, the Nazis began translating their campaign promises into practical action against the Jews. Julius Streicher, Gauleiter of Franconia, and a 13-member Nazi Party committee organized a boycott of Jewish retail businesses and shops to take place during the first days of April. Nazi Brownshirts and black-clad SS men marched back and forth in front of stores warning Germans not to buy from the Jews. Windows were smeared with epithets such as "Jew Pig." Jews were dragged off the streets and beaten up in the Brownshirts' barracks.

All Nazis and members of the government were ordered to obey the boycott, and it took only a small offense to draw stiff punishment. A Nazi named Kurt Prelle was expelled from the party and forbidden to practice his profession as a notary after his wife purchased 10 reichspfennigs' worth of picture postcards from a Jewish shop.

The three-day boycott frightened many Jewish businessmen, and their fears were increased by subsequent government restrictions on the raw materials they needed to stay in business. More and more Jewish entrepreneurs elected to sell their holdings, usually at severely depressed prices. Many fled the country.

On April 7, Hitler issued a decree that prohibited Jews from holding civil-service positions. (Those who had been hired prior to August 1, 1914, and Jewish war veterans were at first excepted, but the exception was canceled before long.) Soon similar decrees were applied to other career fields. Jewish teachers lost their jobs at universities and technical schools. Jewish artists, musicians and actors were forbidden to appear before German audiences. Jews were banned from the field of journalism.

Yet another decree solved the legal problem of defining a Jew. A Jew was anyone who had adhered to the Jewish religion or who had one Jewish grandparent.

The Nazis accelerated their anti-Semitic campaign by passing the Nuremberg Laws on Citizenship and Race on September 15, 1935. The laws revoked the Jews' citizenship in the Reich. Jews could not vote, or marry Aryans or employ "in domestic service female subjects of German or kindred blood who are under the age of 45 years." Jews found themselves excluded from schools, libraries, theaters and public transportation facilities. Passports were stamped with the word "Jew." Name changes were disallowed, but Jewish men had to add the middle name "Israel," Jewish women the name "Sarah." Jewish wills that offended the "sound judgment of the people" could be legally voided.

In spite of all the repressive decrees, only about 30 per cent of Germany's Jews had emigrated by 1938. Many could not obtain visas from foreign countries, which were maintaining normal quota systems. Many feared losing their remaining property if they departed. Still others were unwilling to learn a new language and to adjust to a foreign culture. Besides, the onerous laws against them seemed to taper off after 1936. The remaining German Jews persuaded themselves that the worst had passed, that they might settle down once again as second-class citizens.

Then came the Jews' greatest disaster since Hitler took power. On the night of November 7, 1938, a Jewish refugee in Paris named Herschel Grynzpan, angered by the Nazis' maltreatment of his parents, entered the German embassy and shot Ernst vom Rath, a minor German diplomat. Rath died two days later, his demise coinciding with nationwide party celebrations commemorating the Nazi martyrs of the 1923 Beer Hall Putsch.

Orders went out from party headquarters instructing local leaders to mount violent demonstrations against Jews and Jewish businesses. Using the mass-communication facilities at his disposal, Joseph Goebbels exhorted Germans to express their righteous indignation over the murder of Rath by the Jew Grynzpan.

Throughout the Reich, mobs of Nazis smashed the windows of synagogues and stores owned by Jews, leaving the streets and sidewalks littered with glass shards that gave the night its poetic name—Kristallnacht, or Crystal Night. Nearly 100 Jews were killed, and thousands more were beaten up and tormented. Not to be outdone by Goebbels, Himmler and Heydrich ordered the SS to arrest 20,000 Jews, preferably wealthy ones.

Thousands of Jews arrested on Kristallnacht had a bitter foretaste of things to come. They were herded onto trains bound for Buchenwald, Dachau and other concentration camps. Once in the camps, the prisoners were left for long periods without food or water. Sanitation was nonexistent. Men were ordered to entertain their guards with humiliating acts, and if they refused or performed poorly they were flogged. Many were later released, but only if they swore to keep their mouths shut about what they had seen or experienced in the camp. They had to leave the Reich within a few weeks.

In the aftermath of *Kristallnacht,* the Nazis promulgated the strictest anti-Jewish policies yet. Jews were to be rooted out of the economy, totally segregated, and forced to emigrate. And Hitler made his strongest public statement to date on the subject of annihilating the Jews. In a speech to the Reichstag, he declared: "During my struggle for power, the Jews laughed at my prophecies that I would someday assume the leadership of the state. I suppose that the laughter of Jewry is now choking in their throats.

"Today I will be a prophet again. If international finance Jewry should succeed once more in plunging the peoples into a world war, then the consequence will not be the Bolshevization of the world and a victory of Jewry, but on the contrary, the destruction of the Jewish race in Europe." The German press trumpeted the Führer's statements. Many Jews—and many Germans—assumed that Hitler used the word "destruction" figuratively. There was no clear sign as yet that he meant what he said literally.

For still another year and a half the Nazi government made repeated attempts to deport German and foreign Jews. But other countries, underestimating the desperate plight of the Jews, took no emergency measures to relax their stiff immigration quotas. Poland, which had its own anti-Semitism, even closed its doors to Polish Jews who were living in Germany. Nazi officials rounded up 16,000 Jewish Poles and dumped them across the Polish border, but the Poles sent most of them back.

The Germans turned to France as a potential repository for Jews. Foreign Minister Joachim von Ribbentrop tried to persuade the French to accept shipments of German Jews. But French Foreign Minister Georges Bonnet not only refused, he also urged Ribbentrop to prevent German Jews from coming to France on their own. "I replied to Monsieur Bonnet," wrote Ribbentrop, "that we all wanted to get rid of our Jews but the difficulties lay in the fact that no country wished to receive them."

After the German invasion of Poland on September 1, 1939, the cloak of wartime secrecy descended over Nazi brutalities to the Jews. Inside Germany the patriotism engendered by war reinforced the common tendency to obey orders and to look the other way, to avoid inquiries when people suddenly disappeared in the night or died from unexplained causes.

This atmosphere fostered new programs that would make a large contribution to the technology of the Final Solution. A number of these involved the quiet killing of mental patients and deformed children—"useless eaters," in the Nazi vernacular—usually with poison gas and lethal injections. The Führer had personally taken the lead in this program in 1938 when he received a request from the father of a deformed child asking that the child be put to death. Hitler wrote a letter to the parents concurring in their request and stating that he alone, not they, assumed responsibility for the action. He asked his personal physician, Karl Brandt, to attend to the matter.

In early 1939, the government established the Reich Committee for Scientific Research of Hereditary and Severe Constitutional Diseases. Its function was to organize the killing of deformed and retarded children. Committee experts asked doctors, midwives and hospital administrators to notify them of eligible children. Then the committee established special children's centers in 21 hospitals to carry out the killings.

The work was done primarily by lethal injections, but at Eglfing-Haar, near Munich, a Dr. Pfannmüller made a specialty of starving sick children to death. One visitor to Pfannmüller's hospital reported seeing 15 to 25 children, aged one to five, lying in cots. Pfannmüller explained: "Those creatures represent for me, as a National Socialist, only a burden on our nation. We do not kill by poison injections because foreign newspapers and certain gentlemen from Switzerland—the Red Cross—would get new material for their propaganda. Our method is much simpler and more natural."

Then the doctor yanked one of the children from a cot and, displaying the child aloft, declared, "This one will last another two or three days." Pfannmüller explained to his visitor that his technique was not to withhold food suddenly but rather to impose a gradual reduction of rations.

Of greater scope than the children's program was the killing of the adult insane, established by the National Coordinating Agency for Therapeutic and Medical Establishments. The program was code-named T-4 for the agency's headquarters at 4 Tiergartenstrasse in Berlin. The first center was set up in Brandenburg in late 1939, and experiments were undertaken to find a killing method that would not alarm the victims and that later would permit officials to deceive the families of the victims as to the true cause of death. Hitler's physician, Brandt, reported to the Führer on the gassing of four adult male patients with cyanide gas—a rat killer known by the brand name Zyklon B—and observed further experiments with it and, more often, carbon monoxide. Philipp Bouhler, head of Hitler's personal chancellery, was credited with suggesting that the gas chambers be disguised as shower rooms, complete with toilets.

Five additional centers were equipped along the lines of the one in Brandenburg. Their operation was deceptively simple. Patients judged incurably insane were sent to transit facilities. The Charitable Foundation for Institutional Care provided transportation to the killing center, and later notified the families in a form letter that their loved one had succumbed to heart failure or pneumonia and that the body had been cremated as a health measure.

Typically, attendants at the center dressed groups of 20 to 30 patients in paper smocks and ushered them into the gas chamber under the pretext that they needed to shower. Then the physician on duty gassed them. A conveyor belt removed the bodies.

Though the government tried to keep the T-4 program secret—officials did not want to undermine morale in wartime—word drifted about with the smoke that rose from the crematoriums. School children living close to the Hadamar center near Limburg referred to the bus that brought in patients as the "murder box." Little children taunted friends, "You'll be sent to the baking oven." Young girls vowed they would never "bring children into the world so they can be put into the bottling machine," and old people pleaded with their families not to send them to the nursing home, for "after the feeble-minded have been finished off, the next useless eaters whose turn will come are the old people."

The Nazis produced a film to make the idea of euthanasia acceptable. The film told the story of a devoted husband who kills his terminally ill wife at her request in order to end her suffering. This distorted the T-4 program, but the film makers hoped that people would begin to think about executions as a form of racial mercy for the nation.

Though the film was something of a success at the box office, it was strongly opposed by Catholic and Lutheran bishops, who urged parishioners not to view it. And several bishops openly protested the T-4 killings. As public opposition mounted, Hitler reluctantly instructed Brandt to "stall" the program in August 1941, after some 90,000 patients had been killed. But by then, the gassing techniques used in the killing of mental patients were ready for more general application by the SS.

That summer, Heinrich Himmler's SS killer squads, known as *Einsatzgruppen,* had followed the German armies into the Soviet Union. These roving units now swept into the Ukraine, Belorussia, Latvia and Lithuania, and waited for orders to ply their murderous trade among the two million Jews who quickly fell into Nazi hands.

Some Jews had fled with retreating Red Army units, but most simply stayed in their homes. "The Jews are remarkably ill-informed about our attitude toward them," reported a German agent. "They believe we shall leave them in peace if they mind their own business and work diligently."

At first, the four killer squads prevailed upon local anti-Semites to start the murders, so that, in the words of an offi-

SS Lieut. Colonel Adolf Eichmann, who often traveled in civilian clothes while arranging for the deportation of Jews, professed to admire the Zionist Jews' "idealism" in working to establish a homeland in Palestine. In 1940, he even envisioned himself as the future governor of a Nazi-controlled Jewish province, and dreamed of resettling millions of European Jews on the French East African island of Madagascar.

cial *Einsatzgruppen* report, "direction by the German authorities could not be found out." The SS referred to such actions as "self-cleansing." During one self-cleansing in Kovno, Lithuania, reported a German officer, local sympathizers "did away with more than 1,500 Jews, setting fire to several synagogues or destroying them by other means and burning down a Jewish dwelling district consisting of about 60 houses. During the following nights 2,300 Jews were eliminated in a similar way."

Once the locals had tired of murder, the *Einsatzgruppen* resorted to open-air shootings. They also made use of "gas vans" manufactured by the Saurer Corporation of Berlin. Like most of the stationary gas chambers of the T-4 program, the vans killed by carbon monoxide, but being mobile, they saved the trouble of building permanent installations and transporting the victims to a distant death site. Otto Ohlendorf, commander of Einsatzgruppe D, which eventually killed more than 90,000 Jews, explained that the vans "looked like closed trucks and were so constructed that at the start of the motor the gas was conducted into the van causing death in 10 to 15 minutes." The vans varied in size, with capacities ranging from 15 to 25 persons.

Ohlendorf did not care for the vans, however, because often the victims urinated or defecated in their death throes, "leaving the corpses lying in filth." His men, Ohlendorf said, "complained to me about headaches that appear after each unloading."

Dr. August Becker, an SS lieutenant and the inventor of the vans, considered himself a humanitarian, and in order to eliminate the victims' suffering as well as the resultant filth, he ordered a change in the technique of administering the carbon monoxide. The valves were to be opened slowly instead of all at once, so that "prisoners fall asleep peacefully." The inventor was elated at the results: "Distorted faces and excretions such as could be seen before are no longer noticed."

Even with the improvements, the vans were inadequate for mass murders on the scale that SS chief Himmler envisioned, and most of the *Einsatzgruppen* victims were transported to the nearest feasible execution site. There they were herded into antitank ditches or bomb craters. Then they were shot, normally in groups. In some cases, the victims were forced to kneel at the edge of the pit, then were

shot individually by guards carrying pistols. Such executioners were known as the *Genickschussspezialisten,* or neck-shooting specialists.

On January 31, 1942, Franz Stahlecker, commander of Einsatzgruppe A, sent Himmler an ornate map marking his dozens of executions with tiny coffins. Stahlecker's report showed that his group had already eliminated 136,421 Jews in Lithuania alone, with killings elsewhere that added up to a grand total of 229,052.

To the south, Einsatzgruppe C under Brigadier General Otto Rasch managed to eliminate 95,000 people by December of 1941. Included in those figures were more than 75,000 Jews killed in the Kiev area in a two-week bloodbath that began in the town of Uman and ended at a ravine outside of Kiev at a place known as Old Woman's Gully—in Russian, Babi Yar.

The massacre started on September 16 with the posting of an innocuous document that said: "For the purpose of preparing an exact census of the Jewish population in the town of Uman and its subdistrict, all Jews, of all ages, must appear on the day appointed hereunder at the respective places of registration. Persons failing to comply with this order will be punished most severely."

When the Jews had reported for the "census," they were marched off to a site near the Uman airport, where long ditches had been excavated. Erwin Bingel, a regular Army officer who was on hand to secure the region's transportation facilities, later described what happened next: "When the people had crowded into the square in front of the airport, a few trucks drove up from the direction of the town. From these vehicles, a troop of field police alighted and were immediately led aside. A number of tables were then unloaded from one of the trucks and placed in a line. Meanwhile, a few more trucks with Ukrainian militiamen commanded by SS officers had arrived. These militiamen had work tools with them and one of the trucks also carried chloride of lime."

The Ukrainian militiamen dumped the chloride of lime, used to cause the rapid decomposition of corpses, next to the ditches. Then, Bingel recalled, "a number of Junkers-52 transport planes landed at the airport. Out of these stepped several units of SS soldiers who marched up to the field-police unit, subsequently taking up positions alongside it."

With those *Einsatzkommandos* in place, said Bingel, the killing began. "One row of Jews were ordered to move forward and were then allocated to the different tables where they had to undress completely and hand over everything they wore or carried. Some still carried jewelry, which they had to put on the table. Then, having taken off all their clothes, they were made to stand in line in front of the ditches, irrespective of their sex. The *Kommandos* then marched in behind the line.

"With automatic pistols these men moved down the line with such zealous intent that one could have supposed this activity to have been their lifework."

No one was overlooked. Said Bingel: "Even women carrying children two to three weeks old, sucking at their breasts, were not spared this horrible ordeal. Nor were mothers spared the terrible sight of their children being gripped by their little legs and put to death with one stroke of the pistol butt or club, thereafter to be thrown on the heap of human bodies in the ditch, some of which were not quite dead. Not before these mothers had been exposed to this worst of all tortures did they receive the bullet that released them from this sight."

Row after row of Jews went to their death. "The air resounded with the cries of the children and the tortured," until finally, at 5 p.m., nine hours after the slaughter had begun, "the square lay deserted in deadly desolation and only some dogs, attracted by the scent of blood in the air, were roving the site. The shots were still ringing in our ears. The whole thing might have seemed to me to be a terrifying nightmare but for the sparsely covered ditches which gleamed at us accusingly." In all, the men of Einsatzgruppe C put to death an estimated 24,000 Jews at Uman that day. The killing continued at Babi Yar two weeks later, and there 33,771 people by actual count went to their doom.

But open-air killings were not an entirely satisfactory method of extermination to the SS commanders. For one thing, too many people were privy to the executions—not just the few hundred *Einsatzkommandos* but also the scores of local militiamen who had to be employed to cover up the long, deep common graves. Moreover, the regular soldiers and airmen on duty at the airport and the inhabitants of the surrounding area could not be prevented from learning of the event from the incessant rattle of pistols, rifles and submachine guns. Then too, the executions put a great strain on the killer squads. And despite the *Einsatzkommandos'* marksmanship, the method was not wholly efficient, and the moans and shrieks of the wounded were unnerving.

When Reichsführer-SS Himmler visited one killer squad, its commander urged him, "Look at the eyes of the men of this command, how deeply shaken they are. These men are finished for the rest of their lives." Himmler could see that the commander was right, and he was gravely concerned for the men's well-being.

Eventually, key SS commanders concluded that a much better mode of extermination was the stationary gas chamber, followed by cremation of the corpses in such ovens as the mental-patient program had developed. In secluded killing centers, small highly trained staffs could conduct the executions in relative secrecy, with an efficiency that seemed likely to make for savings in the long run. The physical remains would be slight.

In accord with this conclusion, the SS installed crematoriums in many existing concentration camps and gas chambers in six model death camps that would incorporate all the latest technology.

As the full-scale program of annihilation got under way, it brought to the fore a 35-year-old SS lieutenant colonel who had attended the Wannsee conference but who, with deference appropriate to his position as recording secretary for the meeting, had spoken not a word. He was an industrious functionary named Adolf Eichmann, and he was lucky enough to have as his mentor Reinhard Heydrich himself.

Eichmann had joined the SS in 1932 while pursuing an indifferent career as an Austria-based traveling salesman. In 1933, following Hitler's rise to power, he had moved to Germany and begun a year of training in two SS camps in Bavaria. He applied for a job in the counterintelligence branch of the SS, which Heydrich had recently set up for Reichsführer-SS Himmler.

Eichmann's first assignment was to collect information on the Freemasons and other groups that the Nazis considered potentially subversive. But he soon became fascinated by the Jews, and to study them in depth he went so far as to learn a smattering of Hebrew and Yiddish. Eichmann liked to claim that he was not an anti-Semite; he actually conversed with Jews and took a Jewish mistress. He objected to the Jews only because they were a threat to the health of the Greater German Reich.

Eichmann's SS colleagues came to consider him a "Jewish expert," and after the German take-over of Austria in 1938 he was put in charge of the "forced emigration" of Austrian Jews. This, his first important job, turned out to be a stunning success. He "cleansed" Austria of 45,000 Jews in the same eight-month period that saw only 19,000 Jews evicted from Germany. In 18 months, he reduced Austria's Jewish population by about one half, to 150,000 people. What is more, he showed a tidy profit. His tactic, as Heydrich explained it, was the soul of simplicity: "Through the Jewish community, we extracted a certain amount of money from rich Jews who wanted to emigrate."

In recognition of his excellent performance in Austria, Eichmann was prepped for greater things with a series of broadening assignments, some for Gestapo chief Heinrich Müller, some for Heydrich himself. In 1941 and 1942, for example, Eichmann helped to organize the Theresienstadt ghetto north of Prague to accommodate prominent Jews whose disappearance would prompt embarrassing questions. This was part of an interim program of concentrating and isolating all Jews in convenient ghettos and labor camps. In June of 1941, Eichmann, now a major, learned the reason for the program.

Heydrich, who had just received Hitler's instructions to draft a master plan for the Final Solution, summoned Eichmann to Berlin and told him, "The Führer has ordered the physical extermination of the Jews." Years later, during his war-crimes trial, Eichmann said that he was stunned by Heydrich's announcement. But the shock passed. As he later said, the "Popes of the Third Reich" had spoken and "who am I to have my own thoughts in this matter?"

Heydrich soon gave Eichmann another shock: He put him in charge of organizing and coordinating the transportation of Jews from all over Europe to the death camps that were a-building in Poland. Eichmann, promoted to lieutenant colonel in October 1941, began briefing himself on the problems he would face and looking for ways to assist the camp commandants.

Eichmann was awed and gratified by this momentous opportunity to serve the Reich, and in the next few months he made several study trips to the Soviet Union and Poland. He traveled to Minsk on orders from Müller, who wanted him to observe the shooting of some Jews and to report on how it was done. Eichmann arrived late at the killing site. "They had already started, so I could see only the finish," he reported. "Although I was wearing a leather coat that reached almost to my ankles, it was very cold. I watched the last group of Jews undress, down to their shirts. They walked the last 100 or 200 yards—they were not driven—then they jumped into the pit. Then the men of the squad banged away into the pit with their rifles and machine pistols. I saw a woman hold a child of a year or two, pleading. Then the child was hit. I was so close that later I found bits of brains splattered on my long leather coat. My chauffeur helped me remove them."

During a visit to Lodz, Eichmann witnessed the gassing of 1,000 Jews in sealed buses. He found the spectacle so disconcerting that he forgot to time the gassing procedure. For this he was later chided by Müller. To explain his undue sensitivity, Eichmann said, "I simply cannot look at any suffering without trembling myself."

Of his visit to the Majdanek death camp near Lublin he said: "A German police captain there showed me how they had managed to build airtight chambers disguised as ordinary Polish farmers' huts, seal them hermetically, then inject the exhaust gas from a Russian U-boat motor. I never thought that anything like that would be possible, technically speaking."

During his study period, Eichmann also visited what was to become the biggest and most efficient death camp, Auschwitz. He found Rudolf Höss, the commandant of the camp, in a quandary over design of the gas chambers, which depended on the kind of gas to be used. Eichmann, Höss later said, was extremely helpful. "He told me about the method of killing people with exhaust gases in trucks, but there was no question of being able to use this for these mass transports that were due to arrive in Auschwitz. Killing with showers of carbon monoxide while bathing, as was done with mental patients in some places in the Reich, would necessitate too many buildings. We left the matter unresolved. Eichmann decided to try to find a gas that was in ready supply and that would not entail special installations for its use.''

One possibility was Zyklon B. To be sure, both carbon monoxide and Zyklon B had been proved effective in the T-4 program. But Zyklon B worked faster and was easier to handle, since it came in the form of pellets that dispensed the poison into the air when the canisters were opened. Its only drawback—not a serious problem considering the massive extermination program now getting under way—was a limited shelf life.

On a return trip to Auschwitz, Eichmann was pleased to learn that Commandant Höss had found a quantity of Zyklon B on hand for fumigation, and that one of his assistants had tried it out with satisfactory results on a few prisoners of war. Following a short discussion, Höss and Eichmann agreed that Zyklon B would be employed for the mass extermination operation at Auschwitz.

The man put in charge of supplying Auschwitz and a few other small camps with Zyklon B was SS First Lieutenant Kurt Gerstein, a technical genius who, as it turned out, led a strange and contradictory secret life. His mentally ill sister-in-law had been one of the first victims of Himmler's T-4 program, and upon learning of her death the bitter Gerstein joined the SS in order ''to see clearly into its workings and proclaim them to the world.'' Throughout the War, he dutifully kept Auschwitz supplied with Zyklon B, but he destroyed some of his own shipments and claimed that they had spoiled or were lost. He also passed forbidden information on the gas extermination program to the Catholic Archbishop of Berlin, the Swedish embassy and the Dutch Resistance. It was in vain. The Church apparently ignored him, the Swedes did not pass his report on to the Allies until after the War, and the Dutch Resistance kept the information secret for fear that it would not be believed.

In the end, all that Gerstein accomplished was to have the gas formula modified slightly, removing a chemical that made deaths particularly agonizing. At the end of the War, he turned himself in to the French, handed them his autobiography and then hanged himself in his cell in a military prison in Paris.

While Zyklon B was the chosen gas at Auschwitz, carbon monoxide was employed at Chelmno, Belzec, Sobibor, Treblinka and, for the most part, at Majdanek. That five of the six new death camps chose the less efficient gas apparently was due to Christian Wirth, the overseer of Treblinka, Belzec and Sobibor. He was partial to carbon monoxide because he had helped perfect the carbon monoxide gas chamber during the T-4 program.

At first, it seemed that Wirth would change his mind; under pressure from Eichmann and others who favored the use of Zyklon B, he reluctantly agreed to convert his gas chambers. To see to the conversion, Lieutenant Gerstein and Eichmann's deputy, Rolf Günther, arrived at Belzec bearing 200 pounds of Zyklon B. But before the work began, Wirth asked the visitors to watch a carbon monoxide operation in four gas chambers, each packed with 750 people. Gerstein pulled out a stopwatch and timed the operation. Because of difficulties with the diesel engine that produced the gas, the procedure went on for three hours before the last few Jews died.

Wirth was mortified and begged the men not to report the incident. Out of sympathy for Wirth, the quixotic Gerstein and the obliging Günther agreed. Thereafter, sheer stubbornness kept Wirth using the inferior gas in his camps.

Mopping his forehead on a warm summer's day, SS chief Heinrich Himmler inspects plans for expansion at the Auschwitz death camp in July 1942. Himmler was surprisingly squeamish for a perpetrator of genocide; he once fainted while watching the mass execution of 100 political prisoners.

The pace of Eichmann's work speeded up after the January 1942 conference at Wannsee. The business of organizing the country-by-country deportation of Jews proved hectic and full of imponderables. The hardest part of Eichmann's job was to find enough rolling stock anywhere. In some countries, the railroads were left in the hands of the local administrators, and Eichmann's subordinates had to negotiate with officials who were reluctant to cooperate in the deportation of citizens, even though the Jews' announced destination was only "labor camps."

Eichmann also had to contend with Army supply officers who considered it more important to provide for the fighting fronts than to liquidate the Jews. Such obstructionists fought hard for the limited rolling stock available—a supply that grew ever more limited as Allied bombers took their toll. But some officers recognized the import of his work and cooperated with him.

Eichmann later claimed that he had no desire to see his Jewish charges suffer unnecessarily. He said that "the Jews were always shipped in covered, not open, cars, and always by the quickest possible routes." It annoyed him to hear accusations that he and his staff tolerated the maltreatment of his Jews. When one of his assistants informed him that local Hungarian "police were driving the Jews into the cars like cattle to a slaughterhouse," Eichmann "several times reminded the Hungarian government in writing that we did not want to punish individual Jews." The point was, he said, that the deportation of the Jews was neither personal nor punishment but "work toward a political solution."

In any event, the long rail journeys to the death camps were ghastly. Each boxcar held 60 to 100 Jews, and they would have to stay locked in for as long as 10 days while the train moved along routes that avoided population centers. A small number of armed guards rode on each train and dismounted at stops to make sure that no Jews tried to escape and to prevent civilians from passing food or water into the cars.

The Jews in transit were quick to discover, as one survivor recounted, that "the simplest details of existence would be extremely complicated. Sanitary disposal was out of the question. As the journey stretched on endlessly, the car jerking and jolting, all the forces of nature conspired against us. The torrid sun heated the walls until the air became suffocating. The travelers were mostly persons of culture and position from our community. But as the hours slipped away, the veneers cracked. Soon there were incidents and, later, serious quarrels. The children cried; the sick groaned; the old people lamented. As night fell we lost all concept of human behavior and the wrangling increased until the car was a bedlam."

Once a train disgorged its cargo of Jews at a camp, Eichmann had to make sure that the railroaders returned swiftly to the next pickup point. Nothing was more frustrating than to have one of his trains delayed because its passengers had arrived at a camp that was too crowded to handle them immediately. So Eichmann assembled statistics on the "absorptive capacity" of each camp and tried to see to it that Jews were not deposited at any camp faster than they could be conveniently killed there.

The assembly-line exterminations of Jews had begun by the summer of 1942. Except for the choice of gas the procedure was much the same at all six death camps. A train of boxcars arrived at the camp station. "Special commandos"—Jews who had been lured into service with bounties of food and promises that their lives would be spared—opened the doors, urged the new arrivals onto the platform and carefully instructed them to leave their luggage on the train. The newcomers obeyed, reassured by the fact that the special commandos spoke their own language.

As the new arrivals walked forward along the platform, they passed the camp doctor or an SS officer, who signaled each to step either to the left or to the right with a wave of his finger. Those who were sent to the right—the healthy-looking ones—were taken to one of the camp's work projects, where they labored 12 hours a day and longer in a munitions factory, coal mine, synthetic-rubber works or farm. The life expectancy of these workers was short. Normally, malnutrition weakened them in about three months' time. And as soon as they became too weak or ill to work, they were gassed.

The newcomers who were sent to the left were gassed within an hour or two. Ordinarily, children and most of the women were directed to the left. In all, only about 10 per cent of any trainload were selected for work, but if the workers' barracks were already full, everyone was waved left. At Chelmno and Belzec there was no industry, so the selection step was unnecessary.

The doomed Jews were ordered to undress for a shower. At the more commodious camps, such as Auschwitz, they hung their clothes on numbered hooks, and the special commandos instructed them to remember their numbers in order to reclaim their clothes after their "bath." At smaller camps, like Belzec and Treblinka, they undressed outside, sometimes in freezing weather. Many mothers had to help their small children undress. This caused delays that irritated SS guards. Occasionally, guards would grab the wailing children by the legs and smash their heads against a wall. But at Auschwitz such brutality was unusual; care was taken not to alarm the Jews so they would offer no resistance.

Next, the special commandos urged their charges—up to 2,000 Jews at a time—toward the gas chambers. The special commandos tried to be helpful and good-humored, chatting about camp life and assuring the victims that they would be able to reclaim luggage at a later time. At Auschwitz, the SS organized a small camp orchestra. Groups of musicians accompanied the victims and played popular tunes or light operatic music, often from the *Tales of Hoffmann* or *The Merry Widow*.

These precautions sometimes failed. Occasionally, victims noticed upon stepping into the so-called shower room that it lacked drainage runnels. That caused them to panic. The special commandos then had to use clubs and whips to beat the rest of the victims into the chambers.

Next, the special commandos slammed the doors shut and screwed them tight to their gasproof jambs. Then a camp officer dropped the Zyklon B pellets down the ventilating shafts. The results were dramatic. "It could be observed through the peephole in the door," Commandant Höss reported, "that those who were standing nearest to the induction vents were killed at once. It can be said that about one third died straightaway. The remainder staggered about and began to scream and struggle for air. The screaming, however, soon changed to the death rattle and in a few minutes all lay still."

The process took somewhat longer in the camps that used carbon monoxide. The chambers were smaller and the victims sometimes had to stand tightly packed for an hour or two before the diesel engine roared into life. The gas it delivered killed slowly. One visitor, who put his ear to the wall after the gas had been pumped in, heard wailing sounds "just like a synagogue."

The carbon monoxide killings also left a bigger mess. Thanks to Zyklon B at Auschwitz, Höss reported that "there was no sign of convulsions or discoloration. Soiling through opening of the bowels was also rare." In the camps using carbon monoxide, Gerstein said, the bodies were "blue, wet with sweat and urine, the legs covered with excrement and menstrual blood."

The job of cleaning up fell to the special commandos. Once the gas had been dispelled through the ventilation system, they entered the chambers carrying special hook-tipped poles and pried apart the bodies. Using large ice tongs, which they clamped on the victims' heads, they then dragged the bodies out of the chamber and wrestled them into a rail wagon or elevator, or onto a conveyor belt for transport to a disposal site. With pliers they pulled out teeth containing gold. They shaved the heads of the women and sent the hair to the camp workshop to be made into felt boots for railroadmen and U-boat crews. Every three or four months the special commandos, who had by now seen too much, were themselves sent into the gas chambers.

The SS officers and the technical aides never found a completely satisfactory way to dispose of the bodies. Explosives were tried at least once with unsatisfactory results. Burial, cremation in ovens and mass burning in pits were the most common methods used, but each process had certain disadvantages.

Burial ultimately was rejected because it required too much land and labor, and the earthen cover sometimes collapsed before the quicklime had worked completely, allowing odors to spread for miles. The mass graves, moreover, left telltale scars on the landscape, evidence that many Nazis considered a problem. However, SS Lieut. General Odilo Globocnik could see no objection and on one occasion argued his point with a visitor from Berlin. Dr. Herbert Linden, a sterilization expert of the Ministry of the Interior, opposed the mass graves, remarking, "General Globocnik, a future generation might not understand." Replied Globocnik, "Gentlemen, if ever a generation should arise so slack and soft-boned that it cannot understand the importance of our work, then our entire National Socialism will have been in vain. I am of the opinion that bronze plaques should be erected with inscriptions to show that it was we who had the courage to carry out this great and necessary task."

Though cremation left little evidence, it was slow. At Auschwitz, for example, the two large new crematoriums that went on line in the spring of 1943 could incinerate fewer than 2,000 bodies in 24 hours in their five ovens, each with three retorts. Attempts to increase the capacity damaged them severely and caused them to be shut down for repairs on several occasions.

Commandant Höss ordered two additional four-retort ovens and paired them with new gas chambers. I. A. Topf and Sons, an Erfurt heating-equipment firm, won the contract after highly competitive bidding. Company technical experts calculated that the new units would be able to handle 1,500 bodies a day, but wartime shortages led to shoddy construction and the ovens were a great disappointment. One broke down after only a short time and eventually had to be taken out of service altogether. The second had to be shut down repeatedly because after four to six weeks of continuous use its flimsy fire walls and chimneys would be burned out.

One by-product of incineration caused further delays. So many bodies were burned at Auschwitz and Belzec that periodically a foot or more of human fat had to be scraped off the chimney walls.

When a camp's ovens were inoperative, the commandant had no choice but to order the bodies burned in open pits. Special commandos alternated layers of bodies with layers of railroad ties to assure a good draft, and then soaked the pile with whatever petroleum wastes were available. Sometimes they drew buckets full of human fat from the pit bottoms and hurled the fat back onto the fire to increase the intensity of the blaze. Once the fire was burning properly, more bodies were added. If the fires burned out too soon, the special commandos would complete the incineration with flamethrowers.

Ultimately, the pit fire proved the cheapest and fastest method of disposing of bodies. But the fires burned slowly and gave off dense clouds of smoke that hung unpleasantly low in misty or rainy weather. Townspeople many miles away complained about the stench of the burning flesh. Local air-defense authorities also protested: The fires made dangerous beacons for enemy bombers to use as checkpoints on their way to or from their targets.

The task of processing the property of the deceased Jews went on continuously in an immense operation called Action Reinhard. Large staffs of prisoners, occupying warehouses at the camps, were put to work sorting, cataloguing and distributing the goods—mountains of shoes, shirts, watches, eyeglasses, gold teeth and other effects.

Most of the possessions were turned over to the SS Economic and Administrative Main Office, known by its German initials WVHA. The German paper money collected by the WVHA was bundled off directly to the Reichsbank. Dental gold, jewelry, precious stones, pearls and foreign currency were inventoried at the WVHA, then deposited at the Reichsbank. The bank credited all the value to one Max Heiliger, a code name for the WVHA account.

Soon the bank's vaults were filled to overflowing. Though a bank director sniffed, "the Reichsbank is not a dealer in secondhand goods," trading specialists for the bank began selling the loot through Berlin pawnshops and on the Swiss jewelry market. For a time the Swiss outlets were glutted with such wares.

Less valuable items—watches, clocks, fountain pens, mechanical pencils, razors, pocketknives, scissors, flashlights, wallets and purses—were sent to Army post exchanges for sale to the troops. Other useful commodities went to a second agency, called VOMI, a contraction of Volksdeutsche Mittelstelle, the SS Welfare Organization for Ethnic Germans. Men's and women's clothing was sent by VOMI to needy Germans. Feather beds, quilts, blankets, umbrellas, baby carriages, handbags, leather belts, shopping bags, pipes, mirrors, suitcases and other accessories and possessions were sent by VOMI to distributors throughout the Reich and the occupied lands.

There were a few exceptions. All valuable furs were claimed by the WVHA, while more ordinary furs were allocated to the SS clothing factory at Ravensbrück for alteration and distribution to the Waffen-SS. Miscellaneous items of very low value went to the Ministry of Economics to be sold by weight. The Ministry of Economics also appropriated women's silk underwear and other silk garments, which it distributed as wedding presents to the brides of SS men.

The property of the deceased Jews was enormously valuable. During the two years following the invasion of the Soviet Union, the Germans deported 434,329 Jews from eastern Galicia. That operation alone, according to an Action Reinhard inventory, yielded a booty that included: 97,581 kilograms (214,678 pounds) of gold coins; 167,740 kg. silver coins; 82,600 kg. silver necklaces; 6,640 kg. gold necklaces; 44,655 kg. broken gold; 4,326,780 kg. broken silver; 20,952 kg. gold wedding rings; 20,880 kg. gold rings, with stones; 18,020 kg. silver rings; 11,730 kg. dental gold; 39,917 kg. brooches, earrings, etc.; 2,892 kg. gold watches; 3,133 kg. silver watches; 3,425 kg. silver wrist watches; 1,256 kg. gold wrist watches; 22,740 kg. pearls; and 68 kg. cameras.

Naturally, the huge concentrations of easily pocketable valuables invited petty theft—and large-scale corruption—and required strict supervision. But while the SS officers in Action Reinhard tried to stanch the pilferage, overall they lacked the manpower or the inclination to stand watch over their own staffs. Recounted Höss, "It was demoralizing for the members of the SS, who were not always strong enough to resist the temptation provided by these valuables, which lay within such easy reach. Jewish gold was a catastrophe for the camp."

The possessions of the dead Jews were considered Reich property and individual guards or cataloguers caught stealing or accepting bribes were reduced in rank, sent to prison or, in extreme cases, executed. Such actions were embarrassing to commanders—another reason why they often chose to look the other way.

Corruption on a grand scale was usually investigated sooner or later, but little could be done about it in most instances. The key witnesses were often Jews, and camp commanders naturally sent them to the gas chamber before they could be asked questions that would produce damaging answers. Once an entire work camp of Jews was slaughtered on a hurry-up schedule to prevent a hearing on the guards' open traffic in the inmates' confiscated possessions.

Under the circumstances, SS inspectors sometimes had to take Draconian measures to see that justice was done. One such case involved a camp commandant accused of corruption. Before the trial could be held, an SS officer in protective custody as a material witness was found dead in his cell, and the SS inspector felt sure that the man had been poisoned by the camp doctor at the instigation of the commandant. So the inspector ordered that liquid from the dead man's stomach be administered to four Russian prisoners of war. The POWs died, and that broke the case. The doctor was arrested and forced to testify against the commandant, who was convicted and executed.

Corruption was but one of the morale problems that vexed the men in charge of the Final Solution. A number of death-camp guards showed signs of severe stress, including an excess of gratuitous violence. In 1943, Himmler told a group of top SS officers that the camp personnel in general were bravely withstanding their death-dealing ordeal: "To have gone through this and—apart from a few exceptions caused by human weakness—to have remained decent, that has made us great." But he realized that numerous guards and other camp personnel were becoming savages or neurotics. And since job efficiency was at stake, Himmler repeatedly ordered his adjutants to try any measure that might help keep the camp guards from breakdowns.

SS administrators took several tacks. In the hopes of providing the guards with an outlet for their pent-up tensions, they set up brothels in some camps, making prostitutes of inmates. The only certain result of this practice was that the guards—once they had tired of the women—found it an added chore to dispose of them in the gas chamber.

The SS guards were ordered to follow what Eichmann called "language rules"—euphemisms that would spare them the use of unpleasant terms and also help preserve the secrecy of camp business. The euphemism for the shipment of Jews to the death camps was "evacuation for resettlement." In referring to the gassing process, the guards said "special treatment." Gas chambers were called "special installations." Killing was called "cleansing."

The SS tried to correct the thinking of guards who had moral scruples against their work. The guards were told "all of Jewry rose from criminal roots," that German scientists had proved that the elimination of the Jews was "a matter of political hygiene," necessary for the health of the nation. Their public-spirited work in the camps, it was suggested, like Beethoven's music and Nietzsche's philosophy, was

Finally surrendering after weeks of fierce armed resistance, Jews in the Warsaw ghetto are rounded up for deportation in May of 1943 under the cold gaze of Josef Blösche (right), a brutal guard whom the Jews called Frankenstein. Blösche had helped provoke the uprising: He had roamed the ghetto sniping at people in windows, and raping women and beating men whom he caught out in the street.

somewhat ahead of the time but soon would win the same worldwide acceptance. Therefore, as Himmler said, Germans had the "moral right to annihilate this people," and no objections to the Final Solution would be tolerated unless they dealt with conditions damaging to the war effort or the German people or the SS.

SS leaders ordered camp commandants to use stern discipline as therapy for the guards. Men who violated orders or committed atrocities or killed Jews without authorization were to be punished severely, the thesis being that they would henceforth focus on the job rather than on their feelings. This policy was honored mostly in the breach.

In fact, none of the measures worked. Guards and other death-camp personnel went insane, became alcoholics, committed suicide—and were replaced. Vicious practices of every description were routine. The camps were filled with guards who were sadists to begin with or who became sadists under the crushing horror of the work.

Men were beaten at any time for any reason and for no reason at all. Women were raped. Men and women were forced to abuse themselves and to perform sexual acts for the entertainment of their guards. One SS female guard whipped her prisoners mercilessly, then watched, rocking rhythmically, while doctors sutured the wounds in a painful operation, without anesthetic. One male guard forced his prisoners to immerse their testicles alternately in ice water and boiling water, and then painted their tortured scrotums with tincture of iodine, causing agonizing pains.

A guard who prided himself on his marksmanship periodically selected 20 of the prettiest women prisoners he could find, stripped them, lined them up and used them for target practice. Gustav Franz Wagner, the deputy commandant at Sobibor, killed "like a drunk that needed a drink," said one survivor. "He used an ax, a shovel, a whip, even his bare hands. When he killed he smiled."

Heinrich Himmler insisted that he abhorred such acts of sadism, but he had scientific interests that led to similar tortures in medical experiments. An ambitious doctor named Sigmund Rascher wished to assist the Luftwaffe by researching the effects of extremely high altitudes on fliers. Unfortunately, the physician reported, "no tests with human material had yet been possible as such experiments are very dangerous and nobody volunteers for them." When Himmler found out about the doctor's problem, he offered a supply of prisoners.

Rascher set up a decompression chamber and began his tests. When the atmosphere in the chamber became thin, the prisoners' eardrums would burst and, according to an assistant, the prisoners "would tear their heads and faces with their fingernails in an attempt to maim themselves in their madness." The tests generally ended in the deaths of the subjects. On receiving the doctor's report describing the prisoners' agonies in one fatal test, Himmler jotted "interesting" in the margin.

Rascher also conducted freezing experiments to see how much cold a man could endure. "The business with the

blocks of ice in water was most terrible," said a stretcher-bearer for Dr. Rascher. "As a rule, the experimental people fainted after an hour. But one time there were two Russian officers who were forced into the water naked. The Pole who worked with me heard one of the Russians say to the other after three hours, 'Comrade, tell the German he should shoot us.' The other said, 'No, the dog won't have any pity. We don't want to humiliate ourselves by begging.' Then they bade farewell to each other with a handshake. It lasted five hours before they were dead."

Some of the prisoners did not suffer so silently, and their screams hindered the experiments. Rascher thereafter anesthetized the subjects before exposing them to ice and snow.

Himmler informed the doctor that he would like to know what sort of heat was most effective in reviving the frozen prisoners. Rascher accepted the challenge. He placed naked prisoners, chilled and unconscious, in contact with either one or two naked women prisoners. Rascher and his assistants carefully observed as the prisoners warmed up and regained consciousness, then reported that the test person, if he was able to have sexual intercourse, "warmed up surprisingly fast and also showed a surprisingly rapid return of full bodily well-being."

At Auschwitz, doctors conducted experiments designed to find a production-line method of sterilizing men of "inferior racial stock." Hundreds of healthy young prisoners were brought naked to X-ray machines and their sex organs were exposed to high dosages of radiation. Some men were burned by unskilled technicians and were sent immediately to the gas chamber. Some survived the process, and doctors periodically took study specimens of the affected tissues.

One corner of Auschwitz was the center for gynecological experiments. Doctors sterilized women or injected experimental fluids into their ovaries. These operations were carried out without any effort to spare the women pain, and some would cower in corners, shrieking in terror at the approach of the medical team. Other women had cancer implanted in the uterus. Then doctors removed the womb, piece by piece, to study the effects of the tumor.

Many doctors pursued highly specialized research. Dr. Josef Mengele performed studies on twins in an effort to find ways of improving the quality of German racial stock. A Dr. Dohmen cultivated viruses in animals, then injected them into prisoners in order to observe the effects. Doctors in the pharmaceutical branch of I. G. Farben had prisoners infected with typhus to test new drugs. Dr. Fritz Ernst Fischer tried unsuccessfully to transplant bones between living prisoners.

Tens of thousands of Jews, Poles, Russians and other unwanted peoples died in such experiments. And millions of Poles, Russians and others perished along with the Jews in the enormous extermination dragnet of the Final Solution.

The killings went on and on with only minor interruptions. Every once in a while in the death camps, there were unpleasant scenes at the gas chambers when the Jews, realizing that the shower rooms were not shower rooms at all, panicked and had to be driven inside. There were even a few Jewish uprisings, though of course they were easily put down; the Jews had no weapons, no organization and not much strength. The only really serious Jewish rebellion did not take place in a camp, but in the Warsaw ghetto, and it lasted through the early months of 1943.

By then the Warsaw ghetto had been fairly well depleted of its original population of 160,000 Jews, plus about

"Poison gas" warns the labels on canisters of Zyklon B, a cyanide gas that was used as the killing agent at the death camp at Auschwitz. Business records concerning the supply of the product often referred to the gas with the code phrase "material for Jewish resettlement."

240,000 more Jews who had been rounded up and deposited there in 1940. During 1942 and early 1943, all but about 60,000 of the 400,000 Jews had been herded off without much fuss, most of them ending up in the gas chambers at Treblinka. But those who remained proved to be a nettlesome problem when the Germans came for them. They somehow had managed to acquire weapons, and they put up a resistance that surprised the SS officer in charge, who presumed that Jews were "cowards by nature."

That officer, SS Brigadier General Jürgen Stroop, had been ordered by Himmler to clear out the ghetto by no later than February 15, 1943. It proved to be an impossible demand. Among other problems, the Germans had been defeated at Stalingrad and were now retreating from the southern parts of the Soviet Union; the Wehrmacht desperately needed the rolling stock that would have been used to transport the Jews. Furthermore, Stroop reported, the Jews were now resisting "in every possible way."

On April 19, 1943, Stroop began "a special action" with about 2,000 troops to empty the ghetto in three days. But at the end of that period, Stroop unhappily informed Himmler by telegraph that it was "apparent that the Jews no longer had any intention to resettle voluntarily, but were determined to resist evacuation with all their force and by using all the weapons at their disposal." Stroop was particularly impressed by the fighting of the women. "Not infrequently," he reported, "these women fired pistols with both hands. It happened time and again that these women had pistols or hand grenades—Polish pineapples—concealed in their bloomers up to the last moment to use against the men of the Waffen-SS, police or Wehrmacht."

Eventually, Stroop decided to put the entire ghetto to the torch. Yet even when Stroop's men fired the buildings, the Jews fought on, often escaping into the labyrinth of sewers beneath the ghetto. Eventually, the superiority of arms had to prevail. Said Stroop in his final report: "The large-scale action was terminated on 16 May 1943 with the blowing up of the Warsaw Synagogue. Total numbers of Jews dealt with: 56,065, including both Jews caught and Jews whose extermination can be proved." The survivors were then sent off to Treblinka and Majdanek.

By the time the Warsaw situation had been cleared up satisfactorily, all the death camps were nearing peak efficiency. In each nightmare world, and especially at Auschwitz, killing had taken on an irreversible momentum. In spite of the increasing shortage of rolling stock, Adolf Eichmann's trains kept arriving at Auschwitz, bringing ever larger consignments of people to their deaths. Said an Auschwitz guard to some new arrivals, "You are only numbers. A shot, and the number is gone." The Jews knew that escape was impossible but guards always told them superfluously: "Don't try to escape; the only way to get out of here is by the chimney."

At Auschwitz, the death-making machinery was taxed and overtaxed but kept on working. More and more Zyklon B was required: 7.5 tons in 1942, 12 tons in 1943, and in 1944 a single consignment filled 20 trucks. The canisters of gas-making crystals were hurried to the camp's death center, Birkenau, where the gas chambers could produce 4,000 to 5,000 corpses an hour.

Auschwitz reached peak production in the summer of 1944. The occupied country then being cleared of Jews was Hungary, and by June, Hungarian Jews were arriving in torrents. Adolf Eichmann worked so effectively that his trains full of Jews piled up at the Auschwitz siding and people suffocated in the boxcars before they could be unloaded. Many people were sent under guard into a nearby forest, where they were forced to wait their turn for a day or two without food or water.

To handle the influx, the SS men worked feverishly, tirelessly, around the clock, and 20,000 policemen were called in to help out. On a single day they put to death 24,000 Jews. In their haste they flung many living children onto open-pit fires. By the end of August half of Hungary's 750,000 Jews had been gassed and cremated.

The killing went on and on.

On a bleak plain in the Nazi-occupied East, an SS trooper takes aim at a Jewish mother and child while frightened peasants prepare a grave for them.

THE DEATH OF A PEOPLE

In April 1933, scarcely three months after Adolf Hitler took power in Germany, the Nazis issued a decree ordering the compulsory retirement of "non-Aryans" from the civil service. This edict, petty in itself, was the first spark in what was to become the Holocaust, one of the most ghastly episodes in the modern history of mankind. Before the campaign against the Jews was halted by the defeat of Germany, something like 11 million people had been slaughtered in the name of Nazi racial purity.

The Jews were not the only victims of the Holocaust. Millions of Russians, Poles, gypsies and other "subhumans" were also murdered. But Jews were the favored targets—first and foremost.

It took the Nazis some time to work up to the full fury of their endeavor. In the years following 1933, the Jews were systematically deprived by law of their civil rights, of their jobs and property. Violence and brutality became a part of their everyday lives. Their places of worship were defiled, their windows smashed, their stores ransacked. Old men—and young—were pummeled and clubbed and stomped to death by Nazi jackboots. Jewish women were accosted and ravaged, in broad daylight, on main thoroughfares.

Some Jews fled Germany. But most, with a kind of stubborn belief in God and Fatherland, sought to weather the Nazi terror. It was a forlorn hope. In 1939, after Hitler's conquest of Poland, the Nazis cast aside all restraint. Jews in their millions were now herded into concentration camps, there to starve and perish as slave laborers. Other millions were driven into dismal ghettos, which served as holding pens until the Nazis got around to disposing of them.

The mass killings began in 1941, with the German invasion of the Soviet Union. Nazi murder squads followed behind the Wehrmacht enthusiastically slaying Jews and other conquered peoples. Month by month the horrors escalated. First tens of thousands, then hundreds of thousands of people were led off to remote fields and forests to be slaughtered by SS guns. Assembly-line death camps were established in Poland and trainloads of Jews were collected from all over occupied Europe and sent to their doom.

At some of the camps, the Nazis took pains to disguise their intentions until the last moment. At others, the arriving Jews saw scenes beyond comprehension. "Corpses were strewn all over the road," recalled one survivor. "Starving human skeletons stumbled toward us. They fell right down in front of our eyes and lay there gasping out their last breath." What had begun as a mean little edict against Jewish civil servants was now ending in the death of a people.

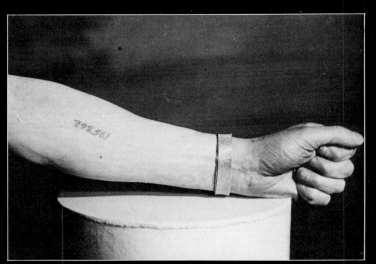

Symbols of the "Final Solution" are a human-skull hood ornament on an SS vehicle and a number tattooed on the arm to identify a camp inmate.

In a town in Poland, an Orthodox Jew, mourning over the bodies of recently executed Jews, is an object of ridicule for passing German soldiers.

A synagogue is left in ruins following Kristallnacht. Orders for the pillaging came directly from Reinhard Heydrich, second only to Heinrich Himmler in the S.

A Berliner carrying a broom surveys broken glass and debris strewn in front of Jewish-owned businesse[s]

THE NIGHT THAT MADE VIOLENCE ROUTINE

For Germany's Jews, the night of November 9, 1938, was a turning point—the time when Nazi measures against them escalated from repressive legislation to organized violence. Using as a pretext the murder of a German official by a Jewish refugee, Nazi Party leaders whipped their followers into a frenzy of destruction.

Throughout the night and the next day, Nazi gangs raged through the cities, towns and villages, methodically vandalizing the property of Jews. They ravaged and des-

ecrated 191 synagogues, set fire to 17[1] apartment houses, and looted 7,500 stor[es] and businesses owned by Jews. The tot[al] property damage was an estimated 25 m[il]lion reichsmarks—about $10 million.

The Jews themselves were flogged an[d] tortured. Some 20,000 men were arreste[d] and sent to concentration camps for a bri[ef] but brutal scourging. About 100 Jews we[re] beaten to death and uncounted Jewi[sh] women were raped.

After the rioting, the streets of German[y's] cities were littered with broken glass fro[m] shattered storefronts. From these shar[ds] came the name the Germans gave the p[o]grom—*Kristallnacht,* or *Crystal Night.*

Preparing for a hasty departur

Ghetto residents in Cracow, Poland, clamber into a boxcar. Their likely destination was a concentration or death camp.

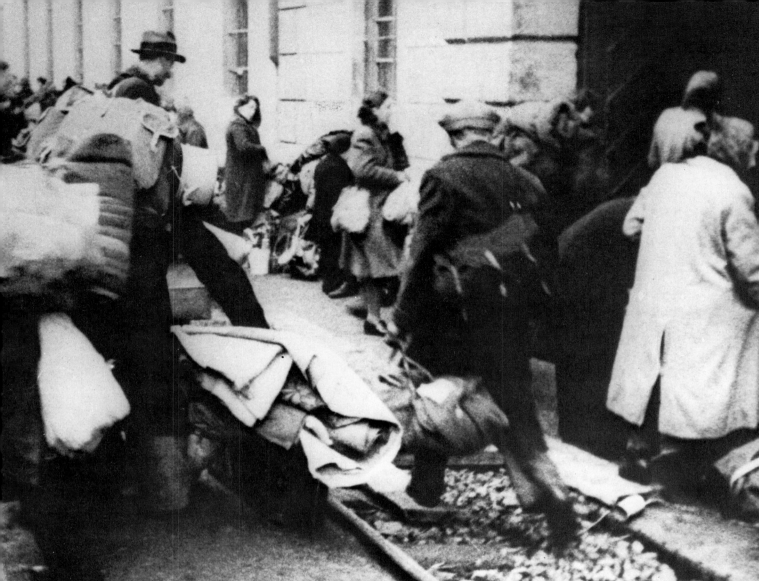

s drag bundles of belongings to an assembly point.

UPROOTED, INTERNED AND DEPORTED

In Germany and later in the conquered countries as well, Jews were uprooted and subjected to bewildering evacuations and relocations. They were forced from their homes into crowded ghettos or local holding camps. They were packed onto trains and moved to labor camps, where many were worked to death.

In the constant upheaval, families were forever separated. One 19-year-old man was ordered from his Polish town to a labor camp. "I barely managed to say goodby to my sister," he said. "She gave me her picture with this inscription: 'If you survive, remember, you live to take revenge.'" He never saw her again.

As troops and townspeople look on, a Russian
is beaten unmercifully by Germans. Many
of the public displays of brutality were simply
calculated to make the people submissive.

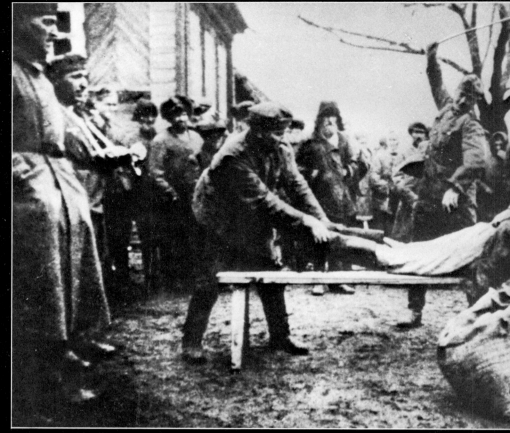

THE FIRST ATROCITIES AFTER THE CONQUEST

All the unfortunates on the Nazis' long list of enemies and "subhuman" *Unter-menschen* were stunned by the violence that erupted with the arrival of victorious German armies in Eastern Europe. But the Jews suffered the worst horrors. They were beaten and humiliated by German soldiers, by local anti-Semites and—most often and most viciously—by the SS.

SS men ripped clumps of hair from the Jews' beards and sometimes set the beards on fire. Terrified Jews in the Polish town of Turck were driven into their synagogue by SS men; they were forced to drop their pants and were lashed with horsewhips. Jewish women and girls were routinely raped in the streets and town squares.

At times, the Jews' Gentile neighbors of only a short time before bade fair to outdo the Nazis in savagery toward the Jews. Under the prod of the SS, latent anti-Semitism exploded into pogroms in which Jews were robbed and beaten and murdered in the most barbaric fashion.

In an occupied town in the Ukraine, a mob of Gentiles tied a Jewish woman's hair to the tail of a horse and drove the animal off. The horse dragged the woman until—said a Jew who watched from a distance—"her whole face was completely disfigured and there wasn't the slightest sign of life from her body. Most of the crowd was hysterical with laughter."

A convict released by the Germans uses a lead
pipe on a Jewish pogrom victim in Lithuania.
The pogrom took place on June 28, 1941, just
days after the invasion of the Soviet Union.

A rape victim in the city of Lvov cries out in rage and anguish as an older woman comforts her. Anti-Semitic citizens rounded up 1,000 Jews and turned them over to the Germans.

"SO MANY BODIES WERE LYING ALL OVER"

In the wake of the German armies, whole communities of Polish and Russian Jews were wiped out by the journeymen killers of the SS *Einsatzgruppen*. In most of the massacres, the procedure was the same. The Jews were marched to a remote execution site. There they were ordered to undress; they did not understand why, but it was partly to facilitate the searching and salvaging of their clothes, and partly because naked people rarely resisted.

"Our father did not want to undress," said Rivka Yosselevscka, who survived a massacre of Russian Jews at Zagrodski in spite of a bullet wound in her head. "He did not want to stand naked. They tore the clothing off the old man and he was shot."

Immobilized by horror, Rivka watched as her mother was shot. Then her 80-year-old grandmother was shot along with the two children she held. "And then there was my father's sister. She also had children in her arms, and she was shot on the spot, with the babies in her arms."

Rivka's younger sister was the next to die. "She went up to the Germans with one of her friends—they were embracing each other—and she asked to be spared, standing there naked. A German looked into her eyes and shot the two of them."

The Germans then shot Rivka's second sister, and finally it was Rivka's turn. "I felt the German take the child from my arms. The child cried out and was shot immediately. And then he aimed at me. He aimed the revolver at me and ordered me to watch and then turned my head around and shot me. Then I fell to the ground into the pit amongst the bodies."

After the Germans left, "I rose, and with my last strength I came up on top of the grave, and when I did, I did not know the place, so many bodies were lying all over. Not all of them dead, but in their last sufferings; naked; shot, but not dead."

A Polish Jew kneels before his SS executioner while other Germans watch. The executed man fell into the common grave below.

Wearing blindfolds and with their arms linked, apprehensive Jews are guided by an SS man to a barren execution site in Poland.

Near the Latvian town of Lijepaja, women and girls huddle together, waiting in fear. Their clothes are scattered about on the ground.

Forced to strip, four Jewish men and a young boy from a town in Poland are brought forward by members of a killing squad.

Barbed-wire fences surround the 15 square miles of the Auschwitz-Birkenau death camp. An estimated two million people from German-occupied countries were killed there in less than three years.

THE FINAL TRAIN TRIP TO POLAND

In the spring of 1942, Jewish leaders in the ghettos of Poland and nearby Slovakia were directed by the Nazi authorities to prepare a specified percentage of their populations for "resettlement." Unaware of the horror that lay ahead, the Jewish communities yielded thousands of deportees. These people would become the first victims of the new death camps in Poland.

Most Jews traveled to their places of death by train. They were marched to the nearest station and packed in boxcars that lacked sanitary facilities, seats and often ventilation. For some the trip took weeks.

In the cramped quarters, people slept in relays or in layers. There was little food or water. Many passengers, already weakened by the privations of ghetto life, fell sick. The stench of vomit and excrement was overpowering.

At length the journey came to an end. On his arrival at a death camp, one Jew later recalled: "The doors were torn ajar. SS men with whips and half-wild Alsatian dogs swarmed all over the place. Parents screamed for lost children."

At death camps where laborers were needed, the Jews were lined up and prodded past an SS officer. With a gesture of his hand, the officer separated out the strongest ones. They would work until they died; the rest would die immediately.

A carload of captives from the Jewish ghetto of Lublin, Poland, rumbles toward the Belzec death camp. The German authorities began liquidating the Lublin Jews on March 17, 1942. By May 9, some 30,000 of them had been deported, and only 4,000 were still left in Lublin.

Jews from Hungary, newly arrived at Auschwitz, pass a camp office whose task it was to determine their fate. About 10 per cent, mostly men, were sent to the work camp. The crippled, the ill, the elderly, and women and young children were automatically sent to the gas chambers.

THE DESTRUCTION OF HUMAN DIGNITY

The long wooden death-camp barracks each held between 500 and 1,000 people lying sometimes six deep in a single bunk. The buildings were infested with billions of fleas and hordes of rats.

A shrill of whistles in the dawn announced line-up for the rag-clad inmates, followed by a day of slave labor. Food consisted of thin broth, a piece of bread and a scrap of potato. The hunger was so intense, a survivor recalled, "that if a bit of soup spilled over, prisoners would converge on the spot, dig their spoons into the mud and stuff the mess in their mouths."

Diarrhea and dysentery were epidemic, but prisoners were denied free access to latrines. Clothing, bunks and floors were fouled, spreading disease. "They had condemned us to die in our own filth," wrote a survivor. "They wished to destroy our human dignity, to fill us with horror and contempt for ourselves and our fellows."

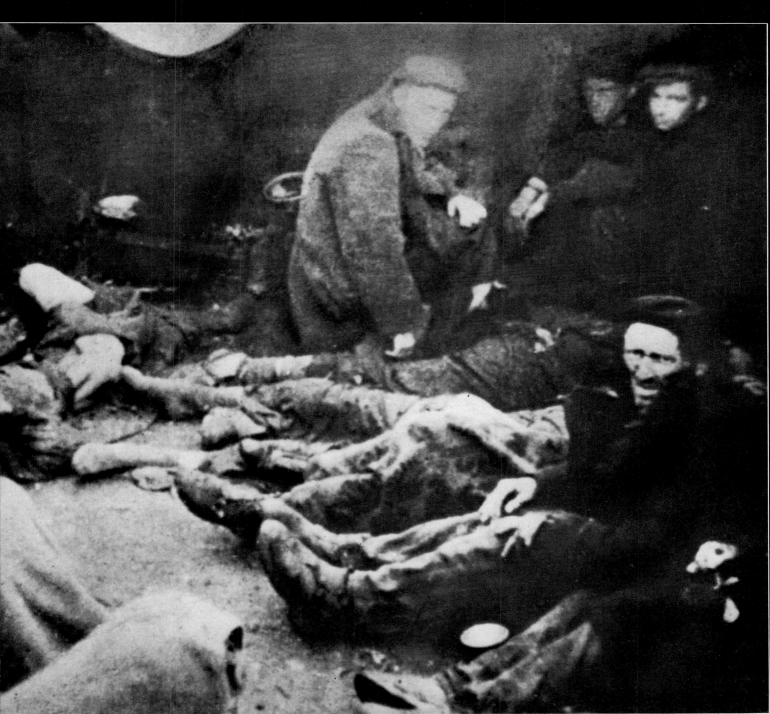

Weakened by hunger and illness, prisoners in Sachsenhausen sprawl in their filthy quarters among the bodies of fellow inmates.

His hands clenched in a death grip, a Mauthausen prisoner who committed suicide hangs from the electrified barbed-wire fence surrounding the compound.

A guard keeps watch on Mauthausen's main square, where inmates were often forced to stand naked for a day and a night. This was common treatment for new prisoners.

VICTIMS OF CASUAL BRUTALITY

Suspended by their wrists, two tortured inmates dangle from trees near Buchenwald. An SS guard stands over a fallen victim.

Every day, Jews and other prisoners were subjected to torture or random cruelty at the whim of the guards. At Auschwitz, women inmates were brutalized by Irma Grese, a guard who liked to pick out buxom ones and flay their breasts with a whip. Kurt Franz, the camp commandant at Treblinka, periodically hung prisoners upside down from a gallows and turned his fierce dog loose to savage them. At every camp, inmates were crippled or beaten to death with cudgels, rifle butts or shovels.

In some cases, beatings and worse were meted out as punishment for imagined breaches in discipline. At Auschwitz, a guard stopped a young girl who seemed to be trying to avoid him, as if she were smuggling something. He aimed his rifle at her but assured her he had no intention of killing her for her "crime." Instead he shot her once in each foot. Her wounds festered and her feet were amputated.

Slave laborers at Auschwitz were frequent victims of large-scale sadism. After the day's work was done, they were forced by SS guards to exercise for hours—to run, fall down in the mud, crawl, get up and run again. Many prisoners died of heart failure during the drill. Others crept away to their barracks and perished there.

Carrying great chunks of granite, prisoners climb steep steps in a quarry near the Mauthausen camp in Austria. Thousands of workers died here.

44 ARCHIV

DESPERATE TOIL TO STAY ALIVE

The incoming Jews and other prisoners at concentration and death camps served as a pool of slave labor for SS enterprises and private German companies. The condemned prisoners drained swamps, built roads, toiled in nearby factories manufacturing benzene or synthetic rubber or munitions. Some prisoners labored to construct or expand the very camps where they would perish.

Prisoners who weakened or sickened to the point where they could no longer work were swiftly sent to the gas chamber. The meager fare fed to the prisoners guaranteed that they would not have the strength to work for more than a few months. Accidents and brutality by SS guards reduced the prisoners' life expectancy still further.

In desperation, sick and crippled prisoners somehow managed to work on and on. One prisoner at a Mauthausen satellite camp, building an airplane-assembly plant, was beaten by his overseer with a shovel, "until he broke both the shovel and my arm." But the man stayed on the job without medical attention. "If they took me to the infirmary," he said, "I'd lose the work and my life."

Emaciated workers at Dachau show the effects of a starvation diet: watery soup, sawdust-filled bread and an occasional putrid sausage.

GUINEA PIGS FOR GRUESOME EXPERIMENTS

Uncounted thousands of Jews and other hapless concentration-camp inmates were used as guinea pigs in a wide range of medical and scientific experiments, most of them of little value.

Victims were infected with typhus to see how different geographical groups reacted; to no one's surprise, all groups perished swiftly. Fluids from diseased animals were injected into humans to observe the effect. Prisoners were forced to exist on sea water to see how long castaways might survive. Gynecology was an area of great interest. Various methods of sterilization were practiced—by massive X-ray, by irritants and drugs, by surgery without benefit of anesthetic. As techniques were perfected, it was determined that a doctor with 10 assistants could sterilize 1,000 women per day.

The "experimental people" were also used by Nazi doctors who needed practice performing various operations. One doctor at Auschwitz perfected his amputation technique on live prisoners; after he had finished, his maimed patients were sent off to the gas chamber.

A few Jews who had studied medicine were allowed to live if they assisted the SS doctors. "I cut the flesh of healthy young girls," recalled a Jewish physician who survived at terrible cost. "I immersed the bodies of dwarfs and cripples in calcium chloride (to preserve them), or had them boiled so the carefully prepared skeletons might safely reach the Third Reich's museums to justify, for future generations, the destruction of an entire race. I could never erase these memories from my mind."

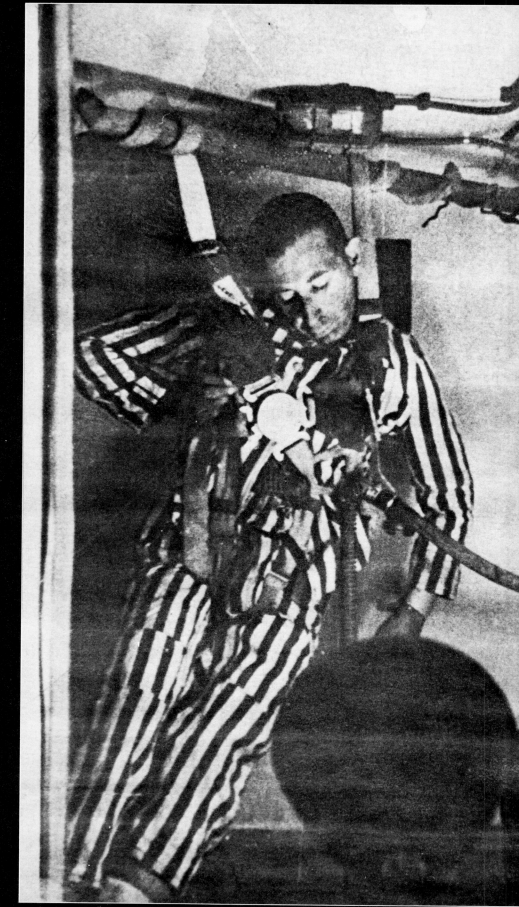

In a pressure chamber at Dachau, a victim of a low-pressure experiment hangs from a pipe. He died when his lungs burst in the thin air. Of 200 test subjects, 70 died this way.

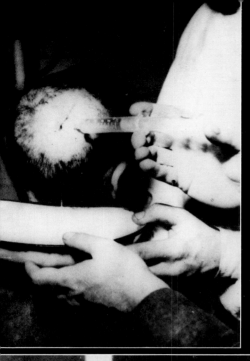

a prisoner through an incision in his skull. The purpose of the experiment is unknown.

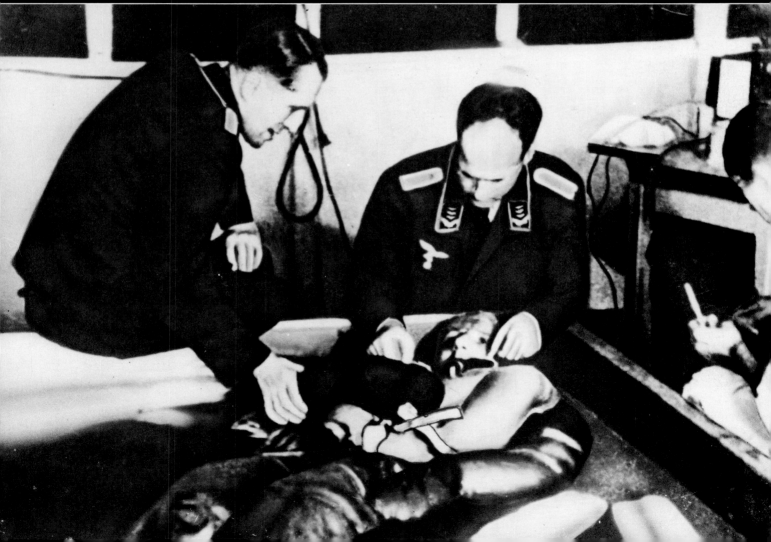

Two Luftwaffe doctors at Dachau observe the reactions of a prisoner who was immersed for three hours in a tub of ice water.

Cavernous in extent, this gas chamber was one of seven installed at the Majdanek camp in Poland, where an estimated 1.3 million prisoners were put to death. The Majdanek camp was in operation for slightly more than two years, from 1942 to 1944; only Auschwitz claimed more lives.

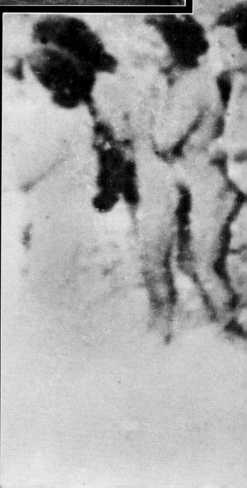

THE "SHOWER BATHS" OF DEATH

After their arrival at a death camp, the Jews who had been chosen to die at once were told that they were to have a shower. Filthied by their long, miserable journey, they sometimes applauded the announcement. Countless Jews and other victims went peacefully to the shower rooms—which were gas chambers in disguise.

In the anterooms to the gas chambers, many of the doomed people found nothing amiss. At Auschwitz, signs in several languages said, "Bath and Disinfectant," and inside the gas chambers other signs admonished, "Don't forget your soap and

willingly. "They got out of their clothes so routinely," said a Sobibor survivor. "What could be more natural?"

In time, rumors about the death camps spread, and underground newspapers in the Warsaw ghetto even ran reports that told of the gas chambers and the crematoriums. But many people did not believe the stories, and those who did were helpless in any case. Facing the guns of the SS guards, they could only hope and pray to survive. As one Jewish leader put it, "We must be patient and a miracle will occur."

There were no miracles. The victims, naked and bewildered, were shoved into a line. Their guards ordered them forward, and flogged those who hung back. The doors to the gas chambers were locked be-

Naked women clutching their children queue up outside the gas chambers at the Treblinka death camp, where about 900,000 Jews were killed. Because women and children were not strong enough to do heavy labor, they were among the first of any group to be gassed.

A hand rests on the sill of an oven door in an unknown Nazi death camp. The photograph may have been taken by an SS officer to record the

operation of the camp, or by an Allied soldier who, after the camp had been liberated, wanted to document the horrors that he found there

6

"The Army and the party," Adolf Hitler announced after ascending to Germany's pinnacle, "are the two pillars of the state." From the beginning to the end of his regime, the Führer *was* the party. But during most of that period, the Army was the only important national institution of which he was less than absolute master. Hitler's frustrating, angry and ultimately savage struggle to impose his will on the Wehrmacht would consume 11 of the Third Reich's 12 fiery years. And that effort would end only after an attempt at assassination and take-over by high-level Army officers was answered by a frightful vengeance that left the Wehrmacht, already sorely wounded on the battlefields, bleeding at its very heart.

From his solitary and highly subjective viewpoint, Hitler had every reason to rail at the ingratitude, and for that matter incompetence, of his generals. He had, in the beginning, considered himself one of the Army's own, a good and courageous soldier. In 1918, he had burned with resentment at what he—and numberless others—regarded as the betrayal by politicians that resulted in surrender and the shame of Versailles. Early in his campaign for power, he had pledged his Nazi Party's troth to the Army: "It has always been my view that we can achieve our goals only with the Army, and never against it." He had decreed in favor of the Army and against the party's own storm troops ("In the state there is only one bearer of arms, and that is the Army"), and he had given baleful effect to his decision in 1934 on the Night of the Long Knives, when he had destroyed the brown-shirted SA as a quasi-military force. No one could argue, either, that Hitler had failed in his vows to rearm Germany and return its Army to a place of power upon the earth.

And what had Hitler received in return for his benefactions? Hesitation and hand wringing. Lectures on the science of warfare. Obstacles thrown up along the paths of conquest. In 1941, even as German troops and tanks were thrusting almost unimpeded across Russia, Hitler revealingly reviewed the history of his relationship with that special culprit, the Army's General Staff. "Before I became Reich Chancellor," he said, recalling the Army as it had existed under the restrictions of Versailles, "I thought the General Staff was like a mastiff that has to be kept on a tight leash because otherwise it threatens to attack everyone else. After I had become Reich Chancellor, I was forced to observe that there is nothing the General Staff less resembles than a mas-

THE ENSLAVEMENT OF THE ARMY

tiff. The General Staff opposed rearmament, the occupation of the Rhineland, the invasion of Austria, the occupation of Czechoslovakia, and finally even the war against Poland. The General Staff advised me not to make war on Russia. It is I who always have first to urge on this mastiff."

By December of that year, with his frozen armies halted in sight of Moscow's spires, Hitler's ever-fragile patience finally snapped. For once and for all, he assumed direct and immediate command of the Wehrmacht, dictating not only its strategy but also its tactical movements.

Under Hitler's flail, the Army drove into Stalingrad, the Soviet armaments center on the Volga. There, with apparent victory in sight, Hitler's 1942 offensive stalled; and there, in the terrible winter of 1942-1943, his obstinacy doomed 300,000 German soldiers to death or Soviet captivity. Inevitably, the dictator blamed his generals. "He passes on the whole body of the generals an annihilating judgment," Joseph Goebbels wrote in his diary. "He can no longer bear the sight of the generals. All generals lie, he says, all generals are against National Socialism, all generals are reactionaries."

The Army's leaders, of course, took a diametrically opposite view. "We German officers used to be called representatives of reaction," said August von Mackensen, last surviving field marshal of the Kaiser's Army. "We were really bearers of tradition."

That tradition, hallowed by centuries of Hohenzollern rule and passed on by generations of professional officers, gave absolute primacy to obedience to the head of state. As was its right and its responsibility, the High Command presented its military advice; whether or not its opinions were accepted, compliance with the sovereign's subsequent decisions was a sacred duty. Inherent in the tradition was the policy of *Überparteilichkeit*—the Army above politics—which, unfortunately for the officers in their relationships with Hitler, rendered them babes in the political jungle.

To that proud if stiff-necked tradition, Germany's senior generals at the outbreak of World War II had given an average of 36 years of devoted service. Drawn mostly from the aristocracy, from long-established military families or from the professional middle class, the officer corps was far from being a champion of civil liberties. Many, but by no means

all, individual officers watched with dismay as the Nazi Party systematically suppressed Germany's civil institutions, as the Gestapo knocked on doors in the night and as genocide became national policy. But these were basically political matters, and while some of the younger, less tradition-bound officers were indeed moved by humanitarian motives to eventual action against the regime, the Army's senior echelons for the most part stood mutely aside—except when their own professional provinces were invaded.

Within a year after taking power in 1933, Hitler had—as was his recognized right—completely reshuffled the Army's High Command. Installed as defense minister and charged with transmitting the Führer's policies for execution by the General Staff was General Werner Eduard Fritz von Blomberg, 54, by every outward sign the very model of the Prussian officer. Tall, perfectly postured, properly bemonocled, with iron-gray hair and steely blue eyes, he had earned imperial Germany's highest military award, the Pour le Mérite, as a planner in World War I. But Blomberg was seriously flawed. "His intelligence," noted one associate, "lacked the foundation of a firm character." Though weak himself, Blomberg respected strength in others—and his admiration for Hitler knew few bounds. "The Führer," he once said, "is cleverer than we are; he will plan and do everything correctly."

Named as Blomberg's deputy was Lieut. General Walther von Reichenau, then 48, as hard as Blomberg was soft, an aristocrat by birth and initially a Nazi supporter. But Reichenau's element was in troop command, and in 1935 he was transferred to the field. His successor, to the infinite misfortune of the German Army, was General Wilhelm Bodewin Johann Gustav Keitel, 53, an undistinguished staff drudge, soon to be dubbed by his brother officers, in a play on his name, as *"Lakaitel,"* or "Lackey." Whatever Keitel's faults, and they were many, in Hitler's eyes he possessed a single surpassing virtue: He was as "loyal as a dog."

Taking rank as the Army's new commander in chief, responsible for carrying out the directives from Blomberg, was General Werner Thomas Ludwig von Fritsch, 53, a superb staff officer and a traditionalist by nature as well as by training. For Hitler, Fritsch felt a personal revulsion. "I wear a monocle," he explained, "so that my face remains stiff, especially when I confront that man." Yet duty was duty, and

Werner von Fritsch would follow it into disgrace and unto death with a helpless fatalism. Even as his doomed career neared its end, he recognized Hitler as the sovereign to whom his allegiance was pledged beyond redemption. "This man," he said, "is Germany's destiny for good and for evil. If he now goes over the abyss, he will drag us all down with him—there is nothing we can do."

Finally, appointed during that first year of the Nazi reign as the Army's top planner was a new chief of the General Staff—of whom Hitler, in an astonishing admission, would one day say: "The only man I fear is Beck."

Ludwig Beck. A Rhinelander. Son of a metallurgical engineer. Entered the Army in 1898 at the age of 18. Married in wartime and left a widower with an infant daughter 18 months later. Twice decorated for outstanding staff work. Author in 1933 of *Die Truppenführung,* the Army's standard infantry tactics manual.

Such were the prosaic facts about the man who would, perhaps beyond all others, come to epitomize the agonizing inner struggle of the Army's officer corps—the conflicts between keeping an oath and breaking a higher trust, between honored tradition and frightful reality, between narrow obedience and a far broader concern. Beck had once viewed National Socialism with hope that it might become the instrument of German resurgence. He ended as the failed leader of a conspiracy to take the life of Adolf Hitler.

Beck was by no means a firebrand. He was quiet, cautious, methodical, an exemplar of the old Army dictum, "First consider, then venture." After his tragically brief marriage, Beck's entire existence melted into that of the Army. During the 1920s, as a planner on the clandestine army-leadership group established to frustrate the Versailles prohibition against a German general staff, Beck was a shadow among shadows. By then, he had settled into the spartan routine that was to endure throughout his military career: up at 5:30 a.m., horseback riding (his only diversion) from 6 to 8, breakfast, at his desk by 9, work without break (lunch was a warm drink) until 7 p.m., dinner, and finally, back in his office from 9 until midnight.

The Reichswehr—the tiny 100,000-man German Army decreed by Versailles—was an incubator for seething resentments, not least at the sluggardly pace of promotion. "People know nothing," a young officer named Richard Scheringer wrote in 1930, "of the tragedy of the four words: 'Twelve years as subalterns.' "

As it happened, Scheringer was in a jail cell at the time. Along with two other subalterns of the 5th Artillery Regiment—commanded by Colonel Ludwig Beck—he faced trial on a charge of high treason for urging fellow officers to refrain from firing on rebels in the event of a Nazi uprising. Although the defendants were ultimately given a remarkably light sentence of only 18 months in fortress detention, the case aroused widespread interest if only because Hitler, called as a witness by defense attorney Hans Frank, used the trial as a podium to attract Army support. "We will see to it," he shouted, "that when we have come to power, out of the present Reichswehr shall rise the great Army of the German people."

Almost unnoticed amid the headlines inspired by Hitler was the fact that a little-known officer named Ludwig Beck not only appeared as a character witness for Scheringer but also expressed approval of National Socialism. The Führer had a keen eye for potential allies, and during his first months as Chancellor, he selected the lieutenant general to be the new chief of the General Staff.

Despite their subsequent displeasure at what they considered to be a reckless policy of foreign expansion, neither Beck nor the other senior officers could complain that Hitler

Army Commander in Chief Werner von Fritsch (left) and Defense Minister Werner von Blomberg confer with Hitler in 1935. Within three years, both generals had been humiliated and driven into retirement by the Führer in his remorseless campaign to bend the Army to his will.

had failed to give them early warning. In a watershed pronouncement, taken down and later paraphrased by General Maximilian von Weichs, Hitler told Army and SA leaders on February 28, 1934, that "an economic recession must ensue. This evil could be remedied only by creating living space for the surplus population. However, the Western powers would not let us do this. Therefore, short, decisive blows to the west and then the east could be necessary."

Rarely has any political leader been more candid about his intentions. Yet the German officer corps was persistent in its misunderstanding of Hitler, and Weichs's own reaction was typical: "One did not take at face value these warlike prophecies."

As for Beck and his General Staff superior, Fritsch, they had more immediate matters to worry about: In a stream of orders issued through the pliant Blomberg, Hitler was inexorably attempting to gain control of the Army. One of the earliest and, as it turned out, most telling moves came on August 2, 1934, the day after Paul von Hindenburg died and Hitler, with Army approval, was officially proclaimed head of the German state. It took the chilling form of an oath of loyalty, required of all officers and men in the armed forces, to Hitler, not only in his role as military commander but also as their personal leader: "I swear by God this holy oath, that I will render to Adolf Hitler, Führer of the German Reich and People, Supreme Commander of the Armed Forces, unconditional obedience, and that I am ready as a brave soldier, to risk my life at any time for this oath."

Without recorded exception, the members of the Army, Navy and Luftwaffe swore this pledge, and thus placed their honor and their lives in Hitler's hands.

Other orders were accepted by the General Staff with no more than murmured complaints. In steady succession, servicemen were required to salute uniformed Nazi Party officials (though not yet with the Nazi salute); the swastika was made part of the Army emblem; Jewish officers and men were dismissed from the services; all ranks underwent instructional courses in Nazi doctrine.

Despite the High Command's apparent acquiescence, a break was inevitable. When it came, the chief issue was, of all things, rearmament, for which the generals had long yearned; the second issue was Hitler's use of the Army as a card face down in his game of international bluff.

No sooner did he become chief of the General Staff than Beck put into motion a tidy plan to increase the number of Army infantry divisions from seven to 11. But that was much too modest an aim for Hitler: In January 1934, he ordered that the Army's size be trebled, surging to 300,000 from the Versailles allowance of 100,000. On April 1 more than 50,000 volunteers reported to Army training centers; on October 1 about 70,000 others entered the Army and on March 16, 1935, Hitler announced the reintroduction of national conscription. His plans now called for a 36-division Army of half a million men.

The Army planners were overwhelmed. They had wished for orderly rearmament and they had been plunged into a frenzied national roundup. Beck insisted that the process was "not a building up of a peacetime army, but a mobilization." Fritsch was beside himself. Hitler, he raged, was "forcing everything, overdoing everything, rushing everything far too much and destroying every healthy development." Even the docile Blomberg fretted, arguing that France and England would step in to prevent such flagrant violation of the Versailles strictures.

However, the Western powers failed to intervene against the German build-up, and Hitler decided to raise the stakes. In February 1936 he instructed the High Command to prepare to march into the Rhineland the following month.

Again, the generals were aghast. In fact, they had long since settled on regaining the Rhineland, with its industrial Ruhr, as their first order of military business once the Army was powerful enough to meet the French retaliation that seemed certain to result. But that time, they estimated, was at least four years away. At this moment the Army, flooded with raw recruits and still pitiably short of equipment, was utterly unprepared for a showdown with France. Still, orders were orders. A newcomer to General Staff councils, Colonel Alfred Jodl, commander of the Home Defense Department, later described the headquarters atmosphere at the time as "like that of a roulette table when a player stakes his fortune on a single number."

The German force, when it moved, consisted of a single more or less combat-ready division, of which only three battalions crossed the Rhine to occupy the industrial cities of Aachen, Trier and Saarbrücken. Even to Hitler, the period of waiting for a French response was "the most nerve-racking in my life. If the French had then marched into the Rhineland we would have had to withdraw with our tails between our legs."

But while the Führer held fast to his resolve, the generals panicked. Even on March 9, two days after Hitler had announced to a roaring Reichstag the successful reoccupation of the Rhineland, Defense Minister von Blomberg, egged on by Fritsch and Beck, urged that the troops should at least be withdrawn from the left bank of the Rhine.

By then, Hitler knew that his game was won. He had been right; his generals had been wrong. In a mental equation that was to have calamitous consequences, Hitler's confidence in his own military judgment soared, while his respect for the opinions of the High Command plunged. As for General von Blomberg, he went down in the Führer's book as "a hysterical maiden."

Since Blomberg clearly could not be counted upon in a crisis, he would have to go. And, for his outspoken opposition to the breakneck pace of the Army's expansion, Fritsch, too, was marked for removal. In the event, the fall from grace of Blomberg and, especially, Fritsch would rank as the major turning point in the entire relationship between Hitler and the German Army. Incredibly, it was brought on not at Hitler's instigation but by a bizarre sequence of events involving a prostitute, a case of mistaken homosexual identity—and the naked ambitions of Heinrich Himmler and Hermann Göring.

Himmler had long cast envious eyes upon the Wehrmacht. His military SS (a forerunner of the Waffen-SS), established in 1933 as a guard company of 120 men, by 1939 had become a full-fledged fighting force, complete with artillery. Hitler, despite his earlier promise that the Army would be Germany's only "bearer of arms," had approved. This caused deep worry in the ranks of the High Command, and the Army's Fritsch was undisguisedly hostile. The SS armed force, he said caustically, "must create an opposition to the Army, simply through its existence."

Against his nemesis, Himmler struck with rumors: Fritsch was preparing a putsch, Fritsch was working to have Göring removed from the Air Ministry, Fritsch was friendly with a subversive professor. "Nothing," Fritsch complained, "is too ridiculous to be used against me." But the worst of the slanderous campaign was yet to come. In 1936, Himmler's deputy, Reinhard Heydrich, presented Hitler with documents incriminating the middle-aged, unmarried Fritsch as a homosexual. Frankly disbelieving, Hitler ordered that the papers be burned. And so they were—but only after the Gestapo made copies for future use.

If Himmler's ambitions were mainly institutional, Göring's were entirely personal. In addition to the multitude of titles he already held, he wished to become commander in chief of the armed forces. As commander of the Luftwaffe, he was Germany's senior officer next only to Blomberg, Fritsch and the Navy's Admiral Erich Raeder. Since the Navy played a relatively minor part in Hitler's plans, Raeder hardly constituted a threat to Göring's hopes. That left Blomberg and Fritsch to be disposed of.

Unwittingly, Blomberg played into Göring's hands. A widower since 1932, he had taken up with one Erna Grühn, a typist for the Reich Egg Marketing Board, and by the beginning of 1938 she was bearing his child. On January 12, in a private ceremony with Hitler and Göring as witnesses, Blomberg and Erna Grühn were married.

Even as the happy couple was honeymooning, a Berlin police officer, rummaging through old files, happened upon a photograph of an unclad female—whom he recognized as the new Frau Blomberg. After further investigation had disclosed a lengthy record of prostitution, the evidence was turned over to the president of the Berlin police court, who eventually turned it over to Göring.

With that, Blomberg was as good as done for. But it is a measure of Göring's hard and calculating mind that before moving against Blomberg, he set about arranging Fritsch's downfall as well. He was aware of the abortive 1936 attempt by the SS to brand Fritsch as a homosexual. Now, with Göring in brief but purposeful alliance with Himmler, the Gestapo files in that case were revived and refurbished.

The case rested on the word of one Otto Schmidt, a small-time felon who specialized in blackmailing homosexuals. While under Gestapo interrogation, he had told of prowling Berlin's streets and spotting a youth engaged in homosexual activity with a man wearing a monocle. Posing as a detective, Schmidt had demanded to see the older man's identification card and then had extorted a sizable sum of money in return for promised silence. Schmidt swore the name on the card had been that of a General von Fritsch.

That was all that Göring needed. On January 24, 1938, armed with evidence against the two Wehrmacht generals who stood in the way of his envisioned advancement, Göring went to Hitler, actually weeping and bemoaning the fact that he had to be the bearer of sorrowful news. The Führer, although he was a master dissembler, seemed genuinely shocked by the disclosures. "I have never seen him so downcast," said an aide. "He paced slowly up and down his room, bent and with his hands behind his back." Nevertheless, Hitler swiftly set about making the most of the opportunities that had been handed him.

There was no question about Blomberg. So gross was his indiscretion that even his fellow generals agreed that he must be sacked. "One cannot tolerate the highest-ranking soldier marrying a whore," Beck said stiffly. But despite his failings, Blomberg had been faithful to Hitler, and the Führer repaid him with remarkably gentle treatment, sending him into "voluntary" exile, giving him 50,000 reichsmarks to augment his salary and holding out the hope that one day Blomberg might return to the Army. "As soon as Germany's hour comes," said Hitler, "you will again be by my side."

Göring's aspirations were almost immediately blighted. During his conversation with Blomberg, Hitler asked for suggestions as to a successor. Still unaware of Göring's role in disgracing him, Blomberg mentioned the Luftwaffe commander as a possibility. In fact, Hitler had already rejected that notion, telling an aide that Göring "does not understand even how to carry out a Luftwaffe inspection."

Then Blomberg came up with an idea that would weigh heavily in the history of the Wehrmacht and the Third Reich: Why did not Hitler himself become defense minister and commander in chief of the armed forces? To that, Hitler said nothing—but his silence was filled with portent.

Next, Hitler asked Blomberg to nominate candidates to head the Führer's personal military staff, a function that the departing general had formerly fulfilled. When Blomberg seemed nonplused, Hitler asked who the Defense Minister's own staff chief had been. Wilhelm Keitel, said Blomberg, but "he's nothing but the man who runs my office."

Cried Hitler: "That's exactly the man I'm looking for!"

Having thus done a monumental disservice to the Army in which he had spent his life, Blomberg left to resume his honeymoon.

The charge against Fritsch had yet to be settled. Though he steadfastly denied his guilt, Fritsch was a broken man. He resigned as Army commander in chief on January 30 and was replaced by Colonel General Walther von Brauchitsch, 56, a distinguished World War I veteran who both admired and feared Hitler. "When I confront this man," he once said, "I feel as if someone were choking me."

At first, Hitler had decreed that Fritsch must be tried before a Gestapo court, but in the face of furious Army opposition, led by Beck, he assented to a military tribunal. The trial began on March 10 and was immediately adjourned to await the outcome of Hitler's latest military adventure.

That very morning, Hitler had informed his new personal staff chief, Wilhelm Keitel, that he intended to invade Austria—within two days. Taken by surprise, Keitel raced to General Staff headquarters in Berlin's Bendlerstrasse, hoping that plans of some sort had been readied. "We have prepared nothing," said Ludwig Beck. "Nothing has been done, nothing at all." Urgently summoned to the Reich Chancellery, Beck and his chief of operations, General Erich von Manstein, later to become one of World War II's great field commanders, estimated that they would have to draft an invasion plan within five hours if they were to meet Hitler's deadline. Somehow, they managed the job.

But it was at best a patchwork. No sooner had they finished it than Beck set about trying to get it canceled, only to find that Keitel was already interposing himself between the Führer and the General Staff. Keitel recorded the events of the night of March 10: "There was telephone call after telephone call from the Army General Staff all imploring me to work on the Führer to give up the move into Austria. I had not the smallest intention even of putting the question to the Führer. I promised to do so and shortly afterward without having done it rang back to say that he had refused. The Führer never knew anything about all this; if he had, his opinion of the Army leadership would have been shattering and I wanted to save both sides that experience."

Although the German march into Austria was badly flawed—the Wehrmacht's tanks had to stop for fuel at commercial gas stations—it met with no opposition. By March

13, Hitler could proclaim another triumph—and the trial of Werner von Fritsch could resume.

It, too, was over in short order. Army and defense investigators had discovered that witness Otto Schmidt had indeed blackmailed an Army officer for a homosexual act. But his name had been Frisch, not Fritsch, and he had been a captain instead of a general. At the instigation of the Gestapo, Schmidt had simply transferred the circumstantial details of the actual case to make his accusation against the Army's commander in chief. When the guilty Frisch was produced to testify, the court swiftly returned a verdict for General von Fritsch: "Acquitted on the ground of proven innocence."

For his false testimony, the hapless Otto Schmidt was shot without trial. Despite outraged Army demands that Fritsch be completely rehabilitated, Hitler would go no further than to name him honorary colonel of his old artillery regiment. In that capacity, Fritsch later accompanied the Army to Poland, where, on September 22, 1939, he was relieved of his misery by a sniper's bullet.

The effects of what came to be known as the Fritsch Crisis reached far beyond the fates of mere individuals. Hitler used it as the occasion for a radical Army house cleaning. Sixteen generals were swept into retirement and 44 others were transferred to posts of lesser importance.

Much more important, Hitler accepted Blomberg's ill-considered suggestion and—in addition to the largely honorific position of Supreme Commander, which he held by reason of being head of state—he appointed himself commander in chief of all the armed forces. Blomberg's War Ministry was abolished, and in its place was established a new Oberkommando der Wehrmacht (OKW), directly and completely subservient to Hitler. Its staff chief was the obsequious Wilhelm Keitel. And in the fateful years to come,

Keitel and his OKW would isolate Hitler almost completely from the parallel General Staff (OKH), which became little more than an agency for drafting operational plans.

And what of Ludwig Beck? Beck was allowed to stay on as chief of the General Staff. During the Fritsch Crisis, he had made a formidable and highly unfavorable impression on Hitler. He had urged Fritsch to challenge Himmler to a duel. He had led the protest against Fritsch's being tried by a Gestapo court. He had directed the Army investigation that discredited Schmidt. Reflecting on Beck's persistent opposition, Hitler remarked to Minister of Justice Franz Guertner that he had actually come to fear Beck. "That man," he said, "would be capable of acting against me."

Not quite yet. The Fritsch Crisis had indeed provoked some generals to contemplation of overthrowing the Führer. Among them were Colonel General Baron Kurt von Hammerstein, a former Army commander in chief; General Erwin von Witzleben, commander of the Berlin military district; Major General Count Walter von Brockdorff-Ahlefeldt, commander of the Potsdam garrison; Erich Hoepner, commander of a panzer division in Thuringia; Karl-Heinrich von Stülpnagel, head of operations of the Army General Staff; and Beck's own deputy, Franz Halder, the scion of a distinguished Bavarian military family. However, when at the height of the Fritsch Crisis, Halder had urged his chief to lead a coup against Hitler, Beck had replied in the truest tradition of the Army: "Mutiny and revolution do not exist in the lexicon of the German soldier."

By summer's end, he would change his mind.

Flushed with his Austrian victory, Hitler now moved with bewildering speed. On April 20, he assigned to Keitel the task of formulating Operation *Green*—the plan for an at-

The Munich beer hall made famous by the 1923 Putsch lies shattered from a powerful explosion that ripped through the building on November 8, 1939, minutes after Hitler had left the annual reunion of Nazi fighters. This attempt on the Führer's life was made by a Communist sympathizer named Georg Elser. But to whip up popular support for his planned invasion of Holland, Belgium and France, Hitler blamed the blast on British agents.

tack on Czechoslovakia. As signed by Hitler on May 28, it began: "It is my unalterable decision to smash Czechoslovakia by military action in the near future."

At General Staff headquarters, the officers were despondent. Czechoslovakia had been the creation of the Versailles powers; they could not possibly continue to stand aside. "An attack on Czechoslovakia," said Beck, "would bring France and Britain into the conflict at once. The outcome would be a general catastrophe for Germany, not only a military defeat."

Beck urged that Brauchitsch organize a *démarche* in which senior generals would frustrate Hitler's planned invasion by threatening to resign en masse. Brauchitsch, torn between his own strong disapproval of Operation *Green* and his fear of Hitler, was in a pitiable state and refused to move. "Why, in heaven's name," he would later ask, "should I, of all men in the world, have been the one required to take action against Hitler?"

With his superior unwilling to lead, Ludwig Beck, at long last, arrived at his personal moment of truth. And in a memo to Brauchitsch he posed a historic dilemma. Writing of Germany's senior officers, he said: "History will burden these leaders with blood-guilt. Their military obedience has a limit where their knowledge, their conscience, and their sense of responsibility forbid the execution of a command." Then he took his stand: "Extraordinary times demand extraordinary measures."

On August 21, 1938, Hitler accepted Beck's resignation from the German Army. Six days later, Beck turned over his office to his former deputy, new chief of the General Staff Franz Halder. Recalling that only a few months before he had rejected Halder's plea that they rise against Hitler, Beck said: "I now realize that you were right."

With that, Beck retired to his modest stucco home at No. 9 Goethe Street, Berlin Lichterfelde, where he grew his own vegetables, began work on a volume of military history—and entered into active conspiracy against Adolf Hitler.

There had been conspirators from the very beginning of the Nazi regime. But they were mostly civilians, woefully lacking an institutional base, and they had spent almost all their time in factional argument. Among them was Fabian von Schlabrendorff, a young lawyer whose miraculous survival would leave him as one of the few conspirators familiar with the plots against Hitler from beginning to end.

By 1938, wrote Schlabrendorff, "it had become amply clear that any resistance to the Nazi rule could be effective and successful only if we managed to win over the top military leaders." Upon his retirement, Ludwig Beck became the vital link between the civilians and the Army and, continued Schlabrendorff, his role as head of the conspiratorial organization "was acknowledged by all and was never in doubt. Whenever controversies or arguments arose—and there were many, both personal and otherwise—Beck was called upon to judge each question."

Before their final failure, Beck and his fellow conspirators would launch half a dozen major efforts and countless lesser ones against Hitler. Their widening ring would encompass top Army commands from the Moscow front to the Atlantic Wall; it would include staff officers in the most sensitive and strategic branches of the Wehrmacht. At first, the intention was to arrest Hitler, place him on trial for crimes against the German people and nation, and take over the government. Later, the conspiratorial resolve hardened into an implacable plan to assassinate the Führer by whatever means at whatever cost.

The difficulties of achievement were enormous. Hitler was protected by a bodyguard of SS sharpshooters headed by a giant major general named Hans Rattenhuber. The dictator's travel plans were kept secret; he would arrive at his destinations late; he would leave early—or he would not appear at all. He carried his own revolver and, as was widely rumored, he wore a bullet-proof vest.

Making matters worse, the conspirators were working under the ever-watchful eye of the Gestapo, which as a matter of routine bugged their telephones, read their mail and pried into their personal lives. History does not relate how much the Gestapo knew about the plotters and their plans. But it seems impossible that such a wide-scale conspiracy, involving scores of officers, could go undetected by Himmler's zealous agents. There are various theories. One is that the conspirators covered their tracks so well that the Gestapo, though realizing something was afoot, never had enough evidence to act on. Another is that the Gestapo knew a great deal about the conspiracy but was playing a game of cat-and-mouse, letting its prey run free while it worked to gather up every last conspirator. Yet another fascinating theory is that Himmler himself was in contact with the plotters—that he had turned against Hitler, wished him dead and hoped to replace him as German chief of state.

In any case, despite all obstacles, the conspirators more than once penetrated to within killing range of Hitler—only to be thwarted by astoundingly bad luck. Hitler knew nothing of these attempts, but he liked to boast that a protective Providence watched over him. The men who wished to slay him could only bitterly agree.

No sooner had Beck retired from the Army in 1938 than he set into motion the first plot, aimed at stopping Hitler before he plunged Germany into war by invading Czechoslovakia. In the effort, Beck had help from an unlikely source: Colonel Hans Oster, chief of staff of Germany's Abwehr, or military intelligence. Oster had dedicated himself to Hitler's downfall since 1934, when his close friend and former Abwehr chief, Major General Ferdinand von Bredow, was unaccountably murdered by the SS during the SA purge. Now, under Abwehr director Wilhelm Canaris, an enigmatic admiral who encouraged plots against Hitler while refusing to participate actively himself, Oster acted as a sort of general manager to Beck's conspiratorial chairmanship.

Before taking direct action against Hitler, the conspirators dispatched an emissary, Ewald von Kleist, a gentleman farmer of distinguished lineage, to London to seek, if not material support, at least political encouragement from British authorities. Kleist—like every conspiratorial representative who followed him—received at best a tepid reception. Said Prime Minister Neville Chamberlain, who did not see Kleist but was informed of his purpose: "I think we must discount a good deal of what he says."

As for the scheme to depose Hitler, it seemed simple enough. Beck's successor as chief of the General Staff, General Halder, then 54, would trigger the uprising. With his close-cropped hair, his pince-nez and his acidulous manner of speaking, Halder seemed a prototypical German general. He was, in fact, a highly emotional man, and he had been outraged by Hitler's treatment of Fritsch.

Now, Halder agreed to provide the conspirators with at least two days' advance notice of Hitler's order to march on Czechoslovakia. Upon receiving that word, General von Witzleben, at the head of his Berlin military district troops, would arrest Hitler. A provisional government would be announced with Beck at its head, and Hitler would go on trial for endangering the German nation.

As it turned out, Neville Chamberlain neutralized the plot. Just as the conspirators were ready to move into action, "the news came," recalled Halder, "that the British Prime Minister had agreed to come to Hitler for further talks. I therefore took back the order of execution because the entire basis for the action had been taken away."

With the capitulation of Chamberlain at Munich, the tyrant whom the conspirators had meant to present as a peril to his nation was transformed into a statesman in his moment of glory. To try to depose him now was inconceivable. The conspirators had no choice but to bide their time.

Their next opportunity was a while in coming. So overwhelmed were Germany's senior officers by the Führer's bloodless victories that they made not a murmur of protest when, on May 23, 1939, Hitler announced to them his next step on the path of aggression: "Further successes can no longer be attained without the shedding of blood. There is no question of sparing Poland, and we are left with the decision to attack Poland at the first suitable opportunity."

Later, General von Manstein would explain the confusion that Hitler by now was able to sow in the minds of his military leaders: "The man seemed to have an infallible instinct. Success had followed success. All these things had been achieved without war. Why, we asked ourselves, should it be different this time?"

Thus, in the predawn darkness of September 1, 1939, a German force of 1.5 million troops—part of an Army now comprising 3.7 million men—began to move across the Polish frontier. Twenty-six days later, Warsaw fell, and on that date Hitler, headlong now in his pursuit of conquest, summoned his military chiefs to the Chancellery to make known his decision to "attack in the West as soon as possible, since the Franco-British Army is not yet prepared." Less than two weeks later, on October 9, Hitler gave his generals more specific marching orders: "I have decided without further loss of time to go over to the offensive on the northern flank of the Western Front, through Luxembourg, Belgium and Holland."

The invasion of Poland had finally aroused France and

Great Britain to a declaration of war. But the Western powers displayed little inclination to attack. The German generals found themselves wishfully thinking that the Allies might yet drop the whole affair. Such plans for the Western Front as the German General Staff had formulated were entirely defensive in nature; incredibly, an order had even been drawn up to begin partial German demobilization.

Hitler's latest adventure was therefore greeted with complete consternation. To invade Poland was one thing. To make aggressive war against France and England was quite another. "The technique of the Polish campaign," Halder wrote in his diary, was "no recipe for the West. No good against a well-knit army." General Georg Thomas, head of the High Command's Economics Department, reported an enormous 600,000-ton monthly shortfall in the steel production required for a long war. Quartermaster Colonel Eduard Wagner wrote in a memo that there was sufficient ammunition to supply only one third of the available German divisions in the field for 14 days. Even Keitel protested—and brought down his Führer's wrath upon his head. "When I publicly told him what I thought," Keitel wrote in his diary, "Hitler violently accused me of obstructing him and conspiring against his plans."

This, then, was the occasion for which the conspirators had been impatiently waiting. Halder agreed to participate in another attempt at a coup much along the lines of the previous plan, which Beck had already directed Oster to bring up to date.

Halder did, however, insist on awaiting the outcome of a meeting at which the Army's commander in chief, Brauchitsch, had finally agreed to place before Hitler the General Staff's objections to the Western offensive. That confrontation, as it turned out, was disastrous. Brauchitsch had scarcely finished speaking when Hitler, screaming, leaped to his feet. In the tirade that followed, Hitler shouted, among other things, that he knew all about the "spirit of Zossen" and was determined to crush it.

Hitler was referring to what he considered to be the cowardly, defeatist mood at Zossen, the General Staff's wartime headquarters. But to Halder, when he was told of the phrase, it could mean only that Hitler was aware of the plot against him. Terrified, he hurriedly burned the plans for the coup, which the generals, in their Prussian thoroughness, had incredibly entrusted to paper. And although Halder would detest Hitler to the end of his days, he would never again participate in a conspiracy.

As before, Hitler's blitzkrieg against France squelched the possibility of any overthrow. Hitler then had made a public display of his regard for the generals by elevating 12 of them to field marshal at the Kroll Opera House celebrations. But his private contempt, if anything, grew stronger. Not once in the second half of 1940 did Hitler call upon the General Staff for the strategic advice it had traditionally given. Rather, he relied almost entirely on Keitel's OKW and, recalled one observer, there was a continuing "atmosphere of tension between these two neighboring high-level headquarters. But on the side of the OKW stood Hitler, dominating everything, impatient and suspicious."

During this period and for several months thereafter, the plotters were necessarily inactive. Hitler seemed invincible. The invasion of the Soviet Union was launched on June 22, 1941. Germany's armies swept eastward, crushing whole Soviet armies. The cause of the conspirators was at its nadir—until, in October, Hitler's offensive was brought to a halt on the outskirts of Moscow. Then and only then did Hitler once again appear to be mortal. And the conspiracy took on new life.

Beck remained senior among the plotters; the Abwehr's Oster was still his energetic deputy. But the most active and lethal opposition now moved to the headquarters of Army Group Center on the Moscow front. There, in the person of the army group's senior operations officer, resided a foe of Hitler and Hitlerism who entertained no notions whatever of overthrow without bloodshed. For Lieut. Colonel Henning von Tresckow, 40, only Hitler's death would do.

The motives for Tresckow's hatred of Hitler were obscure, even to his closest friend and conspiratorial associate, Fabian von Schlabrendorff, who became his aide-de-camp in 1941. But whatever his motives, Tresckow worked relentlessly and single-mindedly to bring about Hitler's downfall. Among those he brought into the movement were Colonel Helmuth Stieff, chief of the Organization Department in the Army's High Command (in 1939, witnessing SS atrocities in Poland, Stieff had cried, "I am ashamed to be a German!"); Erich Fellgiebel, the Wehrmacht head of communications;

Fritz Lindemann, ordnance director; and Friedrich Olbricht, deputy to the commander of the reserve army.

By early 1943, after the surrender of the German Sixth Army at Stalingrad, Hitler's military debacle had, according to Schlabrendorff, "lent an added urgency to our persistent efforts to eliminate Hitler before it was too late to salvage anything from the ruins of the Nazi war."

From then on, in dire and increasingly desperate parade, marched the assassination attempts that led inexorably to final tragedy.

On March 13, 1943, Hitler arrived by airplane for a visit to Army Group Center headquarters at Smolensk. During lunch Tresckow asked Lieut. Colonel Heinz Brandt, a Hitler aide, if he would take to Colonel Helmuth Stieff at High Command headquarters a gift package containing two bottles of brandy. In fact, the parcel contained not brandy, but a bottle-shaped, British-made plastic bomb, which enemy planes had dropped to saboteurs and which had been recovered by Oster's Abwehr. Brandt agreed.

Just before Brandt boarded Hitler's plane to return to East Prussia, Schlabrendorff handed him the package—having already triggered the bomb to explode in 30 minutes. For two awful hours, the conspirators waited for news that Hitler was dead. Instead, they heard that the Führer's plane had landed safely after a flight without incident.

Next day, Schlabrendorff flew to Hitler's headquarters to retrieve the package from Brandt, explaining that a mistake had been made in the parcel and exchanging it for two bottles of real brandy.

The bomb, upon later examination, proved to be a dud.

On March 21, one week after their failure in Smolensk, the conspirators tried again. Hitler was scheduled to speak at the opening of an exhibition of war trophies in Berlin. Colonel Baron von Gersdorff, a conspirator on the staff of Army Group Center, had been added to Hitler's military entourage. In each pocket of his overcoat, Gersdorff had placed a bomb with which he meant to blow both Hitler and himself to smithereens. But the bombs were equipped with 10-minute fuses, and after entering the exhibition building Gersdorff was informed by a Hitler adjutant that the Führer would remain there only eight to 10 minutes. For Gersdorff, that was cutting the time much too close, and he gave up on his attempt.

On November 25, at Rastenburg, Hitler was scheduled to examine new Army uniforms and overcoats especially designed for use on the frigid Eastern Front. This was the sort of military detail that never failed to fascinate Germany's Supreme Commander. The uniforms would be modeled by stalwart representatives of Aryan soldiery—including Captain Axel von dem Bussche, 24, who had once suffered the unnerving experience of watching the SS slaughter 1,600 Jews in a single afternoon. Bussche was carrying a hand grenade with a 4.5-second fuse, and he planned to arm the grenade, then throw his arms around Hitler in a fatal embrace. But the showing was canceled: The shipment of uniforms had been destroyed by an Allied air raid against a Berlin railroad yard.

Enough was enough. The final attempt to assassinate Hitler would be entrusted to a man who among all the conspirators was the most likely to bring it off: Colonel and Count Claus Schenk von Stauffenberg.

Looking vigorous and completely in command, Hitler transfers reports of new German victories onto an operations map in the war room at a field headquarters. Thousands of propaganda photographs like this were distributed nationwide in the summer of 1940 to demonstrate that it was the Führer himself, rather than the General Staff officers clearly fawning around him, who was the architect of the Wehrmacht's lightning conquests of Holland, Belgium and France.

By any standard and by every accounting, Stauffenberg was a rare man. He was born in 1907, the son of a former chamberlain to the last king of Württemberg; on his mother's side, he was descended from a Prussian general in the Napoleonic wars. As a young officer Stauffenberg had, like so many others, accepted the National Socialist government as the least of the many evils then afflicting Germany. By 1939, although thoroughly disillusioned—he remarked to a friend shortly before the invasion of Poland, "The fool is going to make war"—he displayed only an academic interest when approached by conspirators.

As a staff officer, Stauffenberg was superb, and a colleague described him vividly: "I never opened Claus's door without finding him on the telephone. In front of him would be piles of papers, his left hand holding the telephone, in his right a pencil with which he annotated the documents before him. He would be speaking forcibly, laughing a lot (as he always did) or swearing (which he was also not slow to do) or giving orders or instructions. Claus was one of those men who could do several tasks simultaneously with full concentration on each."

In the summer of 1941, while visiting the Russian front, Stauffenberg met Henning von Tresckow and, though he agreed that Germany must somehow rid itself of Hitler, he did not seem interested in doing anything to achieve that desirable end. Instead, he pursued his career and asked for an assignment in North Africa. There, in the Kasserine Pass on April 7, 1943, bullets from a strafing Allied airplane struck him and changed his life.

When he awakened in a hospital, Stauffenberg was blind in his left eye; he had lost part of his right arm and had only three fingers remaining on his left hand. He was in the hospital for several months, during which he did a great deal of thinking. Sometime during May he told his wife, the Countess Nina: "You know, I feel I must do something now, to save Germany."

Slowly, torturously, he taught himself to write with what was left of his only hand; using his teeth to assist his three fingers, he learned to dress himself. And, while still on convalescent leave, he returned to work—for the conspirators.

At the request of Ludwig Beck, Stauffenberg in September 1943 consolidated earlier plans for the seizure of power after Hitler was assassinated. The plan, code-named Operation *Valkyrie,* called for coups at key points. In Berlin, the Guard Battalion and contingents from nearby military training schools were to combine with the Berlin Police Force, under Count Wolf Heinrich von Helldorf, and seize government buildings, radio stations and newspaper offices. In the East, troop uprisings led by Tresckow and others would take command of Army Group Center. In the West, General Karl-Heinrich von Stülpnagel, now commandant at Paris, and General Baron Alexander von Falkenhausen, the military governor of Belgium, would bring their forces into the conspirators' camp. Then after SS resistance was crushed, the conspirators would negotiate a peace with the Allies.

There was another plotter: Field Marshal Erwin Rommel, the famed Desert Fox and hero of North Africa who now commanded an Army group in France. Feeling the War lost, Rommel had been won over to the conspiracy in early 1944. In July, after the Normandy invasion, he had sent Hitler an ultimatum demanding that Germany seek peace terms with the Western Allies. "I have given him his last chance," Rommel remarked to fellow officers. "If he does not take it, we shall act."

After many secret meetings and coded messages, the conspirators were ready to execute Operation *Valkyrie.* All that remained was to select an assassin—preferably one with at least occasional access to Hitler's daily military conferences at Rastenburg where, the conspirators had decided, the Führer was most vulnerable.

On July 1, 1944, Stauffenberg, back on the Army's active roster, reported for duty as chief of staff of the German reserve army. That job would take him to Rastenburg.

Sometime before dawn on the morning of July 20, Colonel Count von Stauffenberg arose and painfully dressed at his home in Berlin. Shortly after 6 a.m., his staff car arrived. Stauffenberg instructed the driver to pick up his adjutant, Lieutenant Werner von Haeften. With Haeften, Stauffenberg drove to the Rangsdorf airport, 45 minutes away. Both men had brief cases—and each brief case carried a bomb.

Like those used in previous attempts against Hitler, these were British-made bombs of a putty-like plastic substance; since there was no metal casing, they depended on blast effect. The fuses were both silent and smokeless. When broken, a small glass capsule released an acid that ate through a wire restraining a spring. After the acid had done its work, the spring propelled a striker into a cap, detonating the bomb. The arming apparatus was set for 10 minutes.

Time and again, holding a pair of pliers in his three fingers, Stauffenberg had practiced breaking the glass capsule. He could now open the brief case, squeeze the pliers and smash the capsule within seconds.

At 7 a.m., Stauffenberg's plane left Rangsdorf for Rastenburg, three hours distant. At Rastenburg, a staff car was waiting, but before Stauffenberg and Haeften left for Hitler's headquarters, Haeften ordered the pilot to be ready to take off at a moment's notice.

The car passed through three checkpoints and arrived at the compound where Hitler now dwelt and worked. Among the structures inside the enclosure were Hitler's bunker and the *Lagebaracke,* or situation hut, where the Führer often held his military conferences.

After a brief meal, Stauffenberg chatted with several officers; one was General Erich Fellgiebel who, as the Army's chief signals officer—and a conspirator—would importantly influence the day's events. Shortly after noon, Stauffenberg entered the office of the OKW's Field Marshal Wilhelm Keitel where he summarized the report he was scheduled to make to Hitler. Stauffenberg's mission, ostensibly, was to brief Hitler about progress in training new divisions. By the time he was done explaining to Keitel, the OKW chief was anxiously glancing at his watch. It would never do to be late to a Hitler conference.

As the two left to go to the *Lagebaracke,* Stauffenberg excused himself on the pretext of returning to Keitel's anteroom for his cap and belt, which he had left hanging there. While there, he opened his brief case and broke the bomb's triggering capsule. Ten minutes now remained before the bomb would explode.

When Stauffenberg emerged, Keitel, although fuming at the delay, thoughtfully asked if he could carry the crippled colonel's brief case. Stauffenberg managed a smile while declining the offer. In the entrance hall of the *Lagebaracke,* Stauffenberg paused to speak to the sergeant major in charge of a small telephone switchboard; he was, he said, expecting a call from Berlin with additional data for his report to Hitler, and he would like to be notified when it came through. When Stauffenberg and Keitel stepped into the conference room, seven minutes remained on the fuse.

Keitel's fretting had been justified: They were late, and the conference had already begun. In the 30-by-15-foot room, 24 men stood around a rectangular oak table. Hitler was at the center of one of the table's long sides, with his back to the door. On the table in front of him were maps and, for his failing eyesight, the magnifying glass he used to follow his briefings.

As Stauffenberg and Keitel entered, Lieut. General Adolf Heusinger, the High Command's chief of the operations section, was reviewing that day's situation on the Russian front. Hitler turned and greeted Stauffenberg. Keitel, who acted as a sort of master of ceremonies at Hitler's conferences, took his usual place at the Führer's left. Stauffenberg squeezed into a place one man down from Hitler's right. He placed his brief case beneath the table, leaning it against one of the two thick oaken supports that ran almost the entire width of the table. While the attention of the audience remained on Heusinger, Stauffenberg slipped out of the room. About five minutes were still left on the bomb.

With Stauffenberg gone, Lieut. Colonel Heinz Brandt—the same Hitler aide who had, unknowingly, once carried a bomb from Smolensk—moved closer to the table to get a better look at the map. He accidentally kicked Stauffenberg's brief case and, since it was still in his way, bent over and moved it—to the side of the table support away from Hitler. Two minutes were left.

About 100 yards from the *Lagebaracke,* Stauffenberg stood with General Fellgiebel outside the signal office. He was smoking a cigarette. Nearby waited his staff car, with Haeften, who had been waiting all this while, already in it.

At 12:42 p.m. on July 20, 1944, the bomb exploded. It was, Stauffenberg later said, as if the *Lagebaracke* had suffered a direct hit from a 150mm shell. The ceiling caved in, glass flew from shattered windows and, from within, came the moans and screams of injured and dying men. Stauffenberg flicked away his cigarette and stepped into his car. Surely, Hitler was dead.

The car got only a few yards before it was stopped at the gate to the inner compound. Stauffenberg explained that he had to get to the airport in a hurry, and the officer on duty, still confused by the nearby explosion, let him through. At the second guard post, Staffenberg jumped out and asked if he could use the telephone in the guardhouse. After a moment of talking into the mouthpiece, he hung up, telling the guard officer: "I'm allowed through." The barrier at the checkpoint swung up.

In the same way Stauffenberg bluffed his way past the remaining checkpoint; then he sped toward the airfield. On the way, Haeften threw his own bomb (whose intended use remains unclear) out the car window—to be found later by searching security forces.

Shortly after 1 p.m., Stauffenberg's plane lifted off from Rastenburg. And during the three hours that he was in the air, isolated and out of touch with the rush of historic events, the conspiracy against the life of Adolf Hitler would completely unravel.

Although Stauffenberg could not have imagined it, Hitler was very much alive. At the instant of the blast, he had been leaning over to examine a map; the table's thick top had served as a buffer against the bomb. Moreover, by moving Stauffenberg's brief case, Lieut. Colonel Brandt had inadvertently converted the table's sturdy support into a further shield for the Führer.

Four persons were killed—including Brandt. But Hitler, supported by Keitel, soon staggered from the building, his hair smoking, his trouser legs shredded, both of his eardrums broken and his right arm severely bruised.

General Fellgiebel, who had remained outside after Stauffenberg's departure, was horrified to see that Hitler had survived. He immediately called a fellow conspirator in Berlin, trying to tell him to warn the other plotters. But since he feared that the Gestapo might be listening in, his words were guarded—and, as it turned out, ambiguous.

Nevertheless, to Fellgiebel's mind, the uprising had already gone so far that there could be no turning back. Assuming that the Berlin conspirators would now send out signals for Operation *Valkyrie* to begin, Fellgiebel carried out his own part of the original plan: He issued orders, which could be countermanded only by Hitler himself, for his signals operators to cut off all communications to and from Rastenburg. Thus, for the next two and a half hours, while Hitler was recovering from the shock of his experience, the Wolf's Lair was virtually isolated from the rest of the world.

In Berlin, Colonel General Erich Hoepner—who had been relieved of his panzer command by Hitler for having made a strategic withdrawal outside Moscow—arrived at the Bendlerstrasse office of the reserve army's deputy commander, Friedrich Olbricht, at about 12:30 p.m. Hoepner and Olbricht went out to lunch and, over a half bottle of wine, drank toasts to the death of Adolf Hitler.

Shortly after they returned at 3:15 p.m., they were told by Fellgiebel's deputy of the last message before silence had fallen on Rastenburg. Because of Fellgiebel's enigmatic language, the Berlin conspirators were uncertain whether Hitler was actually alive or dead. They hesitated and failed to put Operation *Valkyrie* into motion.

After his tense trip in a plane lacking long-range radio, Stauffenberg finally landed at the Rangsdorf airfield at 3:45. Calling Olbricht, he was staggered to learn that nothing whatever had been done. Without wasting words, Stauffenberg assured Olbricht that Hitler was dead, and urged that Operation *Valkyrie* be launched at once.

Olbricht moved fast—in the wrong direction. His first and fateful act was to go to his own superior, Colonel General Friedrich Fromm, commander of the reserve army. The fleshy, florid Fromm had long known that a plot was afoot, and he had often been asked to cooperate in the cause. But Fromm was a hedger. Sometimes indicating his approval, invariably changing his mind, he had waited to pick the winning side. Now, still cautious, he insisted on proof that the assassination had been successful.

Olbricht was unworried. Understandably, he had accepted Stauffenberg's word. Moreover, he assumed that communications with Rastenburg were still silenced. Confident that the dead line would convince Fromm, Olbricht picked up the phone and placed an emergency call to Rastenburg.

Keitel answered.

Only minutes before, at the Führer's command, Rastenburg's communications had been restored; and now, as the dumfounded Olbricht silently handed the receiver to Fromm, Keitel explained that although there had indeed been an attempt on Hitler's life, the Führer was not only alive but was at that moment greeting a guest—Italy's dictator Benito Mussolini.

Twenty minutes later, at about 4:30 p.m., Stauffenberg arrived, hatless and disheveled. Not only had Hitler been assassinated, he reported to Fromm, but he had himself been the assassin. "That's impossible," said Fromm. "Keitel has assured me of the contrary." Snapped Stauffenberg: "Field Marshal Keitel is lying, as usual." And then, stretching the truth: "I myself saw Hitler's body carried out."

But Fromm had finally decided where he stood, and he pronounced the conspirators under arrest. Said Olbricht: "You can't have us arrested. You don't realize what the actual situation is. We are arresting you." At gunpoint, Fromm was taken into an adjoining room and placed under guard. It was 5 o'clock.

By then, retired Colonel General Ludwig Beck, attired somewhat incongruously in a lounge suit, had arrived at the Bendlerstrasse, ready to take over as Germany's new head of state. With Stauffenberg and Beck in charge, squads of soldiers from the Grossdeutschland guard regiment sealed off the Bendlerstrasse headquarters, securing rebel control of the building. Both Stauffenberg and Beck took to the telephone in a belated and desperate effort to spur the entire *Valkyrie* network into action. "At our end of the wire," recalled a conspirator, "Stauffenberg incessantly repeated the same refrain: 'Keitel is lying . . . Don't believe Keitel . . .

Hitler is dead . . . Yes, he is definitely dead . . . Yes, here the action is in full swing.' "

At Rastenburg, Keitel was equally busy, telephoning and sending out signals to commanders throughout Germany and the occupied nations of Europe that the Führer lived. Bewildered, even the commanders most deeply dedicated to the conspiracy hesitated and were lost.

Thus the afternoon and early evening passed—until, shortly after 9 p.m., Berlin radio announced that Adolf Hitler would address the German people later that night. To several junior officers within the Bendlerstrasse building, that news was decisive. For so long as they thought Hitler was dead, they were willing to go along with the uprising. But now, under a Lieut. Colonel Franz Herber, they gathered up submachine guns and burst into Olbricht's office.

Olbricht, Beck, Hoepner and others were overcome and arrested. When Stauffenberg looked in to find out what all the commotion was about, he too was taken prisoner. A few minutes later, taking advantage of the confusion, he made an attempt to escape. And as he ran down a corridor, Count Claus von Stauffenberg was shot in his remaining arm and, with blood spurting from the wound, recaptured.

Fromm was released. Previously indecisive, he was now implacable. But when he demanded that the prisoners surrender their revolvers, Beck pleaded for a more honorable death than execution: "I shall find my own way out of this unhappy situation." Fromm allowed Beck to keep his revolver, but ordered him to point it only at himself.

Beck, weary and defeated, squeezed the trigger—and succeeded only in grazing his temple. Moments later, he tried again, and again he failed. Fromm ordered an officer to "help the old gentleman." The officer begged off—and Ludwig Beck, 64, once the chief of the German General Staff, was led into another room and shot by a sergeant.

General Hoepner, given the same choice as Beck, chose arrest over suicide and later shared the terrible fate meted out to other leaders of the conspiracy. At Fromm's peremptory command, Count von Stauffenberg, Olbricht, Haeften and another conspirator were herded outside into a courtyard. There, in the glare of automobile headlights, they were executed by a firing squad.

As for General Fromm, he had flirted for too long with conspiracy: He was executed in the bloodbath that followed the fateful day of July 20, 1944.

Hitler commanded that the principal plotters be hanged —in such a manner that they would die slowly, in agony. A number of them met that fate. Among the conspirators who were gradually strangled by thin cord were Witzleben, Hoepner and Stieff.

Canaris and Oster were both hanged on April 9, 1945. Henning von Tresckow, when he heard of the failure of July 20, walked into the no man's land between German and Soviet lines and blew off his own head with a grenade. Two German field marshals also committed suicide. One was Günther von Kluge, formerly the commander of Army Group Center and sometimes under Tresckow's influence; when his vacillating role in the conspiracy was disclosed, he swallowed cyanide. The other was Erwin Rommel: In return for the promise that his family would be spared, he too swallowed poison. Rather than let the German people know that one of their authentic heroes had died an enemy of the Nazi regime, Hitler ordered a state funeral. There, Field Marshal Gerd von Rundstedt, senior officer of the German Army, delivered the oration. "His heart," said Rundstedt of Rommel, "belonged to the Führer."

"The family of Count Stauffenberg," vowed Heinrich Himmler, "will be wiped out root and branch." Throughout Germany, everyone bearing the name of Stauffenberg—men, women, children—was arrested. Some died in prison. The children were taken from their parents, given false names and put into concentration camps.

One of the few conspirators who survived was Fabian von Schlabrendorff, whose deliverance came from the sky. He was on trial before the People's Court Hitler had set up as his instrument of vengeance when an American bomber scored a hit on the building and Schlabrendorff's records were destroyed. Returned to prison while the case against him was being reconstructed, he was liberated by American troops shortly before the end of the War.

In all, some 7,000 soldiers and civilians were arrested, and nearly 5,000 were executed. Not all of these had played a part in the plot. But what better opportunity for Hitler to weed out doubters and weaklings—and for loyal Nazis to even old scores? Never again would a member of the Army raise a hand against Hitler. For the first time, he was in absolute command of both pillars of the German state.

But what had he won? Although it would make one more dangerous, desperate offensive lunge in the Battle of the Bulge, the Army that Hitler had finally enslaved was now dying. Weakened by misuse, deprived of its proud traditions, its officer corps brutally reduced by war and the dictator's revenge, it would fight bravely but uselessly to the end.

Doomsday was approaching for Adolf Hitler and the Nazis as well. After his July 20 address to the nation, during which his voice was shaken, the great orator made no further broadcasts. He now remained virtually incommunicado at the Wolf's Lair, seeing only his closest associates—Bormann, Himmler, Goebbels and a few trusted generals.

Within six months, Hitler would go to ground altogether and disappear into the concrete bunker beneath the Reich Chancellery, where he would spend the rest of his days.

Joining in the Nazi salute, thousands of Germans show their loyalty to Hitler just after the July 1944 attempt on his life by high-ranking Army officers. Such rallies took place spontaneously throughout the Reich and proved, as Army Chief of Staff Heinz Guderian put it, that the "people still believed in Hitler and were convinced that his death would have removed the only man able to bring the War to a favorable conclusion."

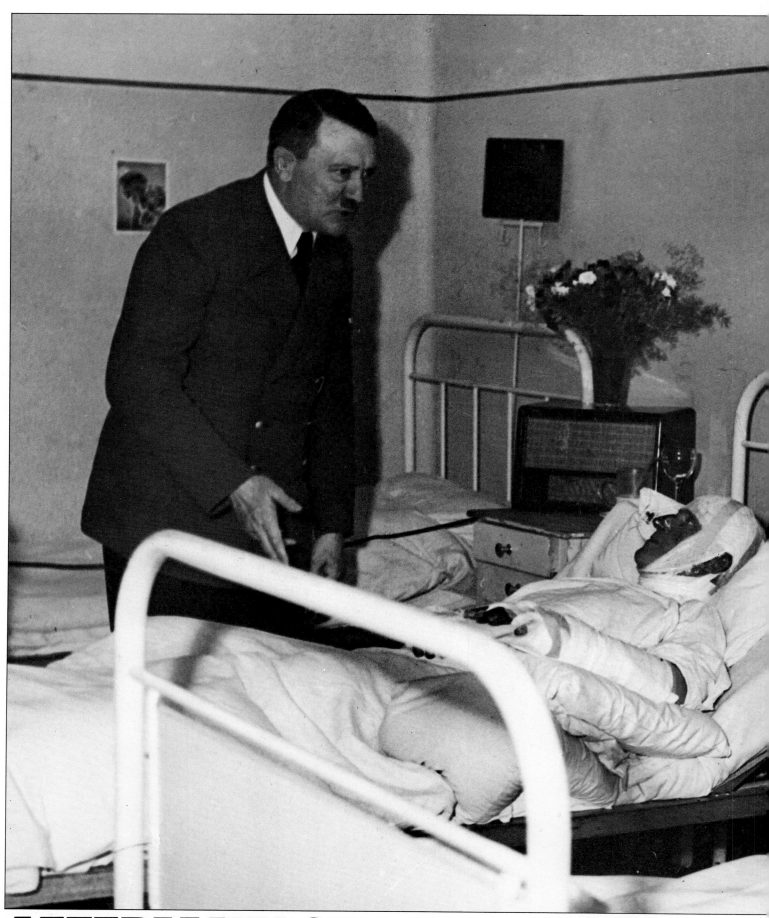

AFTERMATH OF A FAILED COUP

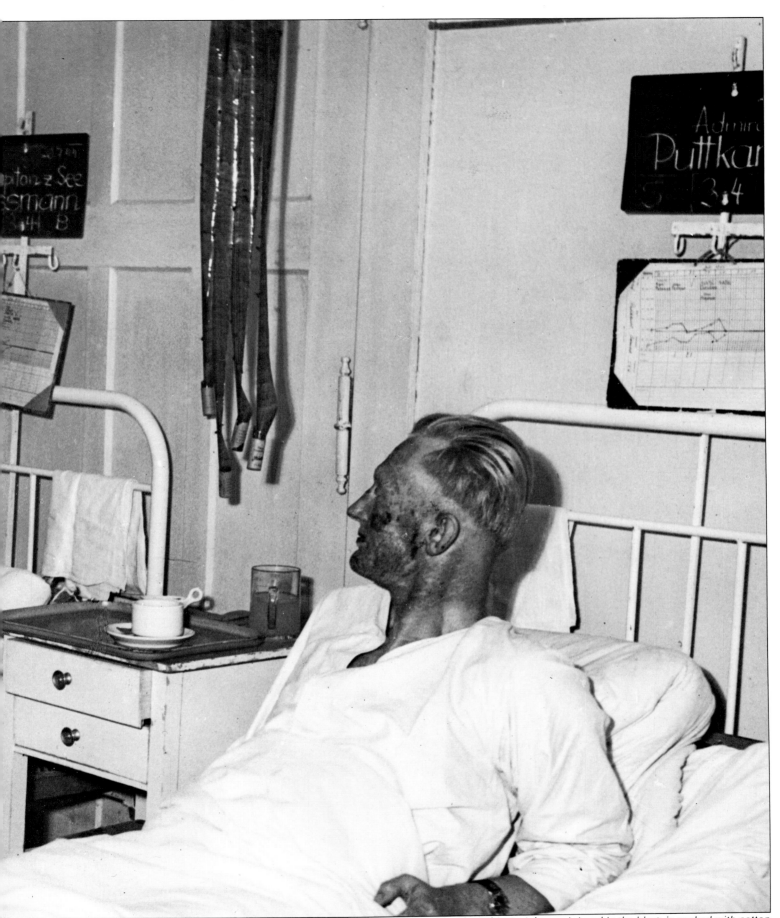

Adolf Hitler pays a visit to aides wounded in the July 20, 1944, bomb attempt on his life. The Führer's right ear, injured in the blast, is packed with cotton.

A GERMAN BOMB INTENDED FOR HITLER

At 1 a.m. on June 21, 1944, Adolf Hitler shocked the Reich with a broadcast from his Wolf's Lair headquarters in East Prussia. He told his countrymen that he had just escaped unhurt from an attempted assassination: "A clique of ambitious and criminal officers concocted a plot to remove me. A bomb planted by Colonel Count von Stauffenberg exploded two meters to my right." It was a crime, said Hitler, "unparalleled in German history."

The attempt to murder Hitler had taken place barely 12 hours before the broadcast and was part of a coup d'état planned by high-ranking Army officers who could no longer tolerate the Führer's destructive efforts to dominate the Army General Staff. Colonel Count Claus von Stauffenberg's bomb, concealed in a brief case and planted under the table at a Hitler conference, almost did the job. One of Hitler's secretaries later described the explosion as "thunder connected with bright yellow flame and thick smoke. The table collapsed. Then I heard a voice saying, 'Where is the Führer?'" Hitler had been knocked clear across the room, and he might well have been killed if a table leg had not blunted the force of the blast.

The assassination attempt triggered swift action by loyal Army units and the loyal legions of Heinrich Himmler's SS. The SS arrested and put to death scores of high-ranking Army officers, their relatives and anyone else vaguely suspected of opposing the Nazi regime. The Army's officer class—the only segment of German society that Hitler had not completely bent to his will—was broken and cowed.

The Führer took further steps to discipline and humiliate the Army. He demanded a pledge of loyalty from the officer corps and enlisted men. He compelled the Army, which had long resisted the stiff-armed Nazi salute, from then on to render that homage instead of the usual cap-touching military courtesy. He overturned a long-standing rule banning political activity in the Army; at his command, the Army Chief of Staff ordered that "every General Staff officer must be a National Socialist officer-leader." Henceforth, the Army would be Hitler's hapless pawn.

Five days before planting a bomb to kill Hitler, Colonel Claus von Stauffenberg (far left) meets with the Führer at the headquarters in East Prussia.

From the Wolf's Lair, Hitler reports the failed plot to the nation, vowing to "settle accounts in the manner to which National Socialists are accustomed."

Outwardly the very soul of calm command, Hitler chats with Field Marshal Wilhelm Keitel and other loyal officers soon after the assassination attempt.

"I WILL SHOW THEM NO MERCY!"

After the bomb blast, Hitler maintained that Divine Providence had spared him to carry on his mission.

He recounted the so-called anti-Nazi plot of Ernst Röhm and other SA leaders in 1934, boasting of the iron will he had summoned to crush that conspiracy, and vowed to show no mercy in the Stauffenberg case. He cried, "I will put their wives and children into concentration camps!"

Less than four hours after the explosion, Hitler greeted Benito Mussolini, arriving on a prearranged visit. The Italian dictator, who had been overthrown by his own people and propped up again by the Nazis as the puppet ruler of German-held northern Italy, was shaken by Hitler's story of the conspiracy. But, Mussolini said, he was reassured by Hitler's invincible spirit.

"What has happened here gives me renewed courage," said Mussolini. "After the miracle today it is inconceivable that our cause should suffer misfortune."

Hitler, his bandaged arm concealed by his coat, cordially welcomes Mussolini to the Wolf's Lair.

Hitler and Mussolini survey the bomb-shattered ruins of the operations room at the Wolf's Lair. Hitler's interpreter, Paul Schmidt, brings up the rear.

This photograph, marked by Hitler, shows his position before (O) and after (X) the bomb exploded.

Flanked by two colleagues, Judge Roland Freisler opens a trial of Army conspirators in his People's Court in Berlin. The accused were stripped of their belts to humiliate them, and Freisler screamed at one defendant, Field Marshal Erwin von Witzleben, who was trying to hold up his trousers, "You dirty old man, why do you keep fiddling with your pants?"

Carl Goerdeler, who had resigned as mayor of Leipzig in 1937 in opposition to the Nazis, was the conspirators' choice to serve as Chancellor of the provisional government following the July coup. After his trial, Goerdeler was executed at Plötzensee prison.

Colonel General Ludwig Beck, who in 1938 had resigned as head of the General Staff to protest Germany's advance into the Sudetenland, was a prime mover in the abortive conspiracy. Beck was shot following his unsuccessful attempt at suicide.

A devout man who thought Nazism was anti-Christian, Major General Hans Oster used his position as deputy controller of the Abwehr, or military intelligence, to get forged papers for the plotters. He was hanged at Flossenbürg concentration camp on April 9, 1945.

Colonel Claus von Stauffenberg, the scion of a noble family, escaped from the Wolf's Lair after the bomb he planted exploded, and immediately flew to Berlin, where he was to have assisted in the coup d'état. He was arrested and shot that same day.

Long a passionate foe of Nazism, Abwehr chief Wilhelm Canaris refused to join the July 20 conspiracy because he was opposed to assassination as a way of deposing the Führer. But he did not inform on the plotters, and for this he was hanged as a traitor.

General Erich Fellgiebel was the conspirator who cut the Wolf's Lair's radio communications after the explosion. Following his arrest he was tortured, but revealed no information about his fellow plotters. Fellgiebel was charged with treason and hanged on September 4.

A MOCKING JUDGE IN A KANGAROO COURT

Hitler made good on his pledge to impose merciless punishment on the conspirators. The SS arrested about 7,000 suspects, including not only officers who took an active part in the plot, but also those who had agreed to support the conspirators' new government after the coup.

The great majority of the traitors, no matter the degree of their complicity, were either killed without trial or summarily drummed out of the Army so they could be put on trial as civilians in the SS-controlled People's Court.

Roland Freisler, the judge, took pleasure in mocking the doomed men in the dock. He shouted them into silence whenever they tried to defend themselves. In no case was the verdict in doubt.

The Führer had ordered that the executions be carried out "two hours after the sentence." In nearly every case, the executioners were punctual.

Major General Helmuth Stieff, whom Himmler mocked as a "little poisonous dwarf," supplied the bomb that went off at the Wolf's Lair. He was one of the first plotters to be tortured by the Gestapo, condemned by the People's Court and executed by the SS.

General Friedrich Olbricht was to have led the coup d'état in Berlin following Hitler's assassination. But he waited several hours for confirmation that the Führer was actually dead, and by the end of the day Olbricht had been captured and killed by the Army.

A BUTCHER'S MEATHOOKS FOR EIGHT CONSPIRATORS

"I want them hung up like carcasses of meat." Such was the fate Hitler commanded for the first batch of conspirators to be executed formally, and his order was carried out to the letter.

Eight conspirators were herded into a small execution chamber at Berlin's Plötzensee prison on the afternoon of August 8. The room was equipped for the occasion with six meathooks borrowed from local slaughterhouses. Floodlights bathed the chamber, and movie cameras whirred, for Hitler had ordered the Ministry of Propaganda to record every last detail.

The executioners looped nooses of thin cord around the necks of the condemned men, then hoisted them until the cords caught on the hooks. The men kicked, writhed and made horrible sounds as they were slowly strangled. As some of them struggled, their beltless trousers fell off.

In spite of his vengeful purge and his subjugation of the generals, Hitler never again trusted the Army. He invested his trusted Himmler with the task of organizing all Army replacements, and he came to rely ever more heavily on Himmler's fanatic armed force, the Waffen-SS. Though the regular Army would serve out the War patriotically against mounting odds, Hitler would see to it that the Waffen-SS got the best equipment, the key attack roles and the lion's share of the glory.

This is the death chamber at Plötzensee prison; on the meathooks at rear th

...nspirators were hanged for their attempted assassination of Hitler. Films of the execution were later shown to Army troops as a warning against disloyalty.

BIBLIOGRAPHY

Arendt, Hannah, *Eichmann in Jerusalem*. The Viking Press, 1963.

Aron, Robert, *The Vichy Regime: 1940-1944*. Beacon Press, 1958.

Bayles, William D., *Caesars in Goose Step*. Kennikat Press, 1940.

Boelcke, Willi A., ed., *The Secret Conferences of Dr. Goebbels: The Nazi Propaganda War, 1939-1943*. E. P. Dutton & Co., 1970.

Bracher, Karl Dietrich, *The German Dictatorship*. Praeger Publishers, 1970.

Bradley, John, *Lidice: Sacrificial Village*. Ballantine Books, 1972.

Bramsted, Ernest K., *Goebbels and National Socialist Propaganda: 1925-1945*. Michigan State University Press, 1965.

Bullock, Alan, *Hitler: A Study in Tyranny*. Harper & Row, 1962.

Bundeszentrale für politische Bildung, ed., *Germans against Hitler: July 20, 1944*. Bonn: Press and Information Office of the Federal Government of Germany, 1969.

Burden, Hamilton T., *The Nuremberg Party Rallies: 1923-1939*. Frederick A. Praeger, 1967.

Butler, Rupert, *The Black Angels: The Story of the Waffen-SS*. Hamlyn Paperbacks, 1978.

Chartock, Roselle, and Jack Spencer, eds., *The Holocaust Years: Society on Trial*. Bantam Books, 1978.

Cooper, Matthew, *The German Army, 1933-1945: Its Political and Military Failure*. London: Macdonald and Jane's, 1978.

Craig, Gordon A., *The Politics of the Prussian Army: 1640-1945*. Clarendon Press, 1955.

Crankshaw, Edward, *Gestapo: Instrument of Tyranny*. The Viking Press, 1957.

Dallin, Alexander, *German Rule in Russia: 1941-1945*. St. Martin's Press, 1957.

Davidson, Eugene, *The Trial of the Germans: An Account of the 22 Defendants before the International Military Tribunal at Nuremberg*. The Macmillan Co., 1966.

Dawidowicz, Lucy S., *The War against the Jews: 1933-1945*. Holt, Rinehart and Winston, 1975.

Des Pres, Terrence, *The Survivor*. Pocket Books, 1976.

Deschner, Günther, *Reinhard Heydrich*. Bechtle, 1977.

Deutsch, Harold C., *Hitler and His Generals: The Hidden Crisis, January-June 1938*. University of Minnesota Press, 1974.

Dietrich, Otto, *Hitler*. Henry Regnery Co., 1955.

Donat, Alexander, *The Holocaust Kingdom: A Memoir*. Holt, Rinehart and Winston, 1963.

Douglas-Hamilton, James, *Motive for a Mission: The Story behind Hess's Flight to Britain*. Macmillan and Co., 1971.

Encyclopaedia Judaica. Keter Publishing House, 1971.

Eschenburg, Theodor, et al.: *The Path to Dictatorship, 1918-1933: Ten Essays*. Doubleday & Co., 1966.

Esh, Shaul, ed., *Yad Vashem Studies on the European Jewish Catastrophe and Resistance*, Vol. 3. Jerusalem: Yad Vashem, 1959.

The Extermination of Jews: Album 1. Lódź: Central Historical Jewish Committee at the Central Commission for Polish Jews, 1945.

Fest, Joachim C.:
The Face of the Third Reich. Pantheon Books, 1970.
Hitler. Vintage Books, 1973.

FitzGibbon, Constantine, *20 July*. W. W. Norton & Co., 1956.

Forstmeier, Hans, and Hans-Erich Volkmann, *Kriegswirschaft und Rüstung: 1939-1945*. Düsseldorf: Dorste Verlag, 1977.

Friedman, Dr. Filip, *This Was Oswiecim: The Story of a Murder Camp*. London: The United Jewish Relief Appeal, 1946.

German Military Uniforms and Insignia: 1933-1945. WE, Inc., 1967.

Gisevius, Hans Bernd, *To the Bitter End*. Greenwood Press, 1975.

Gorlitz, Walter, ed., *The Memoirs of Field-Marshal Keitel*. Stein and Day, 1966.

Graber, G. S., *History of the SS*. David McKay Co., 1978.

Grunberger, Richard:
Hitler's SS. Laurel Editions, 1970.
The 12-Year Reich: A Social History of Nazi Germany, 1933-1945. Holt, Rinehart and Winston, 1971.

Gun, Nerin E., *Eva Braun: Hitler's Mistress*. Meredith Press, 1968.

Halder, Franz, *Hitler As War Lord*. London: Putnam, 1949.

Hassell, Ulrich von, *The Von Hassell Diaries: 1938-1944*. Greenwood Press, 1947.

Heiber, Helmut, *Goebbels*. Hawthorn Books, 1972.

Heiden, Konrad, *Der Führer: Hitler's Rise to Power*. Houghton Mifflin Co., 1944.

Herzstein, Robert Edwin:
Adolf Hitler and the German Trauma: 1913-1945. G. P. Putnam's Sons, 1974.
The War That Hitler Won. G. P. Putnam's Sons, 1978.

Hilberg, Raul:
The Destruction of the European Jews. Octagon Books, 1978.
ed., *Documents of Destruction*. Quadrangle Books, 1971.

Hillel, Marc, and Clarissa Henry, *Of Pure Blood*. McGraw-Hill Book Co., 1976.

Hitler, Adolf, *Mein Kampf*. Houghton Mifflin Co., 1971.

Hoffmann, Heinrich:
Ein Volk Ehrt Seinen Führer. Berlin: Historical Publishing House, 1939.
Hitler Was My Friend. London: Burke, 1955.

Hoffmann, Peter:
The History of the German Resistance: 1933-1945. The MIT Press, 1977.
Hitler's Personal Security. The MIT Press, 1979.

Höhne, Heinz, *The Order of the Death's Head*. Coward-McCann, 1970.

The Holocaust. London: Board of Deputies of British Jews, 1978.

Höss, Rudolf, *Commandant of Auschwitz*. Popular Library, 1951.

Hull, David Stewart, *Film in the Third Reich: A Study of the German Cinema, 1933-1945*. University of California Press, 1969.

Hutton, J. Bernard, *Hess: The Man and His Mission*. The Macmillan Co., 1971.

Infield, Glenn B., *Eva and Adolf*. Grosset & Dunlap, 1974.

Information Department of the Polish Government, *The Polish Territory Occupied by the Germans*. 1940.

Kannik, Preben, *Military Uniforms in Color*. The Macmillan Co., 1968.

Kernan, Thomas, *France on Berlin Time*. J. B. Lippincott Co., 1941.

Kersten, Felix, *The Kersten Memoirs: 1940-1945*. The Macmillan Co., 1957.

Kochan, Lionel, *Pogrom: 10 November 1938*. Andre Deutsch, 1957.

Kogon, Eugen, *The Theory and Practice of Hell*. Berkley Publishing Corp., 1950.

Krausnick, Helmut, et al., *Anatomy of the SS State*. Walker and Co., 1968.

Kris, Ernst, and Hans Speier, *German Radio Propaganda: Report on Home Broadcasts during the War*. Oxford University Press, 1944.

Kurst, Otto, *Auschwitz*. Hillman Books, 1959.

Kurzman, Dan, *The Bravest Battle*. G. P. Putnam's Sons, 1976.

Lang, Jochen von, *The Secretary, Martin Bormann: The Man Who Manipulated Hitler*. Random House, 1979.

League of Fighters for Freedom and Democracy, *1939-1945: We Have Not Forgotten*. 1960.

Levin, Nora, *The Holocaust: The Destruction of European Jewry 1933-1945*. Thomas Y. Crowell Co., 1968.

Ley, Dr. Robert, ed., *Organisationsbuch der NSDAP*. Munich: Zentralverlag der NSDAP, 1943.

Littlejohn, David, *The Patriotic Traitors*. Doubleday & Co., 1972.

Lochner, Louis P., ed., *The Goebbels Diaries: 1942-1943*. Greenwood Press, 1948.

Lorant, Stefan, *Sieg Heil!* W. W. Norton & Co., 1974.

McGovern, James, *Martin Bormann*. William Morrow & Co., 1968.

Majdalany, Fred, *The Fall of Fortress Europe*. Hodder and Stoughton, 1968.

Maltitz, Horst von, *The Evolution of Hitler's Germany*. McGraw-Hill Book Co., 1973.

Manvell, Roger:
The Conspirators: 20th July 1944. Ballantine Books, 1971.
SS and Gestapo: Rule by Terror. Ballantine Books, 1969.

Manvell, Roger, and Heinrich Fraenkel:
The Canaris Conspiracy. David McKay Co., 1969.
Himmler. G. P. Putnam's Sons, 1965.

The Martyrdom, Battle and Destruction of Jews in Poland: 1939-1945. Warsaw: National Defense Ministry, 1960.

Milward, Alan S., *The German Economy at War*. University of London, 1965.

Mitscherlich, Alexander, M.D., *Doctors of Infamy: The Story of the Nazi Medical Crimes*. Henry Schuman, 1949.

Mollo, Andrew, *A Pictorial History of the SS*. Stein and Day, 1976.

Neave, Airey, *On Trial at Nuremberg*. Little, Brown and Co., 1978.

O'Neill, Robert J., *The German Army and the Nazi Party: 1933-1939*. James H. Heineman, 1967.

Orlow, Dietrich, *The History of the Nazi Party: 1933-1945*. University of Pittsburgh Press, 1973.

Passant, E. J., *A Short History of Germany: 1815-1945*. Cambridge University Press, 1962.

Paxton, Robert O., *Vichy France*. W. W. Norton & Co., 1972.

Payne, Robert, *The Life and Death of Adolf Hitler*. Praeger Publishers, 1973.

Peterson, Edward N., *The Limits of Hitler's Power*. Princeton University Press, 1969.

Pia, Jack, *Nazi Regalia*. Ballantine Books, 1971.

Pinson, Koppel S., *Modern Germany: Its History and Civilization*. The Macmillan Co., 1966.

Polish War Losses in the Years 1939-1945. Poznań: Western Press Agency, 1962.

Porter, Roy P., *Uncensored France: An Eyewitness Account of France under the Occupation*. The Dial Press, 1942.

Prittie, Terence, *Germans against Hitler*. Little, Brown and Co., 1964.

Reitlinger, Gerald:
The Final Solution: The Attempt to Exterminate the Jews of Europe, 1939-1945. A. S. Barnes & Co., 1953.
The SS: Alibi of a Nation, 1922-1945. Toronto: Heinemann, 1956.

Ribbentrop, Joachim von, *The Ribbentrop Memoirs*. London: Weidenfeld and Nicolson, 1954.

Rich, Norman, *Hitler's War Aims*:
Vol. 1, *Ideology, The Nazi State and the Course of Expansion*. W. W. Norton & Co., 1973.
Vol. 2, *The Establishment of the New Order*. W. W. Norton & Co., 1974.

Ritter, Gerhard, *The German Resistance*. Books for Libraries Press, 1958.

Roxan, David, and Ken Wanstall, *The Jackdaw of Linz: The Story of Hitler's Art Thefts*. London: Cassell, 1964.

Schellenberg, Walter, *The Labyrinth*. Harper & Brothers, 1956.

Schlabrendorff, Fabian von, *The Secret War against Hitler*. Pitman Publishing Corp., 1965.

Schoenberner, Gerhard, *The Yellow Star: The Persecution of the Jews in Europe, 1933-1945*. Bantam Books, 1979.

Semmler, Rudolf, *Goebbels—the Man Next to Hitler*. London: Westhouse, 1947.

Shirer, William L.:
Berlin Diary. Alfred A. Knopf, 1941.
The Rise and Fall of the Third Reich. Simon and Schuster, 1960.

Smoleń, Kazimierz, *Auschwitz: 1940-1945*. Państwowe Muzeum W Oswiecimiu, 1961.

Snyder, Louis L., *Encyclopedia of the Third Reich*. McGraw-Hill Book Co., 1976.

Speer, Albert:
Inside the Third Reich. The Macmillan Co., 1970.

Spandau: The Secret Diaries. Macmillan Publishing Co., 1976.

Stanić, Dorothea, *Kinder im KZ.* Berlin (West): Elefanten Press Verlag, 1979.

Stein, George H., *The Waffen SS.* Cornell University Press, 1966.

Steiner, Jean-François, *Treblinka.* New American Library, 1966.

Toland, John:
Adolf Hitler. Doubleday & Co., 1976.
Hitler: The Pictorial Documentary of His Life. Doubleday & Co., 1978.

Trevor-Roper, H. R.:
ed., *The Bormann Letters.* London: Weidenfeld and Nicolson, 1954.
ed., *Final Entries 1945: The Diaries of Joseph Goebbels.* Avon, 1979.
ed., *Hitler's Secret Conversations: 1941-1944.* Farrar, Straus and Young, 1953.
The Last Days of Hitler. Berkley Publishing Corp., 1947.

Trials of War Criminals before the Nuremberg Military Tribunals under Control Council Law No. 10, Vol. 4. U.S. Government Printing Office, 1946-1949.

Trunk, Isaiah, *Jewish Responses to Nazi Persecution.* Stein and Day, 1979.

Vagts, Alfred, *Hitler's Second Army.* Infantry Journal, 1943.

Waite, Robert G. L., ed., *Hitler and Nazi Germany.* Holt, Rinehart and Winston, 1965.

Warmbrunn, Werner, *The Dutch under German Occupation: 1940-1945.* Stanford University Press, 1963.

Werth, Alexander:
France: 1940-1955. Beacon Press, 1966.
Russia at War: 1941-1945. E. P. Dutton & Co., 1964.

Wheeler-Bennett, John W., *The Nemesis of Power.* London: Macmillan & Co., 1964.

Wighton, Charles, *Heydrich: Hitler's Most Evil Henchman.* Chilton Co., 1962.

Wroński, Stanislaw, and Maria Zwolakowa, eds., *Poles—Jews: 1939-1945.* Warsaw: Ksiąźka i Wiedza, 1971.

Wykes, Alan:
Himmler. Ballantine Books, 1972.
The Nuremberg Rallies. Ballantine Books, 1970.

Zeman, Z. A. B., *Nazi Propaganda.* Oxford University Press, 1973.

PICTURE CREDITS

Credits from left to right are separated by semicolons, from top to bottom by dashes.

COVER and page 1: Bundesarchiv, Koblenz.

HITLER'S ARTFUL SPECTACLES—6, 7: Hugo Jaeger, *Life,* © Time Inc. 8: National Archives. 9-17: Hugo Jaeger, *Life,* © Time Inc.

THE NEW MEN OF POWER—20: Süddeutscher Verlag, Bilderdienst, Munich. 22: Collection of Stefan Lorant. 25: National Archives. 29: Henry Beville, collection of Glenn Sweeting (3)—Hugo Jaeger, *Life,* © Time Inc. 33: Süddeutscher Verlag, Bilderdienst, Munich.

NAZIFYING A NATION—36, 37: Rijksinstituut voor Oorlogsdocumentatie, Amsterdam. 38: Bildarchiv Preussischer Kulturbesitz, Berlin (West). 39: Bundesarchiv, Koblenz. 40: Heinrich Hoffmann, courtesy Bildarchiv Preussischer Kulturbesitz, Berlin (West). 41: Bildarchiv Preussischer Kulturbesitz, Berlin (West)—Henry Beville, collection of Glenn Sweeting; Imperial War Museum, London. 42: Bildarchiv Preussischer Kulturbesitz, Berlin (West)—Heinrich Hoffmann, courtesy Bildarchiv Preussischer Kulturbesitz, Berlin (West). 43: Gidal, courtesy Bildarchiv Preussischer Kulturbesitz, Berlin (West); Henry Beville, collection of Glenn Sweeting. 44, 45: Collection of Stefan Lorant: Heinrich Hoffmann, from Foreign Records Seized, 1941, National Archives. 46, 47: Collection of Stefan Lorant. 48, 49: Bildarchiv Preussischer Kulturbesitz, Berlin (West)—Bundesarchiv, Koblenz; © Erich Andres, Hamburg. 50, 51: Drawing by Forte, Inc.; Ullstein Bilderdienst, Berlin (West).

ALL THE "LITTLE HITLERS"—54: Foreign Records Seized, 1941, National Archives. 57: Bildarchiv Preussischer Kulturbesitz, Berlin (West). 58-61: Henry Beville, collection of Glenn Sweeting. 64: Ullstein Bilderdienst, Berlin (West). 67: Bundesarchiv, Koblenz.

THE FÜHRER'S PRIVATE WORLD—70-81: National Archives.

THE DARK EMPIRE OF THE SS—85: Bildarchiv Preussischer Kulturbesitz, Berlin (West). 86: Hermann Speer, Schloss-Wolfsbrunnenweg. 87, 88: Ullstein Bilderdienst, Berlin (West). 89: Bildarchiv Preussischer Kulturbesitz, Berlin (West). 90: Süddeutscher Verlag, Bilderdienst, Munich. 92: Süddeutscher Verlag, Bilderdienst, Munich. 94: Bundesarchiv, Koblenz.

BREEDING THE "MASTER RACE"—96, 97: Bildarchiv Preussischer Kulturbesitz, Berlin (West). 98: Süddeutscher Verlag, Bilderdienst, Munich. 99: Bundesarchiv, Koblenz. 100: Bildarchiv Preussischer Kulturbesitz, Berlin (West); National Archives. 102: Bildarchiv Preussischer Kulturbesitz, Berlin (West). 103-105: Bundesarchiv, Koblenz.

A RULE OF PLUNDER—108: Map by Elie Sabban. 111: The University of Michigan Library, Department of Rare Books and Special Collections. 113: Rijksinstituut voor Oorlogsdocumentatie, Amsterdam. 114, 115: Bildarchiv Preussischer Kulturbesitz, Berlin (West). 119: David Rubinger, from the Archives of the Ghetto Fighter's House, Israel.

THE CAMPAIGN OF HATE—122, 123: Bundesarchiv, Koblenz. 124: National Archives. 125: Library of Congress. 126: Süddeutscher Verlag, Bilderdienst, Munich—Henry Beville, collection of Glenn Sweeting (2). 127: Henry Beville, collection of Glenn Sweeting. 128: C. S. Balkin, Berlin. 130, 131: Süddeutscher Verlag, Bilderdienst, Munich. 132, 133: National Archives; Forlag & Antikvariat Sixtus, Copenhagen, inset, Deutsches Institut für Filmkunde, Wiesbaden.

THE "FINAL SOLUTION"—140: Map by Elie Sabban. 144: Bundesarchiv, Koblenz. 149: Henry Beville, collection of Dr. Alexander Bernfes, London. 150: National Archives.

THE HOLOCAUST—152, 153: Henry Beville, Polonia Publishing House, Warsaw. 154: National Archives—L. M. Muller, Boszichtlaan. 155: Bildarchiv Preussischer Kulturbesitz, Berlin (West). 156, 157: Bildarchiv Preussischer Kulturbesitz, Berlin (West); Wide World. 158, 159: from the Archives of YIVO Institute for Jewish Research, except top right, Bildarchiv Preussischer Kulturbesitz, Berlin (West). 160, 161: Fotokhronika-Tass, Moscow—Allgemeine jüdische Wachenzeitung, Düsseldorf; David Rubinger, from the Archives of the Ghetto Fighter's House, Israel. 162: Bildarchiv Preussischer Kulturbesitz, Berlin (West). 163: David Rubinger, Yad Vashem, Jerusalem—Henry Beville, Glavnoye Archivnoye Upravleniye, Moscow—from the Archives of the YIVO Institute for Jewish Research. 164, 165: Dr. Lou de Jong, Amsterdam; Henry Beville, Centre de Documentation Juive Contemporaine, Paris—David Rubinger, Yad Vashem, Jerusalem. 166, 167: Bildarchiv Preussischer Kulturbesitz, Berlin (West)—Rijksinstituut voor Oorlogsdocumentatie, Amsterdam; David Rubinger, Yad Vashem, Jerusalem. 168, 169: Archives Amicale de Mathausen, Paris (2); Rijksinstituut voor Oorlogsdocumentatie, Amsterdam. 171: Bundesarchiv, Koblenz—Peter Hunter, Rijksinstituut voor Oorlogsdocumentatie, Amsterdam. 172: David Rubinger, Yad Vashem, Jerusalem. 173: A. M. Van Bessel-Schiet, courtesy Rijksinstituut voor Oorlogsdocumentatie, Amsterdam—Ullstein Bilderdienst, Berlin (West). 174, 175: Henry Beville, ADN-Zentralbild, Berlin, DDR; Bildarchiv Preussischer Kulturbesitz, Berlin (West). 176, 177: Tass-Photo, Moscow.

THE ENSLAVEMENT OF THE ARMY—180: Heinrich Hoffmann, collection of Al Sherman. 184: Bundesarchiv, Koblenz. 188: Foreign Records Seized, 1941, National Archives. 192: The Hoover Institution on War, Revolution and Peace.

AFTERMATH OF A FAILED COUP—194, 195: Heinrich Hoffmann. 196: National Archives. 197: Heinrich Hoffmann. 198: Photo Archive, Berlin—Heinrich Hoffmann. 199: Bundesarchiv, Koblenz—United Press International. 200: Bildarchiv Preussischer Kulturbesitz, Berlin (West)—Süddeutscher Verlag, Bilderdienst, Munich (2); Ullstein Bilderdienst, Berlin (West). 201: Bildarchiv Preussischer Kulturbesitz, Berlin (West); Süddeutscher Verlag, Bilderdienst, Munich (2)—from *Germans against Hitler,* published by the German Press and Information Office of the Federal Government of Germany; Süddeutscher Verlag, Bilderdienst, Munich. 202, 203: Bildarchiv Preussischer Kulturbesitz, Berlin (West).

ACKNOWLEDGMENTS

For help given in the preparation of this book, the editors wish to thank Chana Abells, Photo Archivist, Yad Vashem, Jerusalem; Hans Becker, ADN-Zentralbild, Berlin, DDR; Eva Bong, Ullstein Bilderdienst, Berlin, West Germany; Carole Boutté, Senior Researcher, U.S. Army Audio-Visual Activity, Pentagon, Arlington, Va.; Cas Oorthuys Archives, Amsterdam; Dr. Georg Deschner, Königswinter, Germany; V. M. Destefano, Chief of Reference Branch, U.S. Army Audio-Visual Activity, Pentagon, Arlington, Va.; Fotokhronika-Tass, Moscow; Ulrich Frodien, Süddeutscher Verlag, Bilderdienst, Munich; Dr. Matthias Haupt, Bundesarchiv, Koblenz, Germany; Werner Haupt, Bibliothek für Zeitgeschichte, Stuttgart; Heinrich Hoffmann, Hamburg; Heinz Höhne, Grosshansdorff, Germany; Imperial War Museum, Department of Photographs, London; Gita Johnson, Wiener Library, London; Heidi Klein, Bildarchiv Preussischer Kulturbesitz, Berlin, West Germany; Dr. Roland Klemig, Bildarchiv Preussischer Kulturbesitz, Berlin, West Germany; Rosemarie Klipp, Bonn; Richard D. Kovar, Reston, Va.; William H. Leary, National Archives and Records Service, Audio-Visual Division, Washington, D.C.; Marianne Loenartz, Bundesarchiv, Koblenz, Germany; Meinhard Nilges, Bundesarchiv, Koblenz, Germany; Susan Patterson, Washington, D.C.; Janusz Piekalkiewicz, Rösrath-Hoffnungsthal, Germany; Dr. Richard Raiber, Hochenssin, Del.; Rijksinstituut voor Oorlogsdocumentatie, Amsterdam; Amy K. Schmidt, Alexandria, Va.; Jost W. Schneider, Wuppertal, Germany; Axel Schulz, Ullstein Bilderdienst, Berlin, West Germany; Albert Speer, Heidelberg; Marina Stütz, Deutsche-Polnische Gesellschaft, Düsseldorf; Glenn Sweeting, National Air and Space Museum, Washington, D.C.; George Wagner, Archives Technician, Modern Military Branch, Military Archives Division, National Archives, Washington, D.C.; Marek Webb, Associate Archivist, YIVO Institute, New York, N.Y.; Paul White, National Archives and Records Service, Audio-Visual Division, Washington, D.C.; Robert Wolfe, Chief, Modern Military Branch, National Archives, Washington, D.C.; Yad Vashem, Jerusalem.

The index for this book was prepared by Nicholas J. Anthony.

Printed in U.S.A.